The Tools of Screenwriting

THE TOOLS OF
Screenwriting

A WRITER'S GUIDE TO
THE CRAFT AND ELEMENTS OF
A SCREENPLAY

■

David Howard

AND

Edward Mabley

ST. MARTIN'S PRESS ■ NEW YORK

Quotes from Paddy Chayevsky, William Goldman, Ernest Lehman, and Robert Towne are taken from *The Craft of the Screenwriter* by John Brady. Copyright © 1981 by John Brady. Reprinted by permission of Simon & Schuster, Inc.

Designed by Beth Tondreau Design / Mary A. Wirth
Production Editor: Suzanne Magida

Library of Congress Cataloging-in-Publication Data

Howard, David
    The tools of screenwriting / David Howard and Edward Mabley :
introduction by Frank Daniel.
        p.   cm.
    ISBN 0-312-09405-1
    1. Motion picture authorship.   2. Television authorship.
I. Mabley, Edward.   II. Title.
PN1996.H73   1993
808.2'3—dc20   93-22787
                                                               CIP

10   9   8   7   6   5   4   3   2

Books are available in quantity for promotional or premium use. Write to Director of Special Sales, St. Martin's Press, 175 Fifth Avenue, New York, NY 10010, for information on discounts and terms, or call toll-free (800) 221–7945. In New York, call (212) 674–5151 (ext. 645).

I count myself in nothing else so happy
as in remembering my good friends
—WILLIAM SHAKESPEARE, *RICHARD II*

TO DAVID JOHNSTONE

ALIVE IN MANY HEARTS

CONTENTS

FOREWORD

*S*ome projects in the motion picture industry spend so much time in the developmental process they seem to be irretrievably entangled there. In that kind of project, observers may begin to wonder if the film will ever reach its final form and its intended audience. Seldom, if ever, does one praise the length of time it takes to create a complex project.

The Tools of Screenwriting, however, is a project that has benefited from its many years in development. Indeed, much of its value comes from the fact that it has been refined over a period of decades. A series of creative minds have distilled the essence of dramatic construction to explain the basics to screenwriters and script analysts.

In New York in the 1960s, Edward Mabley began a train of thought that is the origin of this book. Through his work as a writer and director, he formulated his theories about dramatic construction and used stageplays to illustrate his principles. He applied and refined his ideas as a teacher at the New School for Social Research, and he eventually wrote them down in a book, which was published in 1972.

That book eventually went out of print and lay dormant until another practitioner and teacher, Frank Daniel, discovered and adopted it for his own use in teaching screenwriting. Mr. Daniel has directed many of the world's finest film schools and has for many years used Mabley's book as an excellent and concise introduction to dramatic theory and its application to screenwriting.

One of the individuals to whom Mr. Daniel communicated his enthusiasm and his theoretical approach was David Howard. Mr. Howard, who later became founding director of the Graduate Screenwriting Program at the University of Southern California, added his insight and experience. His students graduated to write scripts for award-winning, profitable, and popular films. The book continued to be a principal resource long after it had gone out of print.

I first encountered the book while I was working at Hometown Films on the Paramount Pictures lot. I had been searching for a good book on screenwriting and found none particularly satisfying. One day a former student of Mr. Howard's walked into my office with a thick stack of pale photocopies. Because I am the son of a publisher, I was curious why he copied an entire book instead of buying one. He told me the book was unavailable in any other way.

It didn't make sense to me that a book that had been the primary text at several of the best film schools had gone out of print and remained unpublished and unrevised for so long. Upon contacting the original publisher, I learned they had narrowed their focus and were not interested in revising it. They released the copyright to the author's estate and I negotiated the rights to the book. Mr. Howard agreed to rewrite the text to reflect the way its principles apply to screenwriting and to substitute analyses of the film scripts as examples.

David Howard dedicated his time, energy, and thought to transforming the original book into *The Tools of Screenwriting*. Keeping the core of Mabley's ideas and concepts intact, he redirected all of the tools, examples, and quotations toward film, expanded and explained the critical elements, and analyzed their use in a variety of important scripts. He has crystallized a highly usable vocabulary to discuss the craft of screenwriting.

The Tools of Screenwriting is what it is because of the extraordinary talents of the contributors who continually refined it over many years. With each script the teachers and students wrote or analyzed, they honed the ideas and the presentation of those ideas. Although this project has been in development for a very long time, the result has become the book I had in mind when I searched for the *perfect* book on screenwriting.

I thank St. Martin's editor George Witte for his vision and his guidance. I thank Adam Belanoff for bringing the Mabley book to my attention. And, I especially thank my father, Wil McKnight, for his invaluable help through all stages of this project.

—GREGORY McKNIGHT

PREFACE

*A*decade ago I had the good fortune to be invited to attend a month-long screenwriting seminar—my first—with the celebrated co-director of the Columbia University Film Division, Frank Daniel. Before the session began, I was told to read a few helpful books, among them *Dramatic Construction* by Edward Mabley. I called every bookstore in the city and discovered that it was out of print, and when I went to the library I found that it had been checked out, presumably by someone else in my seminar. I felt horribly unprepared going to that first session, but found that everyone else had the same problem with the book. The one copy available made the rounds among us throughout that month and the seminar went on without a hitch. In fact, it was a great success.

After that seminar I followed Frank to Columbia for full-time studies in screenwriting and directing, then to the University of Southern California, where I joined the faculty of the School of Cinema-Television where he had become Dean, and where I became the founding director of the Graduate Screenwriting Program. Through all the changes, two things remained constant: even though Mr. Mabley's book was written expressly about playwriting and cited examples primarily from plays, albeit great ones, *Dramatic Construction* was still the book of choice for giving a simple and clearly laid out introduction to dramatic theory to screenwriting students; and the book was still out of print and difficult to find.

When Gregory McKnight first approached me with the idea of updating and orienting the Mabley text to screenwriting, I jumped at the chance to take *Dramatic Construction* and turn it into what you hold in your hands, *The Tools of Screenwriting*. At the outset it looked like an easy task. After all, it was already a very good book, one I was already familiar with and had used extensively for years.

As with all major projects, what appears to be simple is, in reality, complex. Most of Mr. Mabley's essays on dramatic theory needed some degree of rewriting, if only to unify his voice and style of writing with mine. But the essays also needed to be based on examples from film, not theater, and a new set of new essays needed to be developed. Nearly all of the analyses of plays were replaced with analyses of films. *The Tools of Screenwriting* is the product of my recent work and Mr. Mabley's earlier work unified into a single text, although we never had the chance to meet or work together. I hope there aren't too many seams showing.

In part because of the unusual origins of this book, the acknowledgment of credit for ideas, help and, particularly, dramatic theories, also grows more complicated. Much of what is contained here in the form of theory dates much farther back than Mr. Mabley's text. One can't write about dramatic theory without in some way using the ideas of Aristotle. But in addition to Aristotle and his contemporaries, the whole European tradition of theater plays into much of what is discussed in the "Basic Storytelling" and "Screenwriting Tools" sections.

Then, too, there is the problem that one can absorb the ideas of another without ever being aware of appropriating those concepts. Here, at least, I know the source of much that is expounded on in this book. I began my study of drama, film, storytelling, and screenwriting with Frank Daniel, and have gone on to my own career as a screenwriter and teacher largely as a result of the insights given to me by him. Though I am sure that many of "my" ideas really go back to him—my own personal source of the Nile— there are also ideas and dramatic theories that do definitely originate from Frank Daniel. Among these are the notions of "Whose story is it?" and "Whose scene is it?"; the distinction between objective and subjective drama; the entire principle of revelation and recognition was a major discovery of Frank's; the notion of scenes of aftermath and the fact that they often turn into the next scene of preparation; elements of the future; and advertising.

Most important of all of Frank's many contributions to the ideas and theories of storytelling and their use in cinema is the deceptively simple line elaborated on in the text: "Somebody wants something badly and is having difficulty getting it." This most basic of all ideas about what constitutes a story is obviously something that all good dramatists throughout history have understood, yet it took Frank to articulate it and make it so simple. Like the best inventions, the best theories are the ones that seem obvious after they have been created and leave us wondering why no one else saw through the complexity to the simple core at the center.

I would also like to thank Gregory McKnight, who took the initiative to acquire an out-of-print book from the original publisher and Mr. Mabley's estate. When he brought me into the project, we developed the essential features of *The Tools of Screenwriting* together, and then he made the arrangements with St. Martin's Press to publish the revised work.

It is my hope that the ideas and examples in this book will lead the reader/screenwriter to an understanding of the fabric that holds stories together. I hope you will come to comprehend the warp and woof that make up storytelling and learn that it is an incredibly elastic and resilient fabric that is also as translucent as a veil. It is moldable, it can be stretched, twisted, or shrunk, and can even stand up to an occasional hole. The one thing that this fabric underlying all good stories cannot withstand is being discarded. Do that at your own peril.

—DAVID HOWARD

ACKNOWLEDGMENTS

Many of the quotes included in this book come from a series of videotaped interviews made by Cristina Venegas and Roger Christiansen for the Graduate Screenwriting Program at the University of Southern California School of Cinema-Television and Sundance Institute. My special thanks to Cristina and Roger along with the screenwriters they interviewed, Walter Bernstein, Bill Wittliff, Tom Rickman, and Ring Lardner, Jr. And particular thanks to George Witte for his assistance throughout.

Screenwriters' credits:

WALTER BERNSTEIN: *Heller in Pink Tights, Paris Blues, Fail Safe, The Money Trap, The Molly Maguires, An Almost Perfect Affair, The Front, Semi-Tough, The Betsey, Yanks, Little Miss Marker, The House on Carroll Street.*

BILL WITTLIFF: *Thaddeus Rose and Eddy, Honeysuckle Rose, The Black Stallion, Raggedy Man, Country, Barbarosa, Lonesome Dove.*

TOM RICKMAN: *Kansas City Bomber, The Laughing Policeman, The White Dawn, W.W. and the Dixie Dancekings, Hooper, Coal Miner's Daughter, Everybody's All American.*

RING LARDNER, JR.: *Woman of the Year, M*A*S*H, The Cross of Lorraine, Tomorrow the World, Forever Amber, Forbidden Street, Four Days Leave, Cloak and Dagger, Cincinnati Kid, The Greatest.*

INTRODUCTION

—by Frank Daniel

*H*ave you ever been able to understand the theory of relativity? If so, then congratulations. I am one of the mortals who constantly encounters mysterious puzzles and keeps asking, How can one calculate the speed and trajectory that a missile must follow through boundless space to find its way to our little moon? I have a problem balancing my checkbook. Another puzzle is: How come, when you push a little button, some electrons start streaming in lines on your TV in such an orderly manner that you can see something that is happening at this very minute god knows where?

I admit that these (and many other things) are for me still veiled in the mystique of a miracle, although I realize grudgingly that there are people who not only understand it all, but keep adding further miracles every day. Gene splicing, black holes, there's even a bus schedule for New York City!

I know that behind all these things there are people. And for them these miracles are the nuts to crack; they think of them day and night, struggle with them, sleep on them, and finally find solutions, using a heap of accumulated knowledge and a fair amount of their own inventiveness.

I can imagine what an electronics engineer has to master before he is able to add some little improvement to the construction of a TV set. And it is possible to realize that there once was a moment when he decided to enter this field and started learning all that he had to know. He was lucky to select a sphere in which the scope of necessary expertise is generally clear, so that to reach his goal was only a question of his motivation and persistence.

But there are people in this world who—for reasons that only they can tell—set for themselves an entirely different aim. They become obsessed with a desire to sit down and start writing or printing words in order to recount "discoveries." A man affected by this obsession sees these as equal to the discoveries mentioned above, or at least on a level with a New York

City bus schedule, discoveries that members of an audience would be able to follow in their life journeys. They want to write stories.

Nowadays, many of the people thus afflicted are driven to write stories for the screen. They usually possess the derring-do of a Columbus, but very often keep rediscovering America. And as we now all know, Columbus didn't even do that.

"It is a strange thing," Turgenev once said with a sigh. "A composer studies harmony and theory of musical forms; a painter doesn't paint a picture without knowing something about colors and design; architecture requires basic schooling. Only when somebody makes a decision to start writing, he believes that he doesn't need to learn anything and that anybody who has learned to put words on paper can be a writer."

There is so much for any writer to know and learn continuously that one book couldn't cover even the basics. There isn't an area of life, a branch of human knowledge, that couldn't become the object of the writer's interest. But there is one skill that needs to be acquired foremost: the ability to express and shape one's visions. For a screenwriter this skill is a complex one. It means an ability to express and build scenes, sequences, and the whole story in the most effective way that the screen demands.

When people want to know what screenwriting is all about, I have a stock answer: It's simple—it's telling exciting stories about exciting people in an exciting form. That's all there is to it. The only problem is knowing how to make stories and people exciting and how to master all the intricacies of the form—because screenwriting is filmmaking on paper.

There is a nice apocryphal story about an enterprising young man who was made president of a brand-new Hollywood film company. He wanted to convince his investors that the only foolproof and unique way to succeed was to concentrate the company's efforts on stories. He hired a research company to answer the question, What does the public go to see in the movie theater—the story, the stars, the production values, or the special effects, sex, and violence? The research specialists got the message and a few weeks later, and only a little over their already hefty budget, produced a report all wonderfully laid out and nicely bound, full of graphics and tables, with statistics that proved beyond any doubt that it was the story the viewer came seeking in the darkness of the movie house. (As we all know, statistics can prove anything, sometimes even the truth.)

When the company folded, the unsuccessful president wondered what went wrong. And because he never asked the right people, he never found out that viewers go to movies not just to see stories, but to see *stories well told.* The screenwriter's job is called story-*telling*, not story-*making*. Every story can be botched, as we have all seen.

In the area of cinema, "well told" means not only a well-narrated, skillfully structured and plotted tale. The story has to be displayed in rich scenes that use well-conceived (and well-performed) character parts and that inspire the designer, the cinematographer, the composer, the editor, and all the collaborators who add their talents to the final form in which the screenwriter's imagery and words appear in front of the audience.

There are many books on screenwriting. Naturally, as everyone knows, none of them will give someone the things that he has to bring: talent and a zest to tell stories. No book and no school can give you the things that are needed unconditionally: a fresh and never-ending supply of vivid facts of life, observations, impressions, memories of events, and knowledge of people—their life stories, attitudes, whims, quirks, strange tastes, superstitions, ideals, beliefs, dreams—in short, the stuff from which a writer has to, and feels compelled to, write stories.

The poor individual who is under the spell of this desire to write for the screen needs a lot of things besides talent. Fortunately, these are things he or she can learn. He can develop and strengthen his insight and his capacity to conceive and express characters and to create parts that wil. whet the appetite of actors and actresses; he can train his eye to keep discovering graphic and impressive locations; and—most important of all—he can learn from masters of the past, and sometimes even of the present, how to lay out scenes so that they arouse, keep, and intensify audience interest, empathy, involvement, and full participation. We have seen these things happening in our teaching programs.

What the would-be screenwriter needs most is an unbiased, nondogmatic introduction to dramatic structural principles and an understanding of the different narrative techniques and storytelling devices that cinema has learned to use. David Howard has wisely outlined this area for himself and has covered it in a concise, readable, knowledgeable, and intelligible manner. He has also been very generous with his pointers, advice, and admonitions about screenwriting and storytelling.

The worst thing a book on screenwriting can do is to instill in the mind of the beginning writer a set of rules, regulations, formulas, prescriptions, and recipes. Actually, it is even worse when these rules, regulations, prescriptions, and recipes are appropriated by those who don't have any intention of writing, but who are in charge of the development of "properties" (a very special and quite revealing Hollywood term).

In the hands of executives, agents, script readers, and script doctors, these precepts can become cudgels used against those who have the audacity to write something in which a required or expected plot point or turning point doesn't occur on page such-and-such, or where the protagonist, antagonist, or even the whole third act doesn't behave according to the canonized commandments. (This failure to follow "the rules" becomes a sacrilege when the script works anyway.)

In classes and workshops in this country and abroad, at the Sundance Institute and in my work with Hollywood professionals, I have encountered all sorts of skepticism, suspicions, and superstitions. European filmmakers only recently began to admit—reluctantly and with constant apprehension, I must say—that the total abandonment of the screenwriting métier in the past thirty years of unrestricted rule by the director-as-auteur theory has led to an unhappy result. National filmmakers have lost their own audiences, although sporadically some of their films have been able to impress selected festival juries in other countries and have had limited exposure in art theaters.

This loss of audience is why there is such an enormous renewed interest in the theory and practice of writing scripts, and it is why even the term *dramaturgy* has been resurrected. The various national cinemas want to regain their viewers.

It has been said that dilettantes mistrust theoretical knowledge and are afraid that if they understood why and how certain principles work, they would lose their creative freedom if not their creativity.

On the other hand, hacks believe in recipes and stick to them anxiously and injudiciously. They don't know, however, why and how the recipes occasionally work, but they are afraid that without them they would be lost totally.

Professionals, true masters, search for principles. Principles are based on the nature of stories in general and upon the specificity of the medium itself.

David Howard doesn't preach any dogma, but he knows from his own experience, as well as from the lessons his students have learned, that to understand the principles helps, that ignorance is not the best advisor, and that applying the principles actually liberates and broadens creativity and enlarges the available choices. Amanda Silver, who was David's student and wrote *The Hand that Rocks the Cradle* as her thesis script in the Graduate Screenwriting Program, would surely confirm the value of these lessons to her schoolmates.

I once had a student who came to me as a devoted believer in the "method of the premise." According to this precept, a story should prove a premise, a statement, a "truth," a message; the writer should formulate his premise lucidly and rationally before he starts writing. This is supposed to make the writing easier and more organized, but it has unwanted consequences.

This student of mine brought with her a script that she had written according to the dictates of this creed. The result was to be expected: a clean and clear example of a formula story, totally predictable, necessarily boring and two-dimensional, with characters who served the purpose of proving the thesis-premise and did everything to show that it was "true."

She was devastated when she was told why all this had happened. And she grew even more frightened when she was told that she would have to learn to give her characters full freedom so that they would be able to do what *they* wanted and needed instead of being forced by her to perform what the premise required. She had to learn that characters are never our puppets. They have to live their own lives.

"But then . . . " she said, her eyes resembling two black holes, "then it won't be my story!" It took her a long time to understand that *only* then would she be writing truly her story, that it wouldn't be controlled by her rational brain, but would involve the whole of herself, with all her emotional, subconscious, spontaneous, and intuitional insights. It takes courage and it isn't easy. Writing this way is a bit frightening for some people, but it is the only way to write stories that are effective and "organically grown instead of artificially inseminated," to use the contemporary vocabulary. This is the only road to stories that aren't just chewing gum for human minds, but ones that bring some real nutrition to the viewer's imagination and intellect.

The book you are going to study makes this adventure of exploration quite appealing and—apparently owing to David Howard's gentle nature— it doesn't make it look very threatening. My hope is that it will encourage aspiring screenwriters to exert more of their own efforts to learn directly from those who know, or knew, the principles and "secrets" of our art and craft.

With the availability of films on tape and laser disc (as well as scripts to read), there are no obstacles to the enjoyment of these exploratory voyages of discovery.

My other hope is that the reader will take in all the rational and reasonable body of knowledge this book offers, that he or she will digest it and use it in the manner recommended by Lope de Vega, that "wonder of nature," the most prolific playwright of all time, who wrote more than fifteen hundred plays. In his comprehensive study of dramatic theory and practice, *Writing Plays in Our Time* (published in 1609 and written in verse), he stated openly and bravely, after having introduced all the "rules": "When I have to write a play, I lock up the rules with six keys."

ABOUT SCREENWRITING

■

Writing is creating something
out of nothing.

—ROBERT TOWNE

The writer's responsibility, the filmmaker's
responsibility, is to deliver as best he can, the
intention he has.

—BILL WITTLIFF

THE SCREENWRITER'S TASK

I just happen to be one of those irrational persons who think that a film cannot be any good if it isn't well written.
—ERNEST LEHMAN

It's easy to patronize screenwriting, but it's not easy to do. That's proven all the time by all the bad screenplays you see.
—TOM RICKMAN

A movie, I think, is really only four or five moments between two people; the rest of it exists to give those moments their impact and resonance. The script exists for that. Everything does.
—ROBERT TOWNE

The screenplay is certainly one of the most difficult and misunderstood forms of writing in all literature. The film that results from a screenwriter's labors is much more immediate and visceral than prose fiction, yet the process of transforming the writer's words, ideas, and desires into that final product is less direct and involves many more intermediaries between writer and audience than do other forms of literature. As a result, the screenwriter finds his or her path strewn with pitfalls and problems that don't arise in the creation of an essay, a novel, or a poem.

The screenwriter must communicate with a director, actors, costumers, a cinematographer, sound designers, production designers, editors, and a whole host of other filmmaking professionals. At the same time, the screenwriter must be especially aware of audience psychology and the conventions of screen storytelling. And, finally, the screenwriter needs to be attuned to the wants, passions, and limitations of all the characters in the story. These sometimes conflicting demands on the screenwriter are so great that they make the creation of a first-rate screenplay quite rare indeed.

However, the screenwriter has a wealth of dramatic history from which to learn. Screenwriting is the direct outgrowth of playwriting, adapting many of the same tools and conventions of the theater to a newer technology, a new way of delivering the story to the audience. If we examine successful plays (that is, plays that have held the interest of large audiences over a period of time) and compare them with successful films, we find that they seem to share certain features. The technique employed to hold audience interest is strikingly similar in a comedy by Plautus and one by Neil Simon, a Greek tragedy and *The Godfather*, a Shakespearean play and *One Flew Over the Cuckoo's Nest*. In other words, there is a technique of focusing audience interest that can be observed, and it can be learned. (Mastery of the technique will not automatically assure the creation of a viable play or screenplay, but the lack of a deliberate or instinctive technique will almost certainly ensure failure.)

The screenwriter's task is far more than the setting down of dialogue. Indeed, this part of the task may turn out to be the smallest problem. The concept every screenwriter must address is the fundamental vision of a sequence of events, which includes not only the dialogue spoken by the actors, but also their physical activity, their surroundings, the entire context in which the story takes place, the lighting, the music and sounds, the costumes, the whole pace and rhythm of the storytelling. Yet still the screenwriter's job is not done, for, in addition to all these considerations, the script must provide enough clarity that it enables the director, the cinematographer, the sound designer, and all the other film professionals to create a film that resembles the original intentions of the screenwriter.

Although others will eventually interpret the writer's words and story, the original vision of a film is first the exclusive domain of the screenwriter. The writer is the very first to "see" the film, though it is solely in the mind and on the page. The screenwriter must have conscious intentions for what the audience will see and hear and, most important, experience when the script is cast and produced. Without this clarity in the mind of the screen-writer, there is little hope that the script, or a film made from it, will have any of the impact intended by the author.

We can be sure that the author of every great screenplay imagined the activity of the actors as well as their dialogue, envisioning where, as well as when, they would be making their entrances and exists, what the effect of settings, costume, and music would be, the subtle changes of rhythm and pace that would be most effective. This is not to suggest that the screenwriter has to be a sound engineer, cinematographer, set designer, or electrician any more than a director or leading actor; but a screenwriter must know how the various arts of cinema can be utilized to give the impression of reality on film to what was originally born in his head. This vision is contained in the screenplay, a sort of blueprint for an extremely complex art form, an art form recorded in two dimensions that depicts three dimensions, an art form that has the additional dimension of time, which also enters into the arts of music, poetry, and dance.

The screenwriter can hardly anticipate a total fulfillment of this vision, any more than a playwright can. Shakespeare was well acquainted with actors' failings, as is apparent in Hamlet's advice to the players, and his awareness of the limited resources of his playhouse led him to call it an "unworthy scaffold." Still, his plays have endured, and all the elements of dramatic storytelling he employed are just as effective today as they were when his works were first performed. Shakespeare's dialogue, magnificent as it is, was only one element among many in his approach to his story.

Circumstances are much the same with the screenwriter who must relinquish a tenderly nursed and fussed-over vision, his or her "baby," for others to interpret, stage, create, and display to the final audience. With all the steps between a completed screenplay and the first showing of a finished film made from that work, it's amazing that any of the screenwriter's original vision makes it to the screen intact. Yet it does, precisely because the accomplished screenwriter has envisioned the entirety of the production, has communicated with all the collaborators in the process, and, most important of all, has remained attuned to what should be communicated to the audience and when it should be revealed for maximum impact and effectiveness.

What follows are discussions of dramatic construction and the tools of storytelling. Many of them are as ancient as the theater; a few are as new as the technology of filmmaking. In the end, screenwriting comes down to making meticulous plans for a physical representation of a story on real or realistic locations (for the story), and in four dimensions—it is the dimension of time that makes pace and rhythm possible as part of the pattern of telling a story for maximum impact.

STAGE VERSUS SCREEN

A play is manifestly different from a screenplay. You've got a stage, a proscenium; you've got an audience sitting there that knows it's in a theater. They are willing to accept all kinds of conventions that go with the theater. It's a different discipline, almost a different genre. Film is much more permissive—and in that sense, a much more difficult—medium.

—PADDY CHAYEFSKY

There isn't that much difference in the creative process *of writing the two forms of drama, except that one of them is to be put on the screen.*

—ERNEST LEHMAN

*A*lthough the dramaturgy of screenwriting (which is the craft and practice of writing dramatic narrative material for film and television) owes a great deal to the history and development of the theater, the two art forms differ. The problem of describing the ways in which film and theater diverge is a lot like trying to define the difference between a dog and a cat; both are mammals that walk on all fours, have tails, fur, ears that stick up, and snouts. Yet even the quickest glance can determine the difference between them. Once well acquainted with both dramatic forms, most people can usually tell the difference between a work that is cinematic and one that is theatrical.

The most obvious difference is on the page, the format of how the words of the author are laid out. While this is the least important of the differences, it does illustrate the most important distinction. In a play, the bulk of what is on the page is the characters' dialogue; in a screenplay the balance shifts toward scene description, the actions of the characters, and the visuals the audience sees. At the risk of oversimplifying two complex entities to make a point, it can be said that a play depends upon the words of the characters to carry the weight of the storytelling, while a screenplay (and the film made from it) depends on the actions of the characters. That said, it must be emphasized that the actions of the characters in plays are still more crucial to the audience's experience of the work than the dialogue. But consider the strengths and the shortcomings of both live theater and film.

In the theater, the audience watches real, living, breathing human beings interact. In a film there is only the recorded image of the people, the actors. Clearly the former has a much greater possibility for a connection between performer and audience than the latter. An accomplished actor on stage can create an electrifying empathy with the audience that is impossible in film. In other words, the actor on stage can make his or her emotions palpable to the audience in a way the actors on screen cannot. Theater's strength is cinema's weakness.

Yet there is a price for this immediacy, this intimacy between performer and audience. In a play, the storyteller has much less latitude in urging the audience to watch any specific action or reaction, or to register any small bit of information. There are ways of focusing audience attention in the theater, but none is so powerful as the frame of film, which does not allow the audience a choice in looking elsewhere. And in a play, it is much more difficult to change locations and move about through time. Both of course are possible, but can't be done with anything approaching the facility of film, which can jump across town, across the country, or around the world, and get back before any sets have been changed in a play. For major periods of stage time, most plays are locked in one location, in one specific time. Once the screenwriter and the filmmaker have liberated the camera, it can go anywhere; the film story can skip time or go backward and forward in time and come back again in less screen time than the play has spent in one location and time.

So the theater has the advantage of immediacy, of rapport between actors and audience, but the limitations of more cumbersome changes in time and place. Film has incredible latitude in time and place, but suffers from a lack of contact between the actors and the audience. This is not to say that screen acting is a lesser art form than stage acting, just a different one, one with the added obstacle of distance between performer and audience. A great deal of this distance can be made up by the camera, which can bring the audience much closer to a film actor than a seated audience can get to a stage actor. Because the camera magnifies every little gesture and expression, what is a perfectly realistic reaction on stage becomes "too big" on screen. Yet even with the camera's ability to take the audience "inside" a character by participating in the performance, it still cannot bridge the gap between live performance and recorded performance.

The accomplished screenwriter will write for the strengths of film and around its limitations, and the accomplished playwright will do the same in writing for the stage. In the end, this translates into differences in how plays and screenplays distribute the load of telling the story and involving the audience. The playwright can allow the actor long speeches and plenty of time to "strut his stuff," to involve the audience in the performance, while the screenwriter should give the actors more actions that help reveal character, wants, desires, and the whole range of emotion the performance needs to evoke. At the same time, the screenwriter should also write for the strengths of cinema, using its ability to force the audience to see only what the storyteller chooses and its ability to change time and place with ease. While nearly anything that is possible on stage is possible on screen, and even though both film and theater have all the same attributes (but in different proportions), they are, to their core, different animals, just as certainly as cats and dogs share a great many similarities but are not in the least interchangeable.

ADAPTATION

Very often you find that first-rate books don't make first-rate movies. It's often a mistake to try to preserve the literary quality of it.

—WALTER BERNSTEIN

Movies do some things wonderfully well that novels don't do. There's a marvelous narrative thing that movies have; they do size and scope. They are entirely different forms. The only similarity is that very often they both use dialogue. Otherwise the way that one handles a scene in a movie and the way one handles a scene in a book have nothing to do with each other.

—WILLIAM GOLDMAN

*S*tories for film can be adapted from a variety of sources. Plays, novels, short stories, real-life experiences, even poetry and songs have been adapted to the screen. At first glance, this looks like an easier task than developing a whole new story from scratch. Yet adapting a story from another source usually requires greater skill and understanding of the film medium than does creating a new story. Very few stories created for another medium, or stories that have actually been lived through, lend themselves easily and immediately to the needs of a screenplay. We've all heard the term "dramatic license," which comes from the need to alter, simplify, compress, or eliminate material to make the drama work. And we have all had the experience of seeing a film about a real-life event we remember and thinking, "But it wasn't like that."

These discrepancies don't necessarily stem from incompetence on the part of the screenwriter; it could be that license was the only way to solve the dramatic problems. Real people's lives rarely fall into a three-act structure. Novels usually have too much material or are not terribly visual or are decidedly too internal. Plays have been written for the limitations of the stage and must be made more cinematic by the addition of the camera as narrator, expanding beyond the few sets of the play and by dramatizing actions only alluded to in the play. Short stories often don't have a complete first act and sometimes have too little material or, again, are too internal or not very visual. Poems and songs are typically too schematic, too sketchy to be much more than a starting point for a screenwriter.

The moment a writer begins adapting a story from another source, the question comes up: How faithful to that source *must* one and *can* one be? Sometimes the most faithful adaptations make the worst films, because the material wasn't designed for a film story and, as written, doesn't work on screen, however powerful the story is in its original form. Drama in general and certainly in the cinema demands compression, intensification. There is an old saying, "Fiction is gossip, drama is scandal." The two are the same thing except that scandal is more intense and spreads like wildfire, while gossip can meander about and go on much longer. Events that take place in a novel or in real life over months, or even years, will often play much better in a film if they all happen in the same day. But when one is confronted with a story in print or the actual facts of exactly how something happened, there is a natural inclination to go with the facts or the printed page—at the price of the drama. Someone writing an adaptation must constantly weigh these two sides against each other: fidelity to the original source, and the demands of drama for intensity and compression. These are inherently difficult issues.

To the novice screenwriter, then, adaptation from another source is more likely to be a stumbling block than a crutch. Yet adaptation can be a refreshing challenge to an accomplished screenwriter, who will know what to look for, when sections of material can be kept, and when, why, and how others must be altered to make the drama work on screen. The experienced adaptor looks below the surface of the events for the drama that lies underneath, finds ways of bringing disparate elements together to fit thematically and dramatically with the rest of the story, and, at the same time, tries to remain true to the spirit of the original story.

Another major difficulty to overcome in adaptation is translating the voice of the narrator. There is no exact film equivalent of the narrator of a book, whether it's written in the first or third person, and yet in some of the best fiction, the direct one-on-one communication between the author and the reader is the most interesting aspect of the work. The book author can make digressions into philosophy, psychology, personal and regional history, wordplay, and the wizardry of language that can't be brought to the screen in the same way. These aspects of the voice of the author can foil even the most accomplished screenwriter attempting an adaptation, for the very reason they can beguile the reader: the author is provoking the reader's imagination in a way that a film cannot. What is shown on screen is "real" to the audience; the actors *are* their characters, the places and events seem as real as the filmmakers can make them. A reader conjures up images of the people, places, and events in his mind, and delights in the asides and musings of the author. This imaginative conjuring and the leisurely wandering of the reader through the mind of the storyteller are not possible in film, which necessarily has to make visible manifestations in place of the imaginings of the reader.

The beginning screenwriter would be better advised to gain some command over the tools of the craft while pursuing a story that can readily be changed, developed, and emphasized for greatest dramatic impact. Once a screenwriter develops a degree of finesse with the tools discussed at length in this work, an adaptation becomes a worthwhile effort.

THE AUTEUR OF A FILM

Everybody *gets together and* everybody *makes a picture.*

—WILLIAM GOLDMAN

I say this as a writer: there is no more important person on a set than a director. But even then a movie is always collaborative. I believe the auteur *theory is merely one way it is easier for historians to assign credit or blame to individuals. It's a simplistic way of interpreting facts, and it often has very little to do with what actually happened.*

—ROBERT TOWNE

Film is essentially a collaboration.

—BILL WITTLIFF

*W*ho is the real author of a film? Film theorists and film viewers love to wrestle with this question. The popular conception, originated by François Truffaut writing as a film critic in *Cahiers du Cinéma* and first promoted in this country by Andrew Sarris, holds that the director and the director alone is the author of the film, the *auteur.* In the history of film, there have been a number of filmmakers who seem like true *auteurs*—filmmakers whose work shows a consistency of expression and seems to demonstrate primarily the artistry and convictions of one person. Most of these *auteurs* have been directors: D. W. Griffith, Billy Wilder, Alfred Hitchcock, Ingmar Bergman, François Truffaut, and Woody Allen, among others. But it should be noted that Bergman, Wilder, Truffaut, and Allen also have written or co-written most of their scripts, and that Hitchcock worked in very close collaboration with his screenwriters, though he did not take writing credit for his contributions.

Writer-directors or directors who collaborate in considerable depth with their writers only account for a portion of the films created every year. Who is the author of all these other films? The entire team of filmmakers is the *auteur*—the writer and director, but also the producer, the cinematographer, the production designer, and the actors. The director is obviously an important player on the team, but without a script, without actors, without camera, sound, sets, costumes—the whole production—the director is helpless. Close inspection shows the contributions of collaborating writers, the same cinematographer and composer and designer in film after film— even in the films of the great writer-directors listed above. Where does the work of all the others end and the work of the director begin? While the director is undeniably the leader of the team once the game begins, there is no game without the writer, and the director cannot hope to accomplish much without the other team members.

In other words, the question of authorship becomes a moot point. The interdependencies of the family of filmmakers who produce, shoot, and edit a film are much too strong for any one contributor to be the sole author of the work. At the same time, some films have a clear-cut stamp of personality; often this is contributed by the director, but sometimes by the writer, by the cinematographer, or, more often than a lot of auteur theorists care to admit, by the star whose brand is all over the film, no matter who wrote or directed. From the films of Mae West to the *Thin Man* series to James Bond films to Clint Eastwood westerns, many films take their most distinctive quality from the stars in front of the camera. But for most films, the auteur is the team, not any single individual. And the variety, depth, and vividness of any given film is stronger for the efforts of this small group, each adding his or her individual expertise to the enterprise.

THE SCREENWRITER'S RELATIONSHIPS

Basically there are seven people who are essential to a film, and if the film's going to be really any good, all seven have to be at their best. In no particular order, they are the director, the producer, the players, the cinematographer, the production designer, the editor and certainly the writer. Sometimes the composer is essential, absolutely essential.

—WILLIAM GOLDMAN

If everybody does what they do well, then there's a sense in which all the skills tend to merge. You call the writer the writer, the actor the actor, the director the director. But they are really working together in a way that melds their respective jobs.

—ROBERT TOWNE

*T*here is a terrible tendency among film viewers, some critics, and more than a few people in the film industry to think of filmmakers and screenwriters as two separate groups, as if screenwriting were not filmmaking. This fallacy is also perpetuated by a large number of people writing screenplays, who believe they don't need to know anything about filmmaking in order to write a good script. Playwrights, novelists, journalists, actors, waiters, and housewives have all become accomplished screenwriters, but that doesn't mean those occupations have provided training for their screenwriting. Whether a writer went to film school or got hired to write because of some outside work (like novel writing or acting), he or she had to learn what filmmaking was all about. A writer who fails to grasp how films are made, what the needs, limits, and strengths of the film medium are, who the other professionals are, and how to communicate with them, cannot become accomplished at the craft of screenwriting.

One doesn't have to know how to play the oboe to write a symphony, but a classical composer had better know the strengths and limitations of the oboe—as well as of the bassoon, the cello, the violin, and all the other instruments that make up the orchestra. An architect need not know how to build a form for a cement foundation or how to frame a pitched roof, but necessary knowledge for an architect includes knowing what is structurally possible and impossible, plus what the requirements, uses, and pitfalls of various construction techniques are. The same is true of the accomplished screenwriter, who must communicate with producer, director, actors, designers, composer, cinematographer, production manager, sound recordist, editor, mixer, and many more. To become effective at screenwriting, a writer must know not only how to tell a story well, but how to communicate it to a whole host of professionals, each of whom does part of the job of creating the finished film.

Because filmmaking is a group activity, relationships are crucial to effective work. The screenwriter's three most important relationships are with the producer, the director, and the actors. The many other film arts and crafts use the script as a reference and starting point for their work, but these three relationships require a greater degree of understanding by the writer.

The producer of a film asks a great number of questions: Who would want to see this film? How similar is it to other films in current or recent release? Who would want to play the lead and other critical roles? How much would it cost to make this picture? There are many more questions, but these few give an idea of what is going on in the back of a producer's mind when reading a script. It is a bad idea for a screenwriter to propose answers to any of these questions, such as suggesting specific actors or actresses, but it is a very good idea to keep in mind that a producer will be subjecting your work to this kind of questioning. You cannot and should not attempt to second-guess what will be a hit next year (or, more realistically, two years from the writing stage). Instead, write a story that compels you, that you would like to see as a film, and trust that your sensibility will find an audience.

The relationship between the writer and director is so strong that a great many people attempt to do both jobs—and some succeed. These are the only two people involved in a film production who look at the film in nearly the same way; that is, the writer and director look at the totality of the story, how it is told to the audience, how they hope the audience will experience it and react to it. While the producer looks at the whole picture and is concerned with the story and storytelling from early on through release and distribution, the producer's vision must be occupied partly by the practical considerations of getting the film made—budget, scheduling, locations, and all the rest. But the writer and director are potentially each other's greatest allies because these two jobs involve the whole weave and texture of the story, its fabric. If they are both making the same picture— if they both see the same film in their mind's eyes—it can be a wonderfully enriching collaboration. This is why the writer and the director should work together in preproduction, fine-tuning the script until they both are seeing the same story in the same way.

The writer's relationship with the actors is much closer than many people suspect—not necessarily in working closely together, but in similar approaches to the material and work essentials. A great deal of the process of screenwriting begins with character exploration: discovering/inventing who the characters are, what they want, what they hope for, what they fear, what makes them tick. This same process is done by the actors as well, delving into the inner workings of the characters well beyond what will be manifested on screen. The two approaches diverge because a screenwriter must go through this process for every important character, whereas the actor has to do it for only one character. In the end this means that the actor can achieve a lot more depth, can take the character closer to heart than the screenwriter, whose attention and energies are necessarily divided. Because of this, eventually the character "belongs" to the actor even more than it does to the writer; the actor has an even greater depth of understanding of the character. Feedback from actors who have taken their characters to heart can be invaluable to the writer in fine-tuning and polishing the screenplay prior to production. Unfortunately this luxury is not always possible, but it should nonetheless be a goal, because it can help the finished film immensely.

A CAUTIONARY NOTE

One of the great difficulties in film and screenwriting analysis is the confusion of its vocabulary. When a doctor uses the word *appendicitis,* or a lawyer *subpoena,* or an architect *fenestration,* others in the same profession know exactly what is being talked about. When a teacher or screenwriter or producer uses the following words (all of them taken from chapter headings in books on playwriting and screenwriting)—*continuity, progression, premise, theme, forestalling, finger-posts, preparation, anticlimax, complication, scene, catastrophe, resolution, representation, crisis, antagonist, impressionism, adjustment, peripety, irony, attack, focus, suspense, action, recognition, balance, movement, orchestration, unity of opposites, static, jumping, transition, incident*—meanings can become confused, for most of the terms have no precise definitions in the context of the subject matter. They are used to mean different things by different writers. Reading half a dozen books on screenwriting in succession is apt to leave one quite bewildered, unless one ignores the terminology and thinks in terms of concepts.

Anyone venturing another book on the subject must also choose his own vocabulary, and indicate what every imprecise term means to him or her. The reader, to avoid confusion, had best ignore for the moment what others have meant by *premise* and *crisis* and *unity* and so on, and concentrate on the meaning in the context of the work in hand. Unfortunately, there seems to be no other way around this difficulty.

BASIC
STORYTELLING

■

A story starts with a character.

—FRANK DANIEL

WHAT MAKES "A GOOD STORY WELL TOLD"

You just never know. But the audience always does. You can be so damned sure that your film is going to be a smash hit, it's that good in the projection room. And then suddenly the audience tells you what you never knew.

—ERNEST LEHMAN

The biggest sin in movies is being boring.

—FRANK DANIEL

The first thing is content. What does the filmmaker have to say that can mean something that I have not heard before?

—BILL WITTLIFF

*T*here is always room for another really good story. But what is a really good story or, more precisely, "a good story well told"? "A sympathetic hero up against seemingly insurmountable odds who somehow manages to prevail" accounts for a lot of very good stories—from *Shane* to *North by Northwest* to *One Flew Over the Cuckoo's Nest* to *Star Wars*. But there is another whole category of equally successful and riveting films that do not have an inherently sympathetic central character, yet manage to engage an audience—from *The Sweet Smell of Success* to *Amadeus* to *The Godfather*. In each of these, we still manage to care about a character who is far from admirable, far from enviable, yet with whom we still manage to share some small amount of empathy. We see the human heart suffering inside the character whose actions, desires, and possibly whose whole life we find distasteful. A great many good stories revolve around characters who are somewhere in between—not overtly sympathetic, because of some of their thoughts or actions, yet characters we still find compelling. *Casablanca, Five Easy Pieces, The Searchers,* and *Body Heat* all fall into this category.

So our empathy—and its outgrowth, sympathy—need not be absolute with a character; but there must be some amount of empathy, however small. In addition, the character must be attempting to do something; attempting *not* to do something or attempting to stop something from happening are still doing something. Trying to save a life, win a race, avoid being drafted, keep from being touched, or paint a picture are all "wants" that could work for the right character. But there must be obstacles to keep the character from achieving easily whatever he or she wants. If it is easy to save the life, win the race, or paint the picture, then the audience says, "So what?" Audience disinterest is the result of a lack of difficulty to the circumstance.

> *The audience empathize with a character not because they are in pain or oppressed, but because of what they are doing about it.*
>
> —WALTER BERNSTEIN

In 1895, Georges Polti published *Les Trente-six Situations Dramatique* in France. In his work, he sought to identify the thirty-six basic dramatic situations that are possible to tell. Basic and helpful though this identification may be, Polti's work still did not reveal the common thread that *all* stories share. It was Frank Daniel who first formulated a deceptively simple delineation of the basic dramatic circumstance: *Somebody wants something badly and is having difficulty getting it.* If the audience has some empathy with the "somebody," and that character wants urgently to do something, and that something is very difficult to do or get, then we are well on the way to a good story. If the character barely cares whether he or she achieves the goal, or if the achievement is too easy or completely impossible, there is no drama. Thus a good story could be said to be about a character with whom the audience has some measure of empathy, who strongly wants something that is very difficult, yet possible, to achieve.

"A good story well told" includes one more crucial element: the way in which the audience experiences the story. What the audience knows, when they know it, what they know that one or more characters don't know, what they hope for, what they fear, what they can anticipate, what surprises them—all of these are elements in the telling of a story. The management of these and other parts of an audience's involvement in the story is the greatest achievement of the screenwriter. Without these elements, a good story becomes just so many events in a sequence, not an experience the audience craves.

The beginning writer tends to feel that writing with the audience in mind is an evil to be avoided at all costs. But this mistakes writing with the audience in mind for pandering to the audience. Pandering should be avoided; just delivering up, without thought or genuine emotion, so much predigested emotional glop for an audience to consume is a waste of everyone's time and energy. But it is no more sensible, or even possible, to write effective drama without the audience's experience of it in mind than it would be to design clothes without the wearer in mind. Three arm holes, no legs, or a seven-inch waist would be the result; the same would happen in drama—a story no one would want to experience.

The difference between writing with the audience in mind and pandering comes down to who is in control. If the writer panders to the audience, what determines the action is the writer's guess at what the audience wants *a priori* of the story at hand. The control is squarely in the hands of the audience. The writer who writes with the audience in mind, and succeeds in making it care about the characters, circumstances, and events of the story through skillful management of its perceptions of them, is in control; this writer offers an experience and essentially seduces the audience into joining in on it. The storyteller is in control.

The two principal concerns of this book are how to develop a good story and how to tell it well. The two are so intertwined that it would not be possible to deal with them separately. As Frank Daniel says in the introduction to this book, "It's simple—it's telling exciting stories about exciting people in an exciting form." The essential elements of "a good story well told" are:

1. The story is about *somebody* with whom we have some empathy.
2. This somebody wants *something* very badly.
3. This something is *difficult*, but possible to do, get, or achieve.
4. The story is told for maximum *emotional impact* and *audience participation* in the proceedings.
5. The story must come to a *satisfactory ending* (which does not necessarily mean a happy ending).

"A good story well told" is simple, but it's not easy.

THE DIVISION INTO
THREE ACTS

In the first act, it's who are the people and what is the situation of this whole story. The second act is the progression of that situation to a high point of conflict and great problems. And the third act is how the conflicts and problems are resolved.

—ERNEST LEHMAN

*S*ome writers work with a division into five acts, television movies often employ a seven act division, but in this work we deal with dividing the material of a story into three acts. In reality, the only difference in the number of acts results from how the writer organizes his thoughts about the story, not in how the audience experiences it. Used properly and effectively, the three-, five-, or seven-act division would put the same story events and revelations in more or less the same places and sequence.

A great many teachers and authors talk about "the three act structure" rather than about a division into three acts, but the former phrasing gives rise to the implication that the telling of a story is like the building of a bridge, that once the design is complete, it remains unchanged forever. In reality, a story *evolves;* its "structure" changes as the story unfolds; it is constantly in flux. Moreover, there is no fixed structure that works for the telling of a story; each new story is its own prototype, each must be created anew. There is no recipe, there is no blank form that must only have the blanks filled in for a story to take shape. Good storytelling requires a great deal more invention than that.

The reason we employ a three act paradigm is that it is the simplest to understand and it most closely adheres to the phases of an audience's experience of a story. The first act gets the audience involved with the characters and the story. The second act keeps it involved and heightens its emotional commitment to the story. The third act wraps up the story and brings the audience's involvement to a satisfactory end. In other words, a story has a beginning, a middle, and an end.

There are no curtains in a film, no clear-cut changes of act, as there are in most plays. This enables a film story to be told as a continuum, on and on until the end, without stopping, without looking back. The ideal experience a film can give to an audience is that of a seamless dream, one continuously evolving and forward-moving story that engages the audience's mind and emotions, allowing it to "wake up" from the story only at the very end. Because of this attempt by the film storyteller to put the audience into a nearly dreamlike state—a state of being swept up in the story to the exclusion of all outside worries and thoughts—the screenwriter tries to mask the scene divisions, to smooth over the seams where the story is stitched and woven together.

So the division of a film into acts is not something that viewers are consciously aware of, though they feel the emotional shifts that come with pivotal changes in the story. The primary use of the three act division is to help the writer organize ideas about how to tell the story and to aid him in discovering the best places for major moments in the story to fall for maximum impact. Many of the essays in the "Screenwriting Tools" section deal in much more detail with the various components that help the writer achieve this goal of maximum impact.

The first act introduces the audience to the world of the story and its principal characters, and sets up the main conflict around which the story will be built. In most stories, there is a single central character whose life and predicament are focused on by the end of the first act—that is, the character's goal is established and some inkling of the obstacles is given. The second act elaborates in ever greater detail and intensity on those difficulties, the obstacles to the character achieving the goal. At the same time, this character changes and develops during the second act, or at least intense pressure is put on the character to change, and that change is manifested in the third act. Subplots in the story are developed largely in the second act. In the third act, the main story (the central character's story) and the subplots are all resolved in differing ways, but all with some sense of finality—the feeling that the conflict is over. (Even if we might see another storm brewing on the horizon, the conflicts of this story have been completed.)

It is a good idea to think of the three acts not as a mold or formula to be filled in with some kind of batter the writer has concocted, but rather as a set of landmarks an explorer/guide tries to keep sight of when traveling through new and dangerous territory. The travelers (the audience) who follow the guide (the writer) are only aware of the land around them, the potential dangers that may lie ahead of them, the hoped-for benefits, the scary sounds in the night. But the guide must keep track of those landmarks, occasionally losing sight, but then spotting one again and becoming oriented. The wise guide won't point out all the landmarks to the travelers, but will allow them to enjoy the journey as a continuum and to think of the guide as a mystical being with uncanny powers of navigation.

THE WORLD OF THE STORY

I try not to force the characters into some setting or event to accomodate what I want, but rather let them be real enough to dictate to me what setting they want to be in.

—BILL WITTLIFF

There should be some kind of interaction between the people and their milieu.

—WALTER BERNSTEIN

*T*he world of a story in any film is a unique creation, a variation—from very realistic to very fanciful—on the reality of our world, today or in another time period. With the exception of some sequels, two movies usually don't inhabit exactly the same world. Instead, most films take place in a specially designed universe with its own rules, limits, and things that are important. This is true even if at first glance two films appear to take place in exactly the same world. For instance, *The Champ* and *Rocky* are both about struggling prizefighters and the world of professional boxing. Both aspire to a sort of grittiness, but the former is more of a parable, an illustrated moral lesson, and the latter more of a fable, the creation of a legend.

One way to test the specificity of the worlds of individual films is by imagining a scene from one film within another. An extreme but illustrative comparison is between *Moonstruck* and *The Godfather*. Both stories are about several generations of Italian immigrant families in New York City. Yet any single moment from one film would stand out as glaringly inappropriate in the other. Two much more similar films have the same discrepancy. *Chinatown* and *Double Indemnity* both take place in Los Angeles in about the same time period, with hard-boiled characters and dialogue, and both have something of a cynical side. Yet with all these similarities, Jake Gittes no more fits into *Double Indemnity* than Walter Neff fits into *Chinatown;* it's as if they came from a different universe, which of course they do.

Specificity in the world of a story derives from two sources: the nature of the central character (in most films) and the nature of the storyteller. Much of what is important and unimportant in a story's world comes from who the central character is, the qualities of this person and his or her predicament. At the same time, what the storyteller has in mind, what the story is really about (at its core; see the chapter on "Theme") also has considerable influence over the world of the story. What is emphasized and deemphasized, what goals, fears, aspirations, circumstances, realities, and fantasies make up the people who inhabit the story, all come from within the storyteller. These personal (and sometimes unintentional) prejudices and the conscious choices of the storyteller make subtle changes in the proportions, shadings, and views of the world of the story as it is presented to the audience. Another way to look at this is to accept that the world a writer imagines is, to its very core, part of that writer's style.

PROTAGONIST, ANTAGONIST, AND CONFLICT

I never work out the plot apart from the characters. For me to proceed, I have to find who the story is about, the main character . . . When I'm writing something in which there is a villain, I try very hard to give the villain the full benefit of his or her position, to make them formidable and interesting to make the devil persuasive and attractive.

—WALTER BERNSTEIN

Most film stories are told around a single central character, the *protagonist* (see "Protagonist and Objective"). Even in those stories that have many characters or another structural form (see "Unity"), each individual subplot in the overall story has its own protagonist. In the basic dramatic circumstance of "somebody wants something badly and is having difficulty getting it," the "somebody" is the protagonist.

The *antagonist* of a story is the opposing force, the "difficulty" that actively resists the protagonist's efforts to achieve the goal. These two opposing forces form the conflict or conflicts of the story.

Many stories have an antagonist who is another person, the "bad guy." From *North by Northwest* to *Star Wars* to *Chinatown* to *Terminator*, very effective films have been made from stories in which the protagonist and antagonist are clearly and distinctly different people in active opposition to each other. In this sort of a story, the protagonist has what is called an external conflict, a conflict with someone else. But in a great many films the protagonist is his or her own antagonist as well; the central struggle is within the main character, two parts or desires or urges of the same person. Among the clearest cases of an internal conflict are *Hamlet* and *The Strange Case of Dr. Jekyll and Mr. Hyde*, but there are also many examples in film: *The Treasure of the Sierra Madre*, *Bonnie and Clyde*, *Vertigo*, and *Raging*

Bull. In these and many more films, the principal struggle of the story is going on inside the central character.

Even though there is an internal conflict in which protagonist and antagonist are the same person, there is usually outside opposition as well. And in most well-made stories of an external conflict, there is still an element of internal conflict within the main character. Most of the time it is a balance of these two things, but the overriding conflict of the story is either internal or external. In *Casablanca,* Rick's struggle is an internal conflict—to get involved or stay out of it—yet there is Colonel Strasser as a very real manifestation of the pressure on him to take a stand. In *The Sting,* the protagonist, Johnny Hooker, played by Robert Redford, wants to get revenge on the man who had his friend and mentor killed. That man is the antagonist and the conflict is an external one, yet there is still a struggle going on inside the Redford character: Is he up to the task of this revenge? Who can he trust? In *Jaws,* Sheriff Brody is the protagonist and the shark is the antagonist, making an external conflict, yet Brody has his own internal conflicts to overcome as well: his fear of water, his desire not to fight the shark, to get a bigger boat. In *Bonnie and Clyde,* the main conflict is within Clyde, with his own self-destructive impulses, yet there is the sheriff in hot pursuit of him and his gang as an external manifestation of his inner conflict.

An internal conflict in a story with an outside antagonist helps make the protagonist a more complex and interesting human being. An external source of conflict in a story where the main conflict is essentially internal helps make the two sides of the character visible, palpable; it gives them "lives of their own." In fact, this is the nub of the central question of screenwriting, how to show the audience what is going on inside the central—or any—character.

EXTERNALIZING THE INTERNAL

Not what's on the page, but what's on the screen is what counts, even for writers.

—TOM RICKMAN

You have to play the moment, write the moment as fully as you can. If it's done truthfully and honestly and the dramatic situation is a good one, it'll work.

—WALTER BERNSTEIN

*B*ecause there are usually both internal and external conflicts—in whatever proportion—in most films, the screenwriter is constantly confronted with the problem of how to show what is going on inside a character at any given time. Stories would become pretty shallow and boring if we didn't get a window into the inner lives of the characters— their joys, torments, secret desires and aspirations, hidden fears. Clearly this is much easier when there is a character in active opposition to the efforts of another character. Unfortunately, this opposition does not always exist. The beginning screenwriter usually rushes to dialogue to fill the gap, but this is not a very satisfactory solution. What we end up with is a whole host of characters who talk openly and honestly about their feelings; the only drama in the theater is in the audience stampeding for the exits.

It is far better to give the audience a peek at the inner life of a character through his or her actions. One of those actions is speaking, but dialogue can only carry a share of the load. If a character says "I'm very angry with you," it's rather weak and might even be untrue. If the character grabs the other character by the collar and slams him up against the wall, usually we can figure out what is going on inside the first character without the support of dialogue. Finding actions that reveal complex inner emotions is one of the most difficult tasks a screenwriter faces, but it is the difference between a story that works and one that talks about working. In *Annie Hall*, one of the happiest moments Alvy and Annie have is when they are trying to cook lobsters. After they have broken up, Alvy tries the same thing with another woman. This dramatizes what he misses, what he wishes to recapture. And when it goes poorly, it tells us a great deal about how he's doing. Dialogue, while present in both scenes, is really unnecessary for our understanding of the actions, the characters, and the outcome.

Even when dialogue is used, it doesn't always say exactly what it appears to say. If we see a character sneak up on another with a butcher knife hidden behind his back while he speaks of his undying love for the other person, which do we believe, the dialogue or the action? In fact it is the juxtaposition of dialogue and action, very often mismatched, that gives us our clearest picture of the inner world of a character. When a character lies to another character and we know the truth, we learn a second thing about the inner world of the lying character: the truth we already knew, plus how and to whom they lied. Often we are able to fathom why the character lied, which is like a snapshot of that character's motivations, a direct inroad to the internal life of the character.

This use of what appears to be going on between characters and what is really going on is called subtext. The clearest example of subtext occurs when a character lies about something while we know the truth, but subtext is much more complicated than just that. When Ilsa pulls a gun on Rick in *Casablanca*, trying to force him to give her the letters of transit, this act on the surface is one of hostility and aggression. Yet because we know her, because we know the circumstances and we see the way she makes her attempt, we are able to pick up what is going on under the surface: her love for Rick, her admiration/love for Victor, her desire to apologize for what happened in Paris.

By the careful revelation of tidbits of information to the audience, by showing us what various characters know that others do not, by urging us to see an action in a complex light and by making careful choices in how information is revealed on screen—both to the characters and to the audience—the skillful screenwriter can build a scene which is rich in subtext. This not only enriches the scene and reveals a great deal about the characters and how they play with their own knowledge, but it greatly increases the audience's enjoyment and participation in the story. The audience works to understand everything that is happening, and when it grasps the nature of the subtext, it feels like a real participant in the story and understands the inner lives of the characters much more completely.

OBJECTIVE AND
SUBJECTIVE DRAMA

*P*ut a baby just old enough to crawl alone at the top of a cliff and the circumstance is dramatic in itself, without our knowing anything about the baby and its habits, its wants, or its life. The moment is dramatic on its very surface. The use of violent weapons and martial arts, physical assaults, huge piles of cash, an alluring woman sashaying past a gaggle of young men loitering at a corner, the pomp and circumstance of a coronation—all of these are objectively dramatic. That is, their dramatic impact does not depend particularly on our knowing and caring about the characters involved.

But there are a great many moments in nearly all well-crafted films that are dramatic solely because we know something about the characters and care about what happens to them. If we know a man has hysterical claustrophobia, simply having him locked in a closet can create a riveting scene. If we add that he must lock himself into that closet as part of achieving something that he wants even more than avoiding his claustrophobia, the drama of the moment escalates exponentially. This situation is subjectively dramatic, because the drama depends on our knowledge of and participation in the story. The distinction between objective and subjective drama is another of Frank Daniel's contributions to dramatic theory.

Although some films attempt to rely only on objective drama or only on subjective drama, the majority of effective films have a mixture. Reliance on objective drama usually leaves the audience bored and uninterested within a short time. The guns have to get bigger and bigger, the explosions louder, the cliffs taller, and still, if the audience doesn't care about the individual characters in some measure, all the pyrotechnics can amount to wasted effort. On the other end of the spectrum, a film that relies on subjective drama can also lull the audience with a dearth of identifiable and anticipatable danger, a sense of uneventful safety. Often this can lead to a feeling that "too little happens."

For most stories, then, a combination of objective and subjective drama is most effective. One or the other usually dominates, but both are present, often at the same time. Sometimes the most memorable and visceral moments in a film are those that combine both forms. For instance, in *Wait Until Dark,* we know Suzy Hendrix is a self-reliant blind woman who accidentally has drug-dealing killers after her. The combination of our knowing of her disability and our caring about her well-being, and then of our being able to see the attempts made on her before she knows about them, keeps us firmly on the edge of our seats, fully participating in the story. *Amadeus,* which quite effectively uses primarily subjective drama, begins with a suicide scene that is objectively dramatic. And in its very moving end, where Salieri is literally working Mozart to death, the combination of factors—our knowledge of the characters, the allure of the gold to Mozart, and the desperate attempt of his wife to rescue him—makes this richly rewarding scene both subjectively and objectively dramatic.

TIME AND THE STORYTELLER

Try to make the time frame the minimum the story will permit.
—RING LARDNER, JR.

Don't have too much story for the time you have.
—TOM RICKMAN

There are three kinds of time in a film story: real time, screen time, and time frame. Real time is the time an action actually takes—the four minutes it takes a world-class runner to run a mile. Screen time is the time the depiction of an action takes up on screen—perhaps the first thirty seconds, another ten seconds in the middle of the race, and the last fifteen seconds of it, edited together with shots of a significant cheering fan in between, for a total of about a minute. The time frame is a deadline or an end to an action that the audience can anticipate; in the race it is the finish line, the moment we all know the race is leading up to, when the action will be over.

Most scenes take place in real time; that is, the actions we see on screen take the same amount of time as those same actions would take us in our own home. Because we are witnessing the actions of people in (subjectively) realistic circumstances and participating in their actions, major variations from real time usually seem jarring. But a little bit of time can be cut out without marring the scene. This is called *ellipsis*, skipping over small or large amounts of time without shocking the audience out of its seamless dream. For instance it is possible to ellipse the time it actually takes to put on a pair of shoes and socks. In fact, if we don't make it shorter than it would really take, the audience usually gets impatient. At the same time, if the character is in danger of being caught or found out or some other dramatic turn, we might actually prolong the time beyond what it would realistically take to pull on the socks and slip on the shoes. This is called *elaboration*.

Examples of both ellipsis and elaboration can be seen in the final scene of *Chinatown*. When Evelyn is about to make her escape with her daughter, she hops in the car, the engine roars to life, and she speeds off. A small amount of real time has been ellipsed—her fumbling with car keys and starting the engine. After the police shoot and the car comes to a stop with the horn blaring, all the rest of the characters run toward it. When we cut to a shot next to the car, they are still running, but seem a long way off yet. Meanwhile, we're anxious to know what happened and to end the dreadful horn blaring. Real time has been elaborated upon for dramatic impact. Slow motion is sometimes used for the same reason, to prolong our experience of an important moment.

Screen time and real time are thus not necessarily the same thing. A lot of beginning screenwriters "get stuck in real time." That is, they have a character get up, cross a room, unlock the door, lock it behind him, go to his car, unlock it, climb in, put the key in the ignition. . . . Tedium has long since set in, unless all of these actions have new meanings or conflicts of their own. The four-minute mile described above as being depicted on screen in about a minute is an example of the difference, even within one scene. If the mile race is the highest or lowest moment in the whole story, if it is the moment the entire film has been building toward, then we may well choose to make it last four minutes or very nearly. If it is a race someone must win or lose as part of the continuing development of the story, four minutes is a long time to expect an audience to maintain its tension without new actions and information coming into the scene. This is why it becomes necessary to snip out part of the real time while simultaneously making the audience believe it has seen the whole action.

Often an ellipsis of this kind is accomplished by using a parallel action, something happening elsewhere at the same time. For instance, the father of the miler is in the stands, but he has a heart condition. With the strain and excitement of the race, he collapses and the mother must ignore the race for a moment only to discover that he simply slipped off his seat. By the time they right themselves, the race is in the final stretch and all our attention is riveted back to the finish line. The audience won't notice the ellipsis; it has been distracted enough to accept that the four minutes were depicted in one and a half or two minutes. Another way of ellipsing time within a scene is to give the audience something else to look at, to draw its attention away from the action that is being shortened. If we want to boil a three-minute egg in a one-minute scene, it is necessary to draw the audience's attention away from the egg timer and the boiling water. The character boiling the egg either has a significant interaction with another character or does something—such as cutting a finger while chopping onions—that helps us bridge the real time and make the shortened screen time *seem* like real time.

Most major ellipses are done between scenes. A character can walk out of one scene heading for New York from Chicago and walk into the next scene in New York. Optical devices such as fade outs, fade ins, and dissolves are also used to ellipse time, as are montages, but it isn't always necessary or wise to rely on these devices. What is necessary, when one wants to cut directly from one scene to another with any significant jump in time, is to create a transition from one scene to the next. Exiting one scene in Chicago and entering the next in New York is possible, because we have seen the journey begin and end. It is also a good idea to give the audience a breather either at the end of one or at the beginning of the next scene. These ten seconds could be used to help ellipse a day, a week, or a year. In other words, when the character leaves the scene in Chicago, the scene stays with the remaining characters for a few seconds—one last line or reaction or sometimes a gag. Then we can cut to the character in the new place. Or it can be done the other way, giving a few seconds of scene in the new location before the traveling character arrives.

The important part is that the audience is helped to bridge this gap in time with something the writer inserts for that purpose: a verbal or audio transition, a transition based on visual similarities or transformations, making use of costumes, props, or music to carry an action over the ellipsis. For instance, a character says he's going to find so-and-so and punch his lights out, then exits. We can cut right to a punch in the face and show the character satisfied with the completion of his action. Or a character could say he will never wear a tuxedo as long as he lives, and we cut to him being fitted for a tuxedo. Another way of helping the audience bridge the lost time is to start a process in motion, then show it being completed (as discussed above with the race and the parents). This can be done between scenes with great effectiveness. For instance, a character begins painting an apartment. We could dissolve to him completing the task or we could fade out and fade back in as he completes it. But perhaps it would be more cinematic if we cut to the neighbor lady sniffing away at the horrible smell, then cut back to the man completing his painting job.

Time frame is a device the storyteller uses to help the audience store up its emotional energy for the important moments by letting them know there is a deadline or some moment when a crucial action must be completed (see "Elements of the Future and Advertising," page 74). Sometimes the time frame is very obvious, as in the bomb with a timer on it as the hero tries to defuse it. Sometimes it is the title of the story: *48 Hours, Seven Days in May, High Noon, Three Days of the Condor.* We know that this story will have to be told within that time frame. Sometimes the time frame is set up during the course of the story: a deadline, a moment of truth, a battle, a race, or a contest. In *Star Wars* the rebels have to destroy the death star before it destroys their whole planet in x number of minutes. All of *Rocky* builds toward the moment of truth, the big fight. In *The African Queen,* the whole quest is to get down into the lake to sink the battleship *Louisa;* we know that when we have reached that spot, there will be a moment of truth very soon.

Some films have a time frame set from their title on; others are only established within the story, often at the end of the first act; and still others never have an overall time frame, no deadline. But often there will be use of a time frame within smaller portions of a story. For instance, one sequence in *The Sting* involves sneaking into the telegraph office to hold a fake meeting with the target of the sting. It is established that the boss is out to lunch for one hour, and that hour becomes the time frame of that sequence of the story. Use of a time frame—or, as some people call it, a ticking clock—can help intensify a scene or sequence by shortening it, making it more dramatic and focused.

THE POWER OF UNCERTAINTY

You don't want to explain to the audience, because that makes them observers. You want to reveal to them little by little and that makes them participants because then they experience the story in the same way the characters experience it.

—BILL WITTLIFF

For a filmmaker to achieve his or her goals with a narrative film, one essential ingredient is to keep the audience in their seats, paying attention to the story and caring about the outcome and characters. In other words, participation. Without the audience participating in the proceedings, they become mere witnesses, disinterested and unaffected. This can be the death of drama, because a story is not inherently dramatic; it is only dramatic insofar as it has an impact on the audience, as it moves them in some way. Drama (including both comedy and tragedy) requires an emotional response from its audience in order to exist.

Ironically, not all "emotional" stories affect the audience's emotions, and conversely, not all seemingly straightforward, action-packed stories are unemotional as far as the audience is concerned. *Bonnie and Clyde, The Godfather,* and *North by Northwest* are all filled with action, yet each of them generates a strong visceral reaction in the audience. A film of a character crying hysterically won't have an emotional impact unless we know something about the character, the context, and the event or events that prompted the crying.

So what is the trick behind keeping the audience participating in the story and creating in itself the emotional response that drama depends upon? In a word, uncertainty. Uncertainty about the near future, uncertainty about the eventual turn of events. Another way of stating this idea is hope versus fear. If the filmmaker can get the audience to hope for one turn of events and fear another, where the audience truly does not know which way the story will go, this state of uncertainty becomes a very powerful tool indeed. We often find ourselves riveted to a story that has a strong component of hope versus fear.

In *Casablanca,* will Rick stay uninvolved in the complex and dangerous world around him, even though his true love, Ilsa, is involved and implicated? In *The 400 Blows,* will Antoine be able to find a place where he fits in the world? In *The Treasure of the Sierra Madre,* will Fred C. Dobbs succumb to greed, or will he stay true to his word? In *Rear Window,* will L. B. Jefferies prove what happened across the courtyard before the killer finds him? In *Annie Hall,* will Alvy be able to sustain a relationship with Annie?

Sometimes the identical situation can have the opposite hope versus fear under different circumstances. A young couple trying to have a baby would hope that this month the woman is pregnant and simultaneously fear that she was not. An underaged or insufficiently involved couple may fear that the woman is pregnant and hope that she is not. At the same time, the audience's uncertainty is not necessarily the same as the uncertainty of the characters. If the audience feels that the couple trying to have a baby are a bad match, that their break-up is imminent and the baby will suffer as a result, the audience might be hoping that she isn't pregnant and fearing that she is while the characters consciously feel the opposite way.

How is this sense of uncertainty, this hope versus fear, created in the audience? First and foremost, the audience must sympathize, to at least some small degree, with one or more pivotal characters (see "Protagonist and Objective," page 43, for a discussion of sympathy as it relates to the central character). The next most important element in creating hope versus fear is letting the audience know what *potentially might* happen, but not what *will* happen.

In *Modern Times,* Charlie Chaplin is a night watchman in a department store. He straps on a pair of roller skates and shows off his prowess to Paulette Goddard by wearing a blindfold while he skates. The area he is skating in is adjacent to a remodeling project where a huge hole is cut in the floor. He skates close to the hole, then away, closer still, then away, right toward it, then stops. All the while we are both laughing and tense, with a strong hope versus fear being felt. If we didn't know there was a hole in the floor, if we couldn't foresee what *might* happen, there would be no tension, no hope versus fear, hence no drama. But because we know he might career over the side, and yet we don't know for sure if he will, we are in a state of uncertainty, and therefore we are participating.

The basis of this participation, then, is anticipation. Anticipation of what may or may not happen is an informed situation, not one of ignorance. In other words, if we don't know the dangers or benefits that might come about in the near future of the story, we can't anticipate what may or may not happen. A common mistake of the beginning screenwriter is to think that the only way to keep the audience from guessing the ending is to keep it in the dark about what is going on by withholding information. But imagine if we didn't know about the hole in the floor Charlie Chaplin was skating near. Imagine if we didn't know who the real killer was in *Frenzy*. Imagine if we didn't know that mobsters were after the two men dressed up like women in *Some Like It Hot*. Where would the tension and drama come from?

The key to keeping the audience from guessing ahead is not to keep it in the dark about what might happen, but to make it believe that maybe its hope will come about, but that its fear is just as likely to happen. In other words, having two equally plausible outcomes to any given situation keeps the audience both participating and yet still unable to foresee the exact outcome of the scene or story.

This, then, is the furthest extension of audience participation in a story: The audience sympathizes to some degree with a character, it knows what may or may not happen and has taken a vested interest in one outcome or the other (by hoping and fearing), and it truly believes that either outcome is possible. Whether you are analyzing *Amadeus* or *Apocalypse Now*, *Rear Window* or *Gone with the Wind*, *The Third Man* or *Persona*, the key to making the individual scenes and the overall story work is that the film-makers have successfully created this combination of feelings, knowledge, and belief in the audience. This combination must exist on the page for there to be any hope that it will be created in the audience for the eventual film. If creating this relationship with the audience is not taken into consideration in the writing stage, there is virtually no hope of overcoming that shortcoming in the production.

SCREENWRITING TOOLS

∎

Quoting E. M. Forster: *"How do I know what I think until I see what I write?"*

—BILL WITTLIFF

Someone who is involved in self-discovery as a writer is, in a larger sense, discovering for all of us.

—BILL WITTLIFF

PROTAGONIST AND OBJECTIVE

I have to know who the main character is. Where they come from, what their background is. I need to set them socially, intellectually, historically, politically. What do they want? What are they afraid of? What are they taking action for or against?

—WALTER BERNSTEIN

The protagonist of a screenplay is usually the leading character, but this is by no means a definition, nor does it indicate the protagonist's function in the structure of a story. The chief characteristic of the protagonist is a desire, usually intense, to achieve a certain goal, and it is the interest of the audience in watching him move toward that objective that constitutes its absorption in the story. Indeed, it is the movement toward the objective that determines where the film shall begin and end.

Near the beginning of most well-constructed screenplays, the author directs our attention strongly toward one of the characters. The writer does this principally by showing this person, the protagonist, in the grip of some strong desire, some intense need, bent on a course of action from which he is not to be deflected. He wants something—power, revenge, a lady's hand, bread, peace of mind, glory, escape from a pursuer. Whatever it may be, some kind of intense desire is always present.

In *High Noon*, sheriff Will Kane wants to protect the town and do his job. In *Fiddler on the Roof*, Tevye the milkman, who lives precariously, wants merely to provide decently for his family and to see his five daughters properly married. In *It Happened One Night*, Ellie Andrews wants to get back to New York. In *Rear Window*, L. B. Jefferies wants to solve the mystery of what happened across the courtyard. In *The Third Man*, Holly Martins wants to find his old friend, Harry Lime.

The character's want or desire or pursuit usually focuses and intensifies as the story evolves; it is not a static, unchanging want. In other words, the protagonist need not begin with a passionately intense desire to achieve the goal, but that desire must develop during the course of the story. It is the protagonist's pursuit of his objective that we follow as the story unfolds, and it is this pursuit that draws us into the story. The protagonist's pursuit makes us care about the character and the evolution of the events.

A good protagonist arouses a strong emotional response from the audience. He can be sympathetic, like Will Kane or Tevye. He can arouse our pity, like Ellie Andrews, our amusement, like Holly Martins, or our admiration, like L. B. Jefferies. The important thing is that the audience not be indifferent to the protagonist. It must care, in one way or another, whether he achieves the goal. A protagonist incapable of arousing a strong emotional response is almost certain to bore the audience and sink the film.

This does not mean that all central characters must be inherently sympathetic or likable or admirable. Don Corleone in *The Godfather* and Sidney Falco in *The Sweet Smell of Success* are hardly admirable or even likable, yet a riveting story can be told about them. A despicable character with just one shred of salvageability can just as easily be a protagonist as an amusing or admirable one. Conversely, a sympathetic protagonist must have an undesirable side if any tension is to be created in the audience concerning whether he or she will do what it takes to achieve the desired goal.

It should be noted that our interest in whether the protagonist achieves his or her desire is usually proportionate to that character's interest in the same subject. The more intensely he or she desires, the greater our concern. It isn't a question of whether the pursuit is socially desirable, moral or immoral, just or unjust, generous or selfish; it is how fiercely the protagonist wants something that determines our emotional attitude toward him. A protagonist who doesn't know what she wants, or knows but doesn't greatly care whether she gets it or not, is poor dramatic material. Imagine how concerned we would be for Hamlet if somewhere along the line he decided the path he was pursuing was much too dangerous and that he'd better let bygones be bygones. How much would we care about Shane if he hung up his gun, vowed not to fight anymore, and then, at the first sign of trouble, strapped on his gun and reverted back to his old behavior? It is the struggle of a character who is less than perfect but somewhat short of utterly despicable that engages an audience and makes it care about the unfolding events.

In feature films, the role of the protagonist is nearly always the starring part. It is usually the most interesting role, and it is certainly the character most often in focus, for the simple reason that it is this person's fortune we are following. Screenwriters often give their scripts the name of the protagonist: *Mildred Pierce, Citizen Kane, Ninotchka, Shane, Tootsie*—the list is endless. Once in a while we encounter a story where two people want more or less the same thing and strive to achieve approximately the same goal. Yet in these stories, such as *Bonnie and Clyde, Butch Cassidy and the Sundance Kid,* and *Some Like It Hot,* the protagonist is usually the person who makes the decisions that create the story. Clyde, Butch, and Joe/Josephine, while not having more screen time than their partners, do take the role of the protagonist because they are the characters whose actions the partner follows; it is their decisions that determine both characters' actions, and it is their desire that overwhelms the partner's desire.

Only in the light of the protagonist's objective can a screen story be plotted, because the pursuit of that objective determines the course of the action, however straightforward or devious the path may be. Here are the three main points to remember about the objective:

1. There can be only one main objective if the film is to have unity. A story with a protagonist who has more than one ultimate aim must invariably dramatize the success or failure of one effort before going on to the other, and this breaks the spine of the work and dissipates our interest. A screenplay is like a suspension bridge, with one end anchored in what the protagonist wants, and the other end anchored to the disclosure of whether or not he gets it. A bridge that forks in the middle, with branches leading to two different destinations, can never be structurally sound. (The fact that other characters also have desires or objectives must not obscure the fact that the story we are following is the pursuit of the protagonist's objective.)

2. The objective must be capable of arousing opposition in order to produce conflict. Whether the opposition comes from another character, from nature, from the circumstances of the story, or from within the protagonist himself, it is still a much stronger story if the pursuit of an objective is actively opposed than if it is not opposed at all.

3. The nature of the objective is a leading factor in determining the attitude of the audience toward the protagonist and her opposition. If the objective is a heroic one, we will probably admire the protagonist; if it is a quixotic one, he may amuse us; a detestable objective will arouse our hatred or contempt for the leading character; and so on. Protagonist and objective are so closely identified in our minds that it is impossible to consider one without the other.

CONFLICT

The operative word for me is always conflict. What's the conflict of the story? What's the conflict that will tell the story you want to tell?

—WALTER BERNSTEIN

*C*onflict is one element that seems to be an essential ingredient of every forceful dramatic work, on stage or on film. Without conflict we are not going to have a story that will hold an audience. A story depicts a contest in which someone's conscious will is employed to accomplish some specific goal, a goal that is hard to reach, and whose accomplishment is actively resisted. Conflict is the very engine that propels a story forward; it provides the story's energy and movement. Without conflict, the audience remains indifferent to the events depicted on screen. Without conflict, a film story cannot come to life. The necessity of conflict cannot be overstated.

There is a tendency in the beginning screenwriter to think of conflict as always involving shouting, guns, fists, or other forms of extreme behavior. While all of these can convey conflict, they aren't the only means of showing it. A character simply trying to eat lunch can escalate into a conflict sufficient to carry a scene. In a memorable scene from *Five Easy Pieces,* Robert Dupea tries to order toast to go with his meal. What should be a simple and utterly boring moment turns into a fascinating scene when the ordering of toast becomes a test of wills between Dupea and a waitress who sticks to the restaurant rules against substitutions.

Conflict is actually created not by histrionics and excessive behavior, but by a character wanting something that is difficult to get or achieve. This is true in the overall story, and equally so in individual scenes. If no character wants something in a scene, there is no conflict, and the scene itself sags into a shapeless and ineffective mess. If no character wants something in a whole story, the screenplay falls into the same mire.

Wanting something can be either forward or backward, positive or negative. Not wanting to do something is as strong as actively wanting something for the purpose of creating conflict. Trying to get out of a situation or return to a more desirable status quo is wanting something. Trying to do something difficult creates conflict. The want that creates a conflict can be as simple as trying to pull on a pair of boots, as in the opening scene of *Dances with Wolves,* or as a cataclysmic as saving the world from nuclear destruction, as in *Dr. Strangelove* or any number of James Bond films. Not wanting to do something can be a powerful want, as when Rick in *Casablanca* "sticks his neck out for no man." Wanting to return to a better status quo is what powers both the book and the film of *The Wizard of Oz.*

OBSTACLES

When your characters are alive, you find that you aren't so much pushing them around but following them . . . that's when writing and storytelling is really magic.

—BILL WITTLIFF

*I*f the protagonist and his objective constitute the first two important elements in the construction of a story, the various obstacles collectively constitute the third. Without impediments to the attainment of the protagonist's desire there would be no conflict and no story. The protagonist would simply accomplish his objective without difficulty. Delightful as this situation is in real life, it is fatal to drama, for without a struggle to attain a desired goal, audience attention cannot be held.

There may be but one obstacle, and it may be simple and easily identified. A humanoid killing machine from the future is programmed to kill Sarah in *Terminator;* Vandamm's people have mistaken Roger Thornhill for a fictitious spy named George Kaplan in *North by Northwest;* Nurse Ratched is determined to break McMurphy's spirit in *One Flew Over the Cuckoo's Nest.* When there is a clear-cut opposing character, he or she is known as the *antagonist.*

On the other hand, there may be more than one obstacle. Jake's struggle to discover the secrets behind the murder in *Chinatown* are impeded not only by Noah Cross, but by the police and by the reluctance of his chief ally, Evelyn Mulwray, to be honest and forthright with him. Jim's struggle to find himself and his place in the world in *Rebel Without a Cause* is resisted not only by his parents, but by the school, by aspects of the town, and by Jim's own doubts about himself.

There may be several obstacles, arising one after another. Romeo and Juliet cannot openly declare their love because of the enmity of their families, but they also face a series of complications: Romeo is exiled for killing Tybalt; Juliet's parents, unaware of her marriage to Romeo, insist that she wed Paris; Friar Lawrence's message to Romeo that Juliet has taken a potion fails to reach him; supposing her dead, Romeo tries to reach Juliet in her tomb, but must fight a duel with Paris; Juliet, awakening, finds Romeo a suicide. Only by Juliet's killing herself can the lovers be reunited. Richard Blaney in *Frenzy* first gets himself fired from a low-paying job; then he is befriended by a man who turns out to be a vicious serial killer; the killer then targets his ex-wife, with whom Blaney has just had a fight; and then his girlfriend is murdered by the killer after she helps Blaney hide from the police, who now believe that he is the culprit.

Finally, the obstacles may be very subtle and complex, as analyses of *sex, lies and videotape* and *Thelma and Louise* indicate. (See pages 252 and 213.)

The protagonist and the obstacles he or she encounters must be fairly evenly matched. If the obstacle is weak, then the achievement of the objective is too easy, and the story is lifeless. But the obstacle should not be so overwhelming that the protagonist has *no* chance of overcoming it. In other words, the objective must be possible, but very difficult, to accomplish.

This point may seem to be contradicted by such films as *The Third Man* and *Death of a Salesman,* in which the element of a past action poses overwhelming odds against the achievement of the objective. It should be noted that the protagonists do not acknowledge the inevitability of failure until that failure stares them in the face and they must bow to it. They fight against the odds, believing they have a chance of succeeding; it is the character's belief that keeps the story alive, that gives us the needed shred of hope that the goal might still be achieved.

A distinction must also be made between conflicts and hassles. In daily life, flat tires, lost wallets, and faulty phone-answering machines are inconveniences that can seem like formidable conflicts. In drama, each of these could be either a conflict or a mere hassle. The determining factor is whether the inconvenience is truly an obstacle to a preestablished want. A groom trying to get to the church on time has a flat tire and it is an obstacle, it creates a conflict and quite possibly a whole new chain of events. There is something at stake that the flat tire puts in jeopardy. But if there is no want, no goal, nothing at stake for the character, then the flat tire is simply the same hassle for the character it would be for anyone. Without a goal and something at stake for at least one character, there can be no dramatic impact from a given event being depicted in a story, no matter how much of a "conflict" it seems on the surface.

One last point, and an important one: Although the unity of a story depends on there being but one main objective, there is no threat to unity from the use of multiple obstacles to the achievement of that objective.

PREMISE AND OPENING

If you have a lot of action and excitement at the beginning of a picture, there's going to have to be some explanation, some character development somewhere along the line, and there will be a big sag about twenty minutes after you get into a film with a splashy opening. It's made me prefer soft openings for films. It's been my experience that an audience will forgive you almost anything at the beginning of a picture, but almost nothing at the end. If they're not satisfied with the end, nothing that led up to it is going to help.

—ROBERT TOWNE

*T*he beginning of a story is necessarily an arbitrary point, selected by the storyteller, in a larger story. The circumstances that have brought about the conflict with which the screenplay deals can usually be ascribed to things that happened long before the opening FADE IN. Much of *Godfather II* is the telling of the story of Don Corleone prior to events that *The Godfather* covered. The Star Wars trilogy actually comprises episodes four, five, and six of a nine-part series of stories George Lucas developed.

Premise is a particularly misused and misunderstood word in a dramatic context. In logic, a premise is part of a syllogism: All humans have blood in their veins (major premise); I am a human (minor premise); therefore I have blood in my veins (conclusion). In drama, there are close parallels to logic. One way to look at a story is that a protagonist and his goal (major premise) versus an antagonist and the obstacles (minor premise) leads to drama and the audience's emotional response (conclusion). If a story functions primarily through internal conflict, then the protagonist and antagonist are two parts of the personality of the central character. Conversely, if the story functions primarily with external conflict, the protagonist and antagonist are clearly defined as separate characters. Or, in some cases, the antagonist is really the circumstances, as in a man-versus-nature story. The notion to be most wary of is the idea that a premise is something that a story sets out to prove. (See "Theme," page 55 for additional discussion concerning *thesis*, another term that, like *premise*, is often misused.)

The premise, as the term is used here, is simply the entire situation that exists as the protagonist starts moving toward his objective. This includes all background material pertinent to the story. The protagonist, his potential desire for his objective, and the potential obstacles (including the antagonist) to his achieving the goal all predate the story as it is being told. The opening, as distinguished from the premise, is that spot in the extended story selected by the storyteller to begin recounting the story.

Here are the premises and openings of five stories:

> *Rick owns a trendy night spot in Casablanca at the outset of World War II. A man with a past and a former fighter for lost causes, Rick is now hardened and unwilling to stick his neck out for anyone. As an opening, the screenwriters chose to start the story with an encapsulated setup of the world conditions and then a demonstration of the dangers inherent in this world. They quickly get to the point where Ilsa, the critical person from Rick's past, enters Rick's bar.*

> *The Capulets and the Montagues have for years been bitter enemies. Romeo, an impulsive young man and scion of the Montagues, and Juliet, the sensitive daughter of the Capulets, fall deeply in love. Shakespeare chose to open the play with a street brawl dramatizing the enmity of the two families, then moved soon to a ball given by the Capulets, at which Romeo, an uninvited guest, first encounters Juliet.*

> *John Book is a tough and cynical homicide detective in Philadelphia who is called in to investigate the murder of an under-*

cover cop in the train station. His sole witness is an Amish boy traveling with his young widowed mother. The screenwriters of Witness *chose as their opening to introduce us to the Amish world of the boy and his mother, then swiftly demonstrate the horrors of life in the city with the murder.*

Chief Brody is the sheriff of a small island community, a onetime city cop who, despite being afraid of the water, has moved to a bucolic village surrounded by the sea. A great white shark attacks and nearly devours a young woman, then seems to remain near this summer island paradise. For their opening, the screenwriters of Jaws *chose a demonstration of the ferocious and horrifying power of the shark, then quickly moved on land to establish the world of the main character before he learns of this initial shark attack.*

Marty is a butcher, an aging bachelor who lives with his mother and who is constantly being harangued about when he will be getting married. Yet Marty has barely ever been out with a woman, much less contemplated marriage. But he would like to start dating, he just doesn't know how. The screenwriter of Marty *chose as his opening a day with Marty in the butcher shop and the umpteenth time he's asked when he's going to settle down and have a family. The story quickly delves into Marty's "night out with the boys," which proves to be much less than expected.*

Many screenplays are conceived in the writer's mind with a situation that is essentially the premise. A satisfactory premise always contains the potential of conflict and some pertinent and specific information about the main character. (See "Unity," page 58, for other story forms that do not have a single central character.) Once the opening has been selected, the start of that conflict should not be delayed for long.

MAIN TENSION, CULMINATION, AND RESOLUTION

Screenwriting is a piece of carpentry. It's basically putting down some kind of structural form to mess around with. And as long as the structural form is kept, whatever I have written is relatively valid; a scene will hold regardless of the dialogue. It's the thrust of the scene that's kept pure.

—WILLIAM GOLDMAN

In dramatic writing, the very essence is character change. The character at the end is not the same as he was at the beginning. He's changed—psychologically, maybe even physically.

—ROBERT TOWNE

Audiences reject pandering, object to being played to. They're as interested as I am in seeing some real human behavior. They want to be surprised, they want to be delighted, they want to be fulfilled. That doesn't necessarily mean a happy ending, but they want some kind of closure.

—TOM RICKMAN

The average screenplay contains a number of minor culminations and resolutions, scene by scene and sequence by sequence, but here we are concerned only with the main tension of the second act, its culmination and the resolution of the overriding conflict of the story. Beginning screenwriters often confuse the culmination and the resolution and think that there is only one "climax" to a film story. But in fact, in the traditional three act structure, where the second act is approximately half of the story, the main tension is the conflict solely of the second act. When it is resolved at the culmination, this creates a new tension, which, at its simplest, can be stated as "What will happen?" which leads directly (with twists and turns) toward the resolution of the whole story.

For example, in *Chinatown*, the main tension is not "Will Jake help Evelyn and her daughter escape the clutches of Noah Cross?" At the time the main tension is established (at the end of the first act), we don't know enough to hope or fear about that. The main tension is more "Will Jake be able to find out who and what are behind the trick played on him, which led to his embarrassment?" This is what Jake spends the second act trying to unravel; obstacles to this quest to solve the mystery create the bulk of the story. Once the mystery is completely solved and he knows all about Evelyn, Noah, the daughter, and who killed Hollis Mulwray, then a new tension is created: "Will Jake be able to help Evelyn and her daughter escape from the clutches of Noah?" The resolution of that third act tension is that he is not able, Evelyn dies, and Noah takes his daughter.

In *Casablanca*, the main tension might be "Will Rick be able to stay uninvolved in the important world events swirling around him?" This un-involvement is what Rick actively pursues, regardless of how we feel about his detached stance. The obstacles to his quest to stay out of it are that his old lover, Ilsa, has come back into his life, that her husband is a very important man, that the Nazi colonel thinks he is already involved and that he holds the letters of transit. The culmination to this tension comes when he can no longer stay uninvolved and pulls a gun on Louis. At this point it creates a new tension: "Will Rick's help be enough to save Ilsa and Victor, and who will use the letters of transit?" The resolution of the story comes when Ilsa and Victor get on the plane and Rick walks off with Louis.

Although the main tension of a screenplay points in the direction of the overall conflict of the story, it does not directly ask the question, "What will happen at the resolution?" The successful screenwriter has planted this long-term concern somewhere in the back of the audience's mind, concern about the eventual resolution of the story. But what is most pressing, most urgent throughout the second act, is the series of obstacles much closer to home than the resolution, those obstacles which together can be summed up with the main tension. "Will the protagonist stand up for herself?" "Will the protagonist solve the mystery?" "Will the protagonist forgive his brother?" "Will the protagonist come to realize who her true love really is?" Each of these is a viable main tension. Once it is resolved at the culmination of the story, then the question becomes, "What will happen as a result of this change in the character, in his feelings, knowledge, or intentions?"

The changed circumstances and the changed character come into collision and create a new tension (the third act tension), which leads to the resolution of the overall story. A characteristic of the resolution is the disappearance of the will to struggle. Perhaps the protagonist acknowledges defeat and gives up the struggle, or she may achieve her objective and have no further need to struggle. In any case, the conflict subsides, and with it the drama; a fluid situation has become a stable one. The resolution of most stories occurs very near the end, for audience interest and participation cannot be sustained very long without conflict. In other words, the main tension and culmination are fluid situations, while the resolution is a stable one. It requires no further hope versus fear on the part of the audience, even if we are still concerned with the characters and their well-being and future.

Material for the resolution is extremely variable. It can suggest what may happen to characters in the future (as exposition in the beginning of the story has informed us of events in the past). Often it seems to convey, in the mouth of one of the characters, the author's point of view toward the protagonist or the material of the story.

The culmination is the high or low point of the screenplay, the event toward which all that precedes is driving. The resolution is the point after which the audience is allowed to relax; whether things have gone as it hoped or as it feared, the issue is satisfyingly over, resolved. Therefore it is extremely wasteful of a writer's time and energy to begin work on a screenplay before the culmination and resolution are clearly in mind. A story started without knowing these two points invariably wanders into endless revisions and such frustration that the screenplay is often abandoned before it is finished. The culmination is the lighthouse toward which the dramatist steers his ship, and the resolution is the safe harbor toward which that lighthouse guides him.

Given protagonist, objective, and obstacles, the writer should have no difficulty in establishing what his culmination and resolution should be. In deciding on his culmination, the writer will instinctively choose one that correctly interprets his attitude toward his subject matter. (See "Theme," below.)

Knowing the main tension, the culmination, and the resolution are useful to the screenwriter in another way, for they can help him to determine the pertinence and validity of the various scenes in a story. If the omission of a given scene leaves the main tension, culmination, or resolution damaged or altered, then that scene is an essential one and should be kept. On the other hand, if dropping the scene makes no difference at any of these critical points, the screenwriter had better regard that scene with a skeptical eye.

THEME

The best thing that can happen is for the theme to be nice and clear from the beginning.
—PADDY CHAYEFSKY

A good way to destroy a play is to force it to prove something.
—WALTER KERR

The trick with a subplot is what is it doing there anyway? How necessary is it? How does it tie into the main plot? If you take it out, what has the picture lost? How does it relate to the theme?
—WALTER BERNSTEIN

*T*he theme might be defined as the screenwriter's point of view toward the material. Since it hardly seems possible to write a screenplay, even the most frivolous one, without an attitude toward the people and the situations one has created, every story must therefore have a theme of some kind. And there is one spot in the screenplay where this theme can invariably be discerned: the resolution. For here the author reveals, perhaps even unconsciously, what interpretation he or she puts on the material.

This principle is well illustrated by comparing two modern comedies, *When Harry Met Sally* and *Annie Hall.* Both stories are about the difficulties of love and friendship in modern urban settings, with bright and talented people. And both are skillfully written, directed, and performed. Yet Harry and Sally resolve their differences and stay together just as the audience has hoped. But Annie and Alvy go their separate ways, leaving Alvy reliving his relationship with Annie in vain. One is a happy ending and the other a bittersweet ending. Each is valid for its author and its audience, yet the two resolutions reveal the authors' very different attitudes toward the material.

The experienced dramatist or screenwriter seldom begins with a theme, or attempts to fashion a story in order to present a philosophical position, which might be called a *thesis*. This method leads to clichés, propaganda, and lifeless characters, because all the human issues of the drama have been subordinated to this thesis the author is out to prove. Instead, an accomplished screenwriter creates characters and situations, and then chooses a culmination and resolution that seem right and satisfactory to his own feelings about the subject matter. In other words, a good screenwriter lets the theme take care of itself. The theme thus becomes not some point to be proven, but the subject matter itself, that aspect of human existence this story will explore.

The seasoned screenwriter is not apt to put into the mouths of his characters statements that spell out the theme. Those sorts of speeches make the characters sound as if they were on a soapbox and seriously distance the audience from the emotional core of the story. If the writer crossed out every single line that said explicitly what the story "meant," the audience would still know what it meant. The writer can't conceal his own attitude; it's built right into the story, in his treatment of it and how he chooses to resolve it.

In both film and theater, this idea of theme is nearly identical. Listen to one of the world's great playwrights:

> *They try to make me responsible for the opinions certain of the characters express. And yet there is not in the whole work a single opinion, a single utterance, which can be laid to the account of the author. I took good care to avoid this. The very method, the order of technique that imposes its form on the play, forbids the author to appear in the speeches of his characters. My object was to make the reader feel that he was going through a piece of real experience; and nothing could more effectually prevent such an impression than the intrusion of the author's private opinions in the dialogue.*
>
> —HENRIK IBSEN

It's very doubtful that Shakespeare was trying to prove anything about jealousy in *Othello,* or about ambition in *Macbeth.* It is equally doubtful that *Raging Bull* was designed solely to teach the audience the evils of jealousy, or that *Moonstruck* was meant to indict relationships of questionable origin. A theme is that area of the "human dilemma" that the author has chosen to explore from a variety of angles and in a complex, realistic, and believable way. A story can have somewhat different meanings for different people, for each of us brings personal attitudes and experiences to bear on the interpretation of the work. We find the clue to interpretation in the way the story ends.

Another aspect of theme to keep in mind is that it applies to the entirety of the screenplay, not just to the protagonist. Each of the subplots is a variation on the theme of the story, with a different conflict and resolution of its own. Even though the subplot has a different conflict and resolution, the underlying "subject" of the subplot is the same as the theme of the main story line.

For instance, in *Moonstruck*, the title—or, if you wish, infatuation—is the theme. Whether it leads to true romance or not, each of the significant characters in the story is moonstruck. Ronny and Loretta are obviously both infatuated, but so are the mother, the father, and, in an odd sort of way, Johnny, who is more infatuated with the notion of love and devotion than he is with the feeling of it or in following through on it. In *Rocky*, each of the significant characters is striving to prove himself "good enough." Rocky's central story is about being good enough to get in the ring with the heavyweight champion, but his opponent, his coach, his girlfriend, and her brother are all struggling with variations on being good enough.

Each subplot, then, has its own conflict regarding the same subject— the theme and variations—and has its own resolution of that conflict. In this way the author broadens and deepens the meaning and impact of the work, and helps to universalize the drama.

UNITY

The structural unity of the parts is such that, if any one of them is displaced or removed, the whole will be disjointed and disturbed. For a thing whose presence or absence makes no visible difference is not an organic part of the whole.

—ARISTOTLE

Ultimately, what you are trying to do—as I said, structure is crucial—is to find what the story's going to be: the ultimate, basic thread that you can hang everything else on. Once I have the spine of the piece, and everything that can be threaded to hang off that spine, that is it. And if I can use it, super. If I can't use it, no matter how good the material is, it has to go.

—WILLIAM GOLDMAN

O wing perhaps to the physical form of their theater, the Greeks set the entire action of their plays in a single locale, usually the entrance to a royal palace. They also limited the dramatic passage of time to a single day. These practices came to be known as the unities of place and time. Aristotle laid down the rule for unity of action, quoted above, which states that material not essential to the development of the plot should be eliminated.

In building a story for a film, the screenwriter must adhere to one of the three unities, but not all three. One of the great aspects of film is its ability to transport the audience from place to place, and to ellipse, repeat, or even reverse time. Therefore, for most films, the unity that helps give shape to the raw material of the story is the unity of action. At its simplest, this is the reason we need one central character in most film stories. That one character's pursuit of her objective creates this unity of action; the story, then, follows the character in pursuit of her goal.

Thus the telling of a story becomes the sequence of events that happen to a central character in active pursuit of an objective. Even when time is not followed—by means of flashbacks, flash-forwards, reversals of time, recollections, and all the other ways in which the film storyteller can vary time out of the strictly chronological—the unity of the character's pursuit of his goal keeps the audience oriented and makes the story seem "all of a piece." The same can be done with place—we can go halfway around the world and back again from one scene to the next, or we can follow events that are unfolding simultaneously in two different locations. Yet so long as there is unity of action, the audience will be able to stay grounded and participating in the story.

It is entirely possible, though infrequently tried and rarely successful, to build a story around the unities of time or place. (See the analyses of *Rashomon* and *Diner*, pages 240 and 227 respectively, for more detailed discussion.) In these sorts of movies, there is no need for a single central character whose action we follow as the story unfolds. In place of that unity, we can have a location (as in *Diner* or *Nashville*) around which the action is centered. Within this social and atmospheric context, the audience is still able to participate in the various intertwining stories. For the unity of time to focus a story (as in *Rashomon* or its American remake as a western, *The Outrage*), a single overridingly important event becomes the focal center of the story. The various characters' perspectives on that event make the story still seem "all of a piece."

EXPOSITION

One of the tricks is to have the exposition conveyed in a scene of conflict, so that a character is forced to say things you want the audience to know—as, for example, if he is defending himself against somebody's attack, his words of defense seem justified even though his words are actually expository *words. Something appears to be happening, so the audience believes it is witnessing a scene (which it is), not listening to expository speeches. Humor is another way of getting exposition across.*

—ERNEST LEHMAN

*F*acts not evident to the audience from the unfolding events on screen, but facts of which they must be made aware, are handled by the device called *exposition.* These facts may be things that have happened in the past, before the action of the story begins; they may be feelings, desires, shortcomings, or aspirations of the characters; or they may be the specific circumstances and "world of the story" that help create the story's premise.

The problem with exposition is that it is only necessary to the audience; it is not what the characters need to know for themselves in the course of the story. Most exposition reveals what the characters already know (their own past and circumstances), but we must know it too, to get the fullest experience of their story and actions. Exposition should be used sparingly, because it is a narrative device rather than a dramatic one. Overuse of exposition quickly becomes tedious for the audience. The novice screenwriter may be surprised by how little exposition is needed, particularly in the beginning of a film. The audience quickly grasps the essentials of a situation without a lot of preliminary background material.

This is not to say that exposition can be eliminated; it is an essential ingredient in cooking up a good story, but it should be used as a spice, not a filler. Most stories require at least some expository information in order to get moving, and over the centuries, dramatists have been supplying this in a number of ways. Greek plays often opened with a formal chorus in which the historical events leading up to the play were reviewed. The prologue or chorus has survived in the theater in the form of a narrator or character who talks directly to the audience, as in Wilder's *Our Town* and Williams's *The Glass Menagerie*.

The film counterpart of the narrator or chorus is the voice-over narration, often by the central character. When expertly handled, as Billy Wilder did in *Sunset Boulevard* and *Double Indemnity*, this can be a very effective tool, but it is not the tool of first choice under most circumstances. Exposition can usually be made more engrossing if it is revealed in conflict, and this is the most widely practiced method of handling it. The expository information then becomes a sort of by-product of a scene that is dramatically interesting in itself.

For example, in the opening sequence of *Amadeus*, Salieri gives a great deal of background information about himself and Mozart as he is trying to tell the young priest who he is. But because these scenes are about the priest's desire to hear Salieri's confession and to grant him absolution, and because the priest is just as impatient to get on with it as Salieri is anxious to have his tunes remembered, the scenes are dramatically rich and fulfilling for the audience. The exposition is "snuck up" on the audience; it is merely something we learn while we are engrossed in the conflict between two interesting characters.

Another tactic is to thrust the audience into the story and make it work to figure out the past, the relationships, and the circumstances behind the scenes being shown. For example, *The 400 Blows* opens with Antoine already getting himself into trouble, showing the mischief and the humor in his character, and the nature of his friendship with René. At first we can only guess about Antoine's reasons for being mischievous; we are made to work to try to figure it out. Once he is home with his mother and his nightly routine and we see the exposition of his living circumstances, we are already hooked on the boy and his plight.

In other words, the exposition should usually be delayed as long as possible. If, at the same time, the audience is tantalized with little bits of information that point forward to future revelations or information that the audience wants to grasp, this leads to audience interest in the characters and their actions. Using actions of the characters that allow the audience to experience and discover for itself the who, what, where, when, and why of the characters is an extremely useful way of accomplishing exposition.

Another effective technique is to use humor, ideally in conjunction with conflict. For example, in *Chinatown* it becomes necessary for Jake to find out who owns all the land in the valley that is at the center of the mystery. He goes to the hall of records and looks the information up in huge plat books—potentially one of the most boring of all possible scenes, yet one that is essential to the unraveling of the story. When Jake asks for the plat books from an officious and impatient little clerk, a conflict is established between the two characters. The clerk's reluctance to reveal information to Jake (and us) makes him (and us) work to get it. When Jake asks for a ruler, we don't quite understand what he's up to, but when his little trick works and defeats the clerk, we are pleased and amused. And along the way, we learn all the information we need. Instead of being a boring scene of a man looking information up in a book, this scene is turned into an enjoyable and memorable moment, one that expands our affection and admiration for Jake.

The inexperienced screenwriter often tries to crowd a lot of exposition into the beginning of a script. This results in a static opening that bores the audience before the story itself begins to move. A far better tactic is to use hints and partial revelations, little mysteries and puzzles, denials and conflicting opinions of characters about expositional matters. All of these are ways to make the audience work (and therefore participate) to gather its background knowledge of the events on screen. By getting on with the story and letting the audience discover the majority of the exposition as it unfolds, the screenwriter becomes able to put the characters in active pursuit of their daily lives and let us uncover the mysteries behind those lives.

A few rules of thumb might be kept in mind when dealing with the need for exposition:

1. Eliminate exposition that isn't essential or that will soon become clear in the natural course of the story.
2. Present necessary exposition in scenes that contain conflict and, possibly, humor.
3. Postpone using expository material whenever possible until later in the story, and then reveal it at its moment of maximum dramatic impact.
4. Use an eyedropper instead of a ladle whenever you dole out the necessary exposition.

CHARACTERIZATION

When you are drawing characters to serve a plot purpose, you tend to get flat, stereotyped, unliving characters.

—TOM RICKMAN

*C*haracterization and story are interdependent on the screen, and the tie that binds them together is the objective—what a character wants—for that is the foundation on which the writer builds and fleshes out each of the characters. The objectives of the various characters determine the course of events and are the key to understanding the characters and their behavior. But even beyond that, objectives lead directly to the actual plot line of the story, as the people involved try various means of attaining their goals.

In *Casablanca,* Rick's objective is quite clearly stated: "I stick my neck out for no man." The last thing that Rick wants is to get involved; his pursuit of that "personal isolationism" creates many of the events of the story, as his will to remain uninvolved is tested with ever increasing pressure from all those around him. In *Rocky,* Rocky's objective is to be good enough to get in the ring with the heavyweight champion. His pursuit of that goal determines how the plot unfolds and reveals the nature of his character. In *The 400 Blows,* Antoine wants to find his place in the world, someplace he is wanted and appreciated. His pursuit of that objective reveals a great deal about the mischievous side and the troubled side of his character, and helps to create the sequence of events that makes up the story.

There are also superficial traits that help to depict character—language, manner of speaking, dress, gesture, physical condition, mannerisms, and so on. But the key factor still comes back to the character's objective and the means employed to attain it. Many of the less important facets of a personality flow from this central and controlling element, and can be determined to some degree by the actor's interpretation of the role. But only the screenwriter can be responsible for the mainspring of the character's behavior that enables the actor's interpretation. So clearly it is important to have the objectives in mind when attempting to create characters.

A common mistake of the novice screenwriter is to confuse characteristics with characterization, to feel that by giving attributes to a character, one has also given personality. To be tall, short, fat, thin, bald, or wild-haired is merely a characteristic that reveals no more of the inner life of the character than the color of a car reveals the power of its engine. The essential ingredient that these characteristics lack is the attitude of the character toward the attribute. A character can be described as having a big nose, and it tells us nothing of his inner life. But in *Cyrano de Bergerac,* the protagonist's huge nose is very much a part of his characterization for the simple reason that it is crucial to his attitude toward himself. His nose is the source of his sense of inferiority and his sense of superiority; it is a driving force behind what he has excelled at, and behind his fears. We come to see Cyrano's nose as a central formative element of his entire being, thus making the characteristic a window into the inner life of the character. Although not all physical attributes and physical affects are quite so over-riding, the basic lesson remains true: the character's attitude toward any of these conditions is what must be provided in the story if characterization is to flower.

It is not only the protagonist of a story who has an objective that helps form a characterization. Other major characters have their own desires, and conflicting desires are the stuff of drama. Nurse Ratched wants to dominate all of the men in her charge in *One Flew Over the Cuckoo's Nest.* It is the head-to-head conflict between her and the free-spirited McMurphy that creates the story as well as reveals the essential character of each of them. In *Body Heat,* Ned wants to have and sustain an affair with Matty, but she has her own agenda that involves tricks, lies, manipulation, and seduction. At the same time, Oscar and Lowenstein want to unravel the mystery surrounding the death of Matty's husband, Edmund. These forces collide and create the story, putting pressure on the characters to reveal their inner selves. This is the essence of characterization, the revelation of the inner life of the character. Their actions, which are based on their wants or objectives, form our conduit to understanding the inner life of the characters.

Personalities can be depicted on the foundation of such desires, and on conflicting desires scenes can be built. The conflict may be no more than a slight friction of temperaments that grate upon each other, or it may depict an overwhelming clash of willpower; but without at least some measure of conflict a scene will surely be lifeless.

A delightful scene in *Intimate Lighting* (a wonderful film from Czechoslovakia, which unfortunately is not available on video at the time of this writing) is built on a seemingly simple little conflict. A country family of five, of quite modest means, have two dinner guests from the big city whom they wish to treat well and impress. A chicken is cooked and served, but there are only six pieces. As the scene hilariously unfolds, every piece of chicken changes plates several times in the family's attempt to serve the food equitably and with respect to status. In the process, the interrelationships of all the family members, as well as with their guests, are revealed more poetically and cinematically than if there had been a huge family blow-out.

Differing personalities, as well as opposing objectives, can set conflicts in motion. This means the screenwriter must thoroughly understand his characters—everything about them, as if they were close personal acquaintances. In fact, the screenwriter should know a great deal more about the important characters than can possibly fit into the story. Only by understanding the deeply rooted desires of the characters can the writer plausibly depict their motives, making the characters believable and their behavior natural and consistent. And only by knowing more about the characters than can possibly be used in the story can the screenwriter make a script rich and full, lively and lifelike, textured and, ultimately, believable.

It is a good idea to remember that the characters don't know who the protagonist is, who the antagonist is, and who the supporting players are. Each character is the central character of his own life and behaves accordingly. This idea is the genesis of the stage play and subsequent film, *Rosencrantz and Guildenstern are Dead*. These two minor characters from *Hamlet* believe they are at the center of their story, as indeed they are, and their actions based on this belief create their story.

A secondary character who knows her relative unimportance (or, more precisely, is written in such a way as to be aware of her unimportance) is unlikely to come to life on the page and on the screen. But a character who does not know she is secondary is "reluctant" to be part of the protagonist's story and does not easily or readily do all the actions that the plot (and plotter) would like her to do; this conflict fleshes out the character with sometimes amazing economy and simplicity. A character who knows she is subordinate will obediently do what is required to facilitate the objectives of the main character, instead of actively pursuing her own goals. This undermines the potential for conflict, which in turn decreases the possibility of drama.

DEVELOPMENT OF
THE STORY

Pictures are written as well as acted and directed and photographed and edited and scored and all that. The screenwriter determines what scenes are in and what scenes are out; decides whether that bit of information is dramatized or just referred to; whether it takes place on or off screen. There are millions of decisions made by the screenwriter.

—ERNEST LEHMAN

Every little scene that you can cut, you cut.

—WILLIAM GOLDMAN

Write what you do not know, because you will find that there is some part of you that does know. It teaches you something you knew that you didn't know you knew. There's always that sense of discovery, personal discovery.

—BILL WITTLIFF

*T*he protagonist's progress toward his goal is traced in a series of scenes, each of which, even though he may not be present in the scene, moves the central character toward or away from his objective. Put in another way, once the main tension is established, each scene of any significance promotes either the audience's hope or its fear—or causes changes from one to the other in the course of the scene. Even after the main tension has been resolved by the creation of the third act tension, the scenes continue to promote our new hope versus fear. But the scenes don't remain static; the intensity of the audience's feelings should escalate and focus. This idea of rising action involving ever greater hope and ever greater fear is the very nub of what keeps an audience involved throughout the story.

Another aspect of the development of the story, from the time that the main tension is established until it is resolved and turned into the third act tension, has to do with the various possible solutions to the protagonist's predicament. In drama, as in life, we attempt the easiest solution first and try to put off the most difficult or unpleasant solution to any given problem, hoping that we will never need to try that. Often the first recourse is to deny that there is a predicament, and the second is to ask some authority figure to solve it for us (Mom or Dad, a cop, a judge, the principal). Only when those alternative solutions fail do we try to face the problem head-on, to reason with it (if it's a person), or make it go away. In a film, when all the alternatives have been eliminated except the one that is most difficult for our protagonist, the audience is completely focused on an either/or situation. Either Dan accepts his brother's disability and they forgive each other, or Dan will become permanently estranged from his family and everyone he loves. Either the secret agent manages to break into the seemingly impregnable fortress around the nuclear weapon (in order to disarm it), or life on this planet as we know it will end.

The development of a story revolves around the various attempts a protagonist makes at solving his predicament. For instance, in *North by Northwest*, Thornhill's predicament is that he has been mistaken for a secret agent. His first attempt is to deny that he is the agent, but when he is not believed and his opponents try to kill him, he goes to the police. When he is not believed by them, he tries to find the real agent. Then he attempts to face "Lester Townsend" at the UN, only to be suspected of Townsend's unexpected murder. Now on the lam from the police, he tries again to find the real agent. When he is nearly killed in his most desperate attempt to reach him, he turns back on the opposition and faces them directly, now hoping to convince them that he represents no danger to them. When that doesn't work and he finds out the truth about the real agent, he is in an either/or situation: either he goes away and lets the chips fall where they may, including the certain death of a woman with whom he has fallen in love, or he actually becomes the secret agent for a time in order to save her and defeat his unwanted opposition. At the moment he faces the either/or decision, all the alternative solutions but one have been eliminated. This is the end of the second act, and with his decision, the third act tension is created.

But a screen story is not simply the pursuit by a protagonist of a solution to his or her predicament. A good story is not created for the characters or the protagonist. A story is created solely for the audience. Remember, the characters on screen are not the only ones who want something; the audience wants something relative to the protagonist—the main tension. Any scene, revelation, entanglement, or obstacle that impacts on this want of the audience's will very likely dovetail into the overall story, whether it includes the protagonist or not. These are often the sorts of moments in a story that heighten the audience's involvement and make their experience of the story more visceral as well as more meaningful.

DRAMATIC IRONY

*S*uppose we see a man walking slowly along some railroad tracks. There is nothing particularly dramatic about this; no doubt he has a reason for walking that way. But suppose we learn that the man is deaf and there is a train speeding up behind him. Instantly the situation is charged with drama, and we want to shout a warning. In the movie theater we don't shout warnings to the actors on screen, but if we know something that one or more characters don't know, the situation is intrinsically dramatic.

Charlie Chaplin confidently walks a high wire in the circus. He doesn't know, as we do, that his safety belt isn't operative, and we are held in comic suspense.

When Romeo finds Juliet apparently dead in her tomb, but we know that her death is only feigned, we have intense feelings of hope and fear when he is about to take the poison—much more so than if we didn't know Juliet was really still alive and would awaken soon.

Imagine the scene in *North by Northwest* in which Thornhill takes a bus out to the middle of nowhere to meet the fictitious George Kaplan. We know both that Kaplan doesn't exist and the whole meeting is a setup, but Thornhill is aware of neither. Our tension mounts from the very beginning, long before the cropduster first attacks him.

In the incredibly intense scene very late in *Amadeus* where Salieri is transcribing the "Requiem" as Mozart dictates it literally from his deathbed, a great deal of the impact of the scene stems from the fact that we know that Salieri is attempting to work Mozart to death and steal his crowning composition. Without that knowledge, we would have quite the opposite feeling about Salieri at that moment; we would feel the way Mozart does when thanking him for his help.

Try to imagine the telling of the story of Oedipus without revealing to the audience that the king has married his own mother. There would be very little audience involvement indeed until that final revelation, which would be nearly as great a shock to us as it is to him. It would diminish the tragedy beyond all recognition.

Every screenwriter (and every playwright as well) uses the device of dramatic irony, often several times in a story, sometimes from beginning to end. The entire story of *Some Like It Hot* is based on a multiplicity of ironies, from our knowing that Joe and Jerry are men impersonating women to escape the mob, to our knowing that at one point Jerry is actively trying to interfere with the budding romance between Joe (playing Junior) and Sugar.

Yet another of Frank Daniel's contributions to dramatic theory is the understanding of the principle of revelation and recognition. When the audience learns something that at least one person on screen does not know (which creates a dramatic irony), that moment is called the *revelation*. Whenever there is a revelation of this kind to the audience, it creates an obligation for the storyteller to create a moment of *recognition*, when the character finds out what we already know. Revelation puts the audience into a superior position—knowing more than someone on screen—and this translates into a feeling of participation. Revelation and recognition go right to the heart of what makes drama; without them a story becomes more narrative than dramatic. Without use of these crucial tools in the telling of a story, the audience is relegated to the position of witnesses who watch the sequence of events, but don't enjoy the anticipation of future events that is at the core of the dramatic experience.

For example, look at *Some Like It Hot*. From the moment we know that Joe and Jerry are dressing up like women to save their lives, we are awaiting their unmasking. If we didn't get that moment of recognition that these two "girls" are really men, we would feel such a strong resentment and disappointment that it could quite possibly destroy our entire experience of the story. It would be like Oedipus never finding out he has married his mother or Charlie Chaplin never learning how close he roller-skated to an open hole in *Modern Times*. Imagine the ending of *Romeo and Juliet* if we didn't know that Juliet was really alive when Romeo finds her seemingly dead. Imagine the ending of *E.T.* if we didn't know that E.T. was really alive in that iron lung.

Frequently the screenwriter must choose between the device of dramatic irony and the use of surprise; that is, between letting the spectators in on the secret and startling them with it later. Surprise can be very effective dramatically. In the famous scene from *Chinatown* in which Evelyn says, "She's my sister, my daughter, my sister *and* my daughter," we are shocked.

This moment of surprise would be spoiled if we had known this all along. But take another scene from the same film, when Jake is telling a dirty joke and Evelyn is standing behind him. We know she's there, but Jake doesn't; in fact, he is the only one who doesn't know. It is the use of irony that gives this scene its power.

Although surprise can create a very powerful moment, and most assuredly has its place in any narrative film, it is a less effective tool overall than suspense, which is created through irony. The famous example that Alfred Hitchcock gave concerns a bomb that is placed under a table. If a group of characters are sitting around a table and there is a bomb under it, but we don't know it's there and neither do the characters, there is one major moment of surprise—when the bomb goes off. If we know the bomb is there and the characters don't, we can sustain the audience's participation in hoping and fearing for a considerable time, solely because of the audience's knowledge and the characters' ignorance. In the case of surprise, the audience will lose interest in the scene in very short order, but in the case of suspense, it will sit through otherwise boring details with bated breath, waiting for the characters to discover the bomb or perish for failing to. Clearly, suspense is the stronger tool, and it is based on revealing some things to the audience before they are revealed to one or more of the characters on screen.

PREPARATION AND AFTERMATH

*P*reparation and aftermath, two more dramatic tools Frank Daniel has refined, are unnecessary in the development of the plot of a story, but they are very effective tools for heightening the audience's experience of the story. A scene of *preparation* is one in which the audience, and often the character or characters, braces for an upcoming dramatic scene. War movies and sports movies depend heavily on this sort of scene to get all of us, characters and audience alike, prepared for the big battle or game. A scene of *aftermath* is one in which the character and audience are allowed to "digest" a dramatic scene immediately afterwards.

In both sorts of scene, music and atmosphere, along with visual and audio poetry, are used to appeal directly to the emotions of the audience.

When the young priest first enters the sanatorium where Salieri is being kept in *Amadeus*, it is a scene of preparation for the apparent madness we are about to encounter when the two men interview. The famous title number from *Singin' in the Rain* is really a long scene of aftermath, one in which the character's emotions are expounded upon and we are made to feel the same way. After Rocky loses the fight to Apollo Creed and dances around the ring crying out for Adrienne, it is a scene of aftermath that helps us digest his triumph despite the loss of the fight. Very atmospheric films, such as *Taxi Driver* and *Red River*, have numerous scenes of preparation and aftermath from beginning to end. In the latter, the famous "Yeehaw!" scene is a scene of preparation.

Another form of preparation is preparation by contrast. In this kind of scene, the audience is built up to an emotional expectation that is opposite from the effect the forthcoming dramatic scene will actually deliver. Just prior to bad news or an unwanted turn of events, preparation by contrast can be used to make the audience feel good or hopeful or positive. The reverse also works quite effectively. Preparation by contrast increases the impact of the upcoming dramatic moment by making the emotional swing of the audience that much greater. For example, in *Kramer vs. Kramer*, Ted Kramer comes home from "one of the five best days of my life," only to find his wife leaving him without warning and giving him custody of their son. In *Annie Hall*, when Alvy and Annie are separated, Alvy goes on a date with a *Rolling Stone* reporter and is told his lovemaking is "really a Kafkaesque experience." Feeling more lonely than if he were alone, Alvy is distressed, but just at this moment Annie calls him to battle a spider in her bathroom. Soon they are in bed together, vowing never to break up again.

Inexperienced screenwriters often overlook the potential of scenes of preparation and aftermath, to the detriment of the stories being told and the audience's experience of them. These two types of scene are valuable tools in keeping the audience's interest and participation exactly where the storyteller wants them. The plot alone does not make the screenplay or the film. Often a story's plot is neither new nor particularly innovative, but that fact doesn't necessarily diminish the film if the story is told well. It is how a story is told that truly matters, which means that preparation and aftermath are very important parts of the script, even when they don't advance the plot or story line.

PLANTING AND PAYOFF

A "plant" is a preparatory device that helps to weave the fabric of a screenplay together. It can be a line of dialogue, a character's gesture, a mannerism, a prop, a costume, or a combination of these. As the story unfolds, this plant is repeated, thus keeping it alive in the audience's mind. Usually near the resolution of the story, when the circumstances of the characters and the audience have changed, there is a "payoff" on this plant in which the gesture, prop, or whatever takes on a new meaning. This resembles a poetic metaphor, when the plant takes on new meaning at the payoff.

An expert use of planting and payoff is the potted palm tree in *Mister Roberts*. The container is labeled "Property of Captain, Keep Away." The first piece of business in the film and the play is to call our attention to the tree and to the crew's low opinion of it and, by reflection, their attitude toward the captain. Moments later, Roberts explains his hatred of the tree, awarded to this supply ship for "delivering more toothpaste and toilet paper than any other cargo ship," because it represents their lack of involvement in the real war. During the story we are never permitted for long to forget the palm tree or the tyrannical captain's pride in it. We see him watering it; we see how the crew detests it. Late in the story Roberts, in exuberant rebellion, jerks the palm tree from the container and throws it over the side. And when the angry captain is trying to learn who did it, he remarks that it couldn't have been Ensign Pulver, because "he hasn't the guts." Soon the captain has replaced the missing palm with two small ones. In the final moments of the story, after Roberts has been killed, Pulver throws the two palms overboard and confronts the captain. In this symbolic gesture Pulver has replaced Roberts, and the audience roars with pleasure. It is the careful preparation all through the story, of course, that makes the gesture so effective and turns the palm into a metaphor.

The technique of planting and payoff also serves to increase the audience's feeling of involvement in the story, for we sense we have special, inside information, we know secrets and have discovered new or hidden meanings in the very fabric of the story. Another advantage of planting and payoff is that, by requiring the audience to grasp and retain information for later use and by having an effective "wrapping up" of the plant at the time of the payoff, it makes the whole story seem more unified, more of a piece.

Planting and payoff can also have a more mundane use in the telling of a story. It can provide us with a bit of information that is relatively meaningless at the time, but that becomes much more critical later in the story. For example, if a handgun is "planted" in the bedroom night-stand early in a story—that is, the gun is revealed to us—and then later our protagonist is trying to escape from or subdue someone bent on homicide, we remember the gun and hope the protagonist will also remember and manage to get to it. This payoff on the thing planted earlier increases our involvement and strengthens our hope-versus-fear response.

In general, it is a good idea to separate plants and their payoffs with as much screen time as possible. If we learn that a character has a hundred dollars in her purse in one scene, and in the very next scene she needs ninety-five dollars to buy the train ticket that will secure her escape, it just seems too easy, too false to the audience. Sometimes it isn't possible to separate a plant and a payoff by very much screen time, because the location or costume or prop hasn't appeared earlier in the story. In this kind of situation, it is best to attempt to distract the audience from the plant with a major dramatic or exciting event that takes its mind off the plant before the payoff.

ELEMENTS OF THE
FUTURE AND
ADVERTISING

*O*ne of the important jobs of the screen storyteller is to keep the audience looking forward, worrying about the future, hoping something might happen, fearing something else might happen. In a way, planting and payoff work on this area, because at the time of the payoff the audience becomes aware that it has been anticipating, looking forward to a moment, but without realizing why. But if the audience is looking for the payoff from the moment something is planted, the plant is too obvious, too superficial, or emphasized out of proportion. *Advertising* and *elements of the future,* on the other hand, are two tools that more overtly help push the audience into the future, making it continue to think in terms of what *might* happen without knowing what *will* happen.

Advertising is the indication to the audience of some upcoming experience a character might have. If, early in a story, a mother and daughter are having a fitting for the daughter's wedding dress and the daughter is a significant character in the story, we suspect that the wedding will take place as a future event in the story. It is advertising anytime a principal character sets up a rendezvous or indicates a deadline or appointment, anytime a character is dying or is about to give birth, has a test, "heads into town," goes out searching for someone or for the Holy Grail, intends to get something, make something, see someone, go somewhere. The central element of advertising is that the character intends to have this moment, and if it seems important to the story, we expect to have that moment as well. Sometimes things change, we see the daughter and her fiancé break up and call the wedding off, but that means the future event is still dealt with in its own way. Anytime we are told or shown that the characters expect that there will be an event in the future of a story, it is advertising, and the effect is to encourage the audience to look forward, to anticipate— which is the key to getting them to participate.

Elements of the future were first delineated as storytelling tools by Frank Daniel. They are hopes and fears of the characters—sometimes realistic, sometimes merely fanciful—which also encourage the audience to look to the future of the story. Predictions, omens, daydreams, and assurances are all elements of the future. If a fortune-teller tells a character she will meet a man who is tall, dark, and handsome, we begin to look out for that possibility. It might be that she meets the exact opposite of the prediction, but the important thing is that the audience will be looking forward to something that may or may not happen the way the character hopes or fears. Expectations, premonitions, promises, doubts, plans, warnings, forebodings, faith, and aspirations are all elements of the future.

In *The Treasure of the Sierra Madre,* when Fred C. Dobbs assures his partners he will reach his limit and not take a penny more in gold, it is an element of the future. He has made a prediction about his future behavior, and we wonder if it will happen the way he predicted. In *Bonnie and Clyde,* when the gang picks up the delightful couple of Eugene and Velma, any form of prediction seems the farthest thing from our minds. But when Clyde finds out Eugene is a mortician and dumps the pair at the side of the road, his dreadful fear of mortality is made evident. It is a subtle but effective pointer into the future of the story. In *Red River,* when Valence, one of Groot's men, and Dunson both show how good they are with a gun, Groot predicts the two will eventually face each other in a showdown. Later they do face each other, and Valence shoots Dunson in the hand, disarming him, and Dunson declares he will kill Valence someday. In the end they face each other again, and wound each other, before Dunson's big fight with Garth. Each of these moments is an element of the future that gives us something to anticipate without our being able to guess what the outcome really will be. In a famous scene from *Annie Hall,* when Alvy and Annie talk superficially while subtitles tell their real thoughts, there are examples of both advertising and elements of the future. Annie talks about her grandmother who hates Jews, and we wonder if the two will ever meet. At the end of the scene, Alvy asks Annie for a date, which comes up quite soon. In *Shane,* when Joey asks his father if he could "whip" Shane in a fight, it is an element of the future that presages the actual fight the two men have later on.

A good storyteller pulls out all the stops when it comes to urging the audience into the future of the story, to worry, to hope, to fear, to anticipate. Advertising works to point the audience forward, using the intentions of the characters to have or make future events. Elements of the future push the audience forward by using the hopes and fears of the characters, whether they actually expect them to materialize or not. Both are very effective tools for keeping the audience in their seats and making them participate.

THE OUTLINE AND THE STEP OUTLINE

I usually work from an outline. I will know first in a general sense where I'm going. What is it I want to say? Who do I want to say it through? What is the story about? What's the conflict of the story? What is the resolution?

—WALTER BERNSTEIN

I'll write down a list of scenes—thirty, forty, eighty scenes. They won't be scenes really, but key words—like fifty words, and each word is supposed to remind me of a scene that promotes *the story. Since we are dealing with structure, that is crucial.*

—WILLIAM GOLDMAN

A lot of the time what happens is that the little impulse that gets me started on a story leads to something that's more interesting—and the little impulse disappears.

—BILL WITTLIFF

*I*nexperienced screenwriters often say, "Oh, I couldn't work from an outline. My writing would lose its spontaneity." The experienced writer knows that whether she has committed the outline to paper or whether (in very rare instances) it is all in her head, she is following a preconceived framework on which the story will be built. To begin writing without knowing where one is going is to head for the wilderness, with very little prospect of finding one's way out again. A screenplay begun in such a way is almost always wasted effort, abandoned long before the project nears conclusion, for the screenwriter has lost her way. The result is a great deal of discarded material, some of which may be very good by itself, but doesn't fit within the story being told.

For the rare writer who can formulate a plan in his head and keep it there without going to the trouble of putting it on paper, working without a formal outline may be possible. Most mortals, including most accomplished screenwriters, find an outline essential. For one thing, an outline permits a critical scrutiny of the skeleton before the flesh of action and dialogue are applied. In fact, the very act of putting the "spine" down on paper reveals things about the story that wouldn't be evident without outlining. It is obvious that changes are easier to make in an outline—and a lot easier for a writer to accept—than in a first draft, when a lot of work must be discarded if plans change.

Once the screenwriter is satisfied that she has a sound foundation on which to build, her creative faculties are free to concentrate on the fine points of characterization, action, and dialogue. In other words, outlining actually makes the writer *more* spontaneous. There is no longer the worry (which impedes spontaneity) that a scene might not fit into the story, and there is no necessity for clouding one's mind with thoughts about where a story might be heading and whether a scene being written is leading the right direction. Those decisions have been made during the outlining phase—at least for the first draft.

All that is left after an effective outline has been created is writing the scenes—fleshing out the characters, determining their specific actions and short-term motivations, creating atmosphere and specific circumstances, and, of course, writing the dialogue. But at any given moment, the writer is only working on those things for a single scene, not the entirety of the story or an act or even a whole sequence. Stated simply, once the writer has established the macrocosm of the story (by outlining), he or she is able to focus all energy and creativity on the microcosm, one scene at a time.

The most rudimentary plan for a screenplay should contain the following elements: who the central character is (if the unity of action is used; see "Unity," page 58) and what he or she wants; who the other principal characters are and what they each want; the actual outline of the general sequence of events and the act divisions; and formulations of the main tension, the culmination, and the resolution. Many screenwriters take the outlining further. Once the bare-bones skeleton of the story exists in outline form, more and more detail can be added prior to the actual scene writing. This is a relatively easy way of maintaining perspective on the whole story while fleshing it out. The outline of the story with a listing of all of the scenes that the writer plans to use to tell the story (each with some indication of who is involved, and what happens where and when), is known as a *step outline*. This method of story development encourages a kind of organic growth of the work, and helps to achieve the balance and unity that are essential if the screenplay is to be successfully completed.

Once a step outline is completed and the writer knows exactly where this story is heading, the actual scene writing can begin. It can progress with surprising speed. The quickness of writing a first draft in this way actually contributes to the quality and the unity of the script, because the writing is not spread out over time and subjected to uncertainties, second thoughts, and major changes in plan.

But a step outline should not be thought of as being chiseled in stone. It is a plan for the writing of the first draft of the screenplay, no more than that. As the writing of the first draft progresses, the writer inevitably learns more about the characters as they "get up on their feet," that is, as they interact with each other in complete scenes. As the writer's knowledge of the characters deepens and broadens, aspects of the step outline may need to be altered or adjusted, but it is still there as a guide, luring the writer ever onward toward the resolution of the story. The outline can keep the writer safely on track and enable more freedom in the writing of individual scenes and more latitude in making minor adjustments to the outline on the fly.

PLAUSIBILITY

Dramatic effect derives from what is probable, and not from what is possible.

—ARISTOTLE

*D*eus ex machina, Latin for "the god from the machine," identifies a Greek invention. Frequently a Greek play ended with a god being lowered to the acting area by means of a crane from above. This god would then tie up all the loose ends of the story. But the *deus ex machina* is of little use to modern playwrights and of no use to screenwriters, for we no longer accept the notion that a supernatural being will intercede in human affairs. The Greek dramatist could disentangle the knotted threads of his plot by introducing a god to take charge of the action, but the modern dramatist must be more resourceful in resolving a plot's complexities.

We have modern equivalents for the device, but they must still be avoided. The unexpected arrival of a powerful figure, the conveniently timed heart attack, the sudden inheritance, anything introduced by the writer from outside the boundaries of the story to help resolve the plot, must be shunned. Audiences recognize shoddy craftsmanship and refuse to accept a resolution that doesn't evolve naturally from the circumstances of the story.

When Bonnie and Clyde are ambushed and riddled with bullets at the end of that film, it is not *deus ex machina* because the quest of the sheriff they humiliated is part of the very fabric of the story. When George Bailey finally changes and is ecstatic to get back to his family at the end of *It's a Wonderful Life*, even though an angel has been a crucial part of the story, it is not *deus ex machina*. In this case, the change comes from inside George and the angel is an intrinsic part of the story, not tacked on at the end to clear everything up. When Evelyn is shot dead at the end of *Chinatown*, it is the inevitable extension of the overall story, the nature of the Noah Cross character and the impossibility of Jake changing his will or Evelyn's fate. Even in *The African Queen*, where the hand of God seems very close to the surface, both in terms of the rain that floats the boat onto the lake and at the very end, when the sunken boat resurfaces, it isn't really *deus ex machina*. Faith and prayer, the idea that "God helps those who help themselves," and Rosie's belief in both Charlie and the boat itself have all been part of the story's development, and these elements all come to fruition at the end through the design of the story.

Many stories have what is on the surface an unbelievable premise or circumstance: ghosts, cars that fly, thought transference, creatures that won't die or come from another planet—the list goes on and on. These things don't exist in the world we all inhabit, but they are very often the stuff of superb storytelling. In any story that contains an element of the unbelievable, even if all the other circumstances are very realistic, there is a crucial moment the screenwriter must create. This is the moment when the audience willingly suspends its disbelief; when the audience "buys into" the unbelievable part for the purpose of enjoying the story being told. If the storyteller fails to bring the audience along, to get it to suspend its disbelief in order to enjoy the story, all that follows that failure will play as just so much hokum to the audience.

In any successful film of this type—from *King Kong* to *Star Wars* to *Back to the Future* to *Frankenstein*—the willing suspension of disbelief is carefully created and nurtured by the storyteller. At its simplest, the method comes down to facing the disbelief head-on rather than trying to gloss it over. The audience will usually spot the latter and decline to participate in the story being told. Usually the best approach is to have a principal character—very often the protagonist, but not always—voice a disbelief the audience shares. As this character becomes convinced of the truth of the unbelievable thing, so does the audience. In *Back to the Future*, the protagonist doesn't believe in the time machine at first, but when he travels in it and comes to believe, we suspend our own disbelief and sign on for the rest of the story. In *King Kong*, the giant ape already exists; he merely has to be found. But there is very careful preparation for the moment of revelation of the title character, and considerable resistance to belief among the crew until this monster is before their very eyes. Sometimes, as in *Star Wars*, the unbelievable things are part of the everyday life of our protagonist, so we don't have his disbelief to use. In this instance, it is the audience's own world experience that must be used and built upon. We know spaceships now exist, though none so big and sophisticated as the ones in the film. We know computerized robots can move, and we've seen holograms. On and on until finally Luke gets into a car that flies, and we have no trouble accepting the world of this story and all the glorious things in it. Each of the early examples in the film is based on something we know to be possible; it's simply a bit better in the film than what is possible right now. We are even given time to adjust to the notion of space creatures. The first ones we meet are small and hooded, and the only really odd thing about them is that their eyes glow red. By the time we get into the bar with the full variety of creatures, we have bought into the story completely and do not resist believing.

One critical component of the audience's willing suspension of disbelief is that it can only happen once in a story. In other words, we will sign on to believe, but at that moment, what we have decided to accept also includes a sort of set of rules. These rules of a fictitious universe must then be scrupulously obeyed, or the audience will flee from the story. For instance, if we establish early on that cars can fly but buses cannot, we better not see a bus flying later on, or we'll quit trusting the storyteller and stop participating in the story. We often feel that the storyteller is "cheating" when this happens. For instance, in *Back to the Future* a great deal is made of how fast the car must be going to travel through time. It becomes one of the "rules" of this new world we have entered. If, in the end, the car manages to time-travel while standing still or going slower than the speed that we've been told is crucial, we would feel cheated and would rebel against the film, the story, and the storyteller.

Another characteristic of the finest stories is the effect of inevitability the writer has been able to achieve. The course of events the screenwriter sets in motion has not only followed the plausible path; the audience comes to believe there could not possibly have been any other outcome. This feeling of inevitability—a combination of characters moving along a course from which there is no possible turning—is perhaps a screenwriter's finest achievement.

Inevitability should not be confused with predictability. Inevitability is the sense, as the events unfold, that they couldn't have happened another way, while predictability relates to the audience's capacity to guess what is about to happen. So long as there are two equally plausible outcomes preventing the audience from guessing what is going to happen in the next scene or sequence or at the resolution, the story is not predictable. And if, at the same time, each step along the journey of the story feels probable and the hand of neither God nor the writer is visible, the story's unfolding events will seem inevitable.

ACTIVITY AND ACTION

The difference between activity and action: if there's lots of running around with no conflict between the characters, it means there is no dramatic action.

—FRANK DANIEL

*T*he neophyte screenwriter often thinks of a screenplay as endless dialogue instead of as a plan of action. Those who don't fully understand screenwriting think that the writing of dialogue is the whole craft. While characters do talk as part of their attempts to reach their goals and achieve their objectives, their dialogue is ultimately less important than the actions they take. The bulk of a screenplay is the description of the actions and activities of the characters—in addition, of course, to the whole set of circumstances and the premise of the story. The skillful dramatist thinks of what is happening on the stage, and the effective screenwriter thinks of the actions of the characters and how they should be seen by the audience. This is the heart of dramatic writing.

Action and activity are not interchangeable in this context. An activity is anything that a character might be doing in a scene, from knitting to filleting a fish to typing to memorizing song lyrics out loud; this is often called "business." On the other hand, an action is an activity with a purpose behind it, an activity that furthers a character's pursuit of an objective. Sometimes the exact same action is merely an activity in one set of circumstances and an action in another. For example, a character might be chopping onions in a scene solely as an activity. But another time, when the character wants to elicit sympathy from another character, he may chop onions to make himself cry. The latter, then, is clearly an action, because there is a goal behind it.

Another example could be the memorizing of song lyrics. In one scene the character is simply repeating the lyrics to commit them to memory because she likes the song. In another scene she might repeat the same lines in an attempt to warn or woo another character, or to gird up her courage for some particularly difficult moment she is facing. The words take on a meaning when connected with the purpose behind them that they don't have on their own. In fact, in this sort of scene, the dialogue itself can be completely meaningless, but still necessary and effective because of the purpose behind it.

A skillful screenwriter can cause dialogue to become either an activity or an action, depending on the intentions of the character performing it. Often the most effective scenes consist of activity, action, and minimal or even no dialogue. Truly significant actions must be determined before the dialogue is written. Purposeful activity that expresses the emotion and the desire of the character must be known in order to create effective and revealing scenes.

The experienced screenwriter tries first of all to determine what a character wants and what actions he or she takes to try to achieve it. This is true both of short-term objectives and the long-term objective of the whole story. In other words, first determine the actions that reveal character and carry the story forward, then invent the activities and dialogue that support those actions.

Effective actions and activities are visual elements, things the audience can *see*, because our memories and experiences of what we see are far stronger than of what we hear. The degree of hostility between the Capulets and the Montagues is shown by dueling and street brawling. In *Body Heat,* Racine's passion for Matty is effectively demonstrated when he throws a chair through the window and essentially breaks into her house to make love with her. In *Ninotchka,* the transformation in the title character is clearly shown with her action of buying the "decadent" hat seen earlier in the shop window. The action stays with us more effectively than if any of these characters had simply spoken dialogue expressing their hatred, passion, or change.

Examples of this kind could be repeated endlessly. It must be clear, however, that the dialogue for any of these particular scenes could not have been written unless the action was known first—at least by the writer. Often the beginning screenwriter feels that a character doesn't want anything or doesn't know what he or she wants. This may be true of the character at any given moment, but it shouldn't be true of the writer. The writer must know what a character wants, consciously or unconsciously, and the writer must know what a character is in pursuit of at any given moment, even if the character is oblivious to it.

Effective activities for characters need the addition of an action to move the story forward. The best procedure is first to find the action or actions that create the scene and/or are part of the pursuit of a longer-term objective, then find activities that would be natural in the given situation, activities that help to reveal the nature of the characters. Once these elements have been found, whatever dialogue is necessary and appropriate can be added. The weakest scenes are ones in which dialogue is expected to carry all of the dramatic weight by itself.

Activities that reveal character, but that aren't really part of the pursuit of any character's goal, can be effective tools for enriching the audience's experience of a story. For example, in *Chinatown,* when Evelyn cleanses Jake's horribly cut nose, she has no objective other than to clean the wound, yet the tenderness she demonstrates in the activity reveals a side of her character we haven't seen before. In *Annie Hall,* when Alvy and Annie cook lobsters, it is an activity; there is no purposeful action behind it. Yet the way in which they battle the creatures and share the moment of intimacy with each other reveals aspects of both of their characters as well as showing their bond with each other. These activities don't move the story forward, yet they expand our involvement and understanding of the lives of the characters and, in this way, enrich the storytelling.

DIALOGUE

Dialogue comes because I know what I want my characters to say. I envision the scene; I can imagine them up on the screen; I try to imagine what they would be saying and how they would be saying it, and I keep it in character. And the dialogue comes out of that. I think that goes for every writer in the world. Then I rewrite it. Then I cut it. Then I refine it until I get the scene as precise as I can get it.

—PADDY CHAYEFSKY

Most people think screenwriting is only dialogue, and that we're those people who write those dreadful lines that all those nice, wonderful actors have to say. And the reality is that the single most important thing contributed by the screenwriter is the structure.

—WILLIAM GOLDMAN

If you have a facility with writing dialogue, it can be a trap. You write exchanges, things that sound great, but are not really doing anything. Dialogue has to be functional.

—WALTER BERNSTEIN

Dialogue works the least well when it's telling you what's going on.

—TOM RICKMAN

The amazing thing about screenwriting is that the screenwriter does not, like the stage dramatist, hear his dialogue spoken until it's too late [for him] to know whether it plays or not.

—ERNEST LEHMAN

*T*here is endless variety in the dialogue of different periods and different writers. There are the humor and easy charm of Preston Sturges or Billy Wilder writing with I. A. L. Diamond; the hard-boiled but richly textured voice of Raymond Chandler and his many imitators;

the angst-ridden, self-deprecating humor of Woody Allen; or the angst-ridden wealth of image and feeling of Ingmar Bergman. There is the urban, "realistic" voice of David Mamet or Martin Scorcese and his collaborators. There is the literary realism of Mario Puzo and Francis Ford Coppola in the *Godfather* trilogy. And there is the heartfelt earnestness of Frank Capra and his collaborators.

No two screenwriters write exactly the same kind of dialogue, though obviously the differences are not always so wide as those listed above. But there are certain characteristics that are common to good dialogue from any writer. Good, effective dialogue arises out of character, situation, and conflict; it reveals character and moves the story forward. The character on screen is usually more articulate than he would be in life—even when a naturally inarticulate character is being presented—for good dialogue is an intensification of normal speech. So-called realistic speech is hardly real at all; although it may create that illusion, the confusion, excesses, fumblings, and backtracking of ordinary conversation have been trimmed away, and the dialogue has been given direction and a pattern. In addition, most everyday social niceties are dispensed with unless they serve some useful purpose in the scene at hand.

Dialogue carries a tremendous burden. Consider all it must accomplish for the screenwriter:

1. It must characterize the speaker, and perhaps the person addressed.
2. It must be idiomatic, maintaining the individuality of the speaker, yet still blend into the style of the screenplay as a whole.
3. It must reflect the speaker's mood, convey his or her emotion, or provide some window into his or her inner life.
4. It must often reveal the speaker's motivation or an attempt to hide his or her motivation.
5. It must reflect the relationship of the speaker to the other characters.
6. It must be connective, that is, grow out of a preceding speech or action and lead into another.
7. It must advance the action.
8. It must sometimes carry information or exposition.
9. Often it must foreshadow what is to come.
10. It must be clear and comprehensible to the audience.

In addition to fulfilling these functions, some other characteristics of good dialogue are:

1. Actors must be able to speak it without stumbling over the words. It must avoid tongue-twisters and too much alliteration, unless it is used (sparingly) for effect.

2. When long speeches are necessary, they should build toward the end, with the strongest idea or image saved for last. The most emphatic position in a speech is at the end, the second strongest at the beginning. Putting a modifying clause at the end of a speech, or the name of the character addressed, invariably weakens the impact of the speech.

3. The concrete image, one that can be visualized by the actor and the audience, is more effective than an abstract one. *Mountain* is a more vivid word than *grandeur, hurricane* is more visceral than *turmoil, roller-coaster* is more evocative than *bumpy.* Giving actors "visions" in their dialogue makes them better able to deliver the performance intended by the writer.

One of the major problems inexperienced screenwriters run into is overwriting. Their screenplays contain too much dialogue, which makes them too long; this is a bad combination because it allows the audience to "get ahead of the story." It is rarely a good idea to make the audience wait for the story to catch up with it. A principal reason for long and tedious scripts from beginning screenwriters is that they haven't yet learned the secret of compressing the dialogue, of making it do several things at once. They will use one section of dialogue solely to characterize the speaker and another to give needed exposition, instead of accomplishing both goals at once. Beginning screenwriters also tend to cover the same ground in both the dialogue and the scene description. In general, if a writer finds a redundancy between a described action and the accompanying dialogue, it is a good idea to trim or cut out the dialogue and let the action and visual image carry the moment.

In writing dialogue, the screenwriter should remember not only that action is going to carry a significant part of the burden, but that the actors themselves, with their physical presence and their voices, will also make an immense contribution. Even a single line or an entire speech can be spoken in a score of ways—with indifference or passion, with respect or suspicion, with hope, with anger, facetiously or with great earnestness. A skillful actor, aided by the guidance of a perceptive director, supports and reinforces the screenwriter's intent and illuminates the lines with his own understanding of the inner life of the character. Good dialogue leaves room for the actor to contribute in this way. In other words, the lines are not so explicit as to put the actor in an interpretive straitjacket.

Dialogue is the one area where a screenwriter has anything approaching the direct communication with the audience that the novelist enjoys. A good line, a well-turned phrase delivered in just the right way by an actor, can have a very powerful impact on the audience. Though rumors always circulate that the great lines were made up on the set by the actor, this is rarely accurate. More often than not, these are the lines that survived from the script through the production and editing processes, and thus are a reasonably direct link between the screenwriter and the audience. From "Frankly, my dear, I don't give a damn," to "I made him an offer he couldn't refuse," completely effective and memorable moments delivered in dialogue have two things in common—they are short and sweet. They have all the attributes listed above, and in addition, they are to the point and enjoy a simplicity that is inspiration itself.

Dialogue, because it is the only part of the screenplay the audience experiences directly, is the area where a screenwriter can express his inner poetry to greatest advantage. Scene descriptions (including characters' actions) are there for the makers of the film—the actors, the director, the cinematographer, the costume designer, and so on—and thus should be straightforward, clear, concise, and workmanlike. While the expression of visual and audio poetry is both possible and desirable in the scene description, the ultimate arbiter of how they are given to the audience is not the screenwriter but the director. But the screenwriter can use all of the burdens of dialogue listed above to great advantage with the delicate infusion of wit, cadence, word choice, rhythm, and "visions"—all the characteristics of poetry.

It cannot be stated too emphatically: *Dialogue alone cannot sustain a film or screenplay for very long.* "Talking heads" and an overdependence on performance are the result. Even when performance is superb, it is still better to give actors *actions,* to allow them to act, not just talk. Talk is a small part what we do as human beings, and it should be a small part of how we expect to tell our stories to the audience. And very often, by giving the actor an effective and clear-cut action, the screenwriter can make the necessity for dialogue diminish or even disappear.

VISUALS

In a book you might start with some dialogue, and then describe the room, and start with some more dialogue, and then describe your clothing, and more dialogue. The camera gets that in an instant. Boom, *and you're on. Get on, get on. The camera is relentless. Makes you keep running.*

—WILLIAM GOLDMAN

When I started out, I was writing scripts by putting in shots all over the place until I realized directors paid absolutely no attention to it. So now I very rarely do that except if I want to make a specific point.

—WALTER BERNSTEIN

The main thing is I write master scenes. And I write stage directions in, as I would on a stage play: He crosses the room quickly, opens the window and leaps out. *I do not describe what setups the camera should be set up for in order to pick up that action.*

—PADDY CHAYEFSKY

I see everything. It's almost like I'm playing the scene in my head. I never, just never, put down only dialogue; I'm always acting it out in my head.

—ERNEST LEHMAN

*W*e have discussed at length the importance of giving actions to the characters and of creating vivid and succinct dialogue, but there is yet another aspect of the screenplay that must be dealt with—what the audience sees, and how it sees it. In a word, the *visuals*. Although many directors and more than a few film reviewers may bristle at the notion that the visuals of a film begin on the page, or, more precisely, in the mind of the screenwriter, the director must either become his own writer or become helpless without the starting point given by the screenwriter. There is a famous story about Frank Capra, a superb director who was widely renowned in the 1930s and 1940s for his "Capra touch." A screenwriter once handed him 120 blank pages neatly bound as a script and said, "Go ahead, give it that old Capra touch."

It's inaccurate to say that the director has no role in the visuals or is incapable of inventing visuals. However, the starting point of how a film story is shown to the audience is the script, and a wise director looks there first for clues on how to compose individual shots, or for the overall visual design. At this point the director must, of necessity, take over responsibility for the visuals, as with most other interpretive aspects of creating the film, but at the very least the director has the suggestion of the writer right there on the page.

But these suggestions have to be put there by the writer, with forethought, knowledge, and more than a little delicacy. There are few things directors hate more than to have the screenwriter dictating the size of a shot, when to move the camera, or how to compose an image. Instead, the skillful screenwriter will imply his intentions through sentence construction, choice of words, and the details described.

For instance, the writer may write, "Maggie toys nervously with her wedding ring, then slips it off and pockets it." The wedding ring is clearly important, and a good director will know that it won't show up in a long shot or perhaps not even in a medium shot. But the director has the choice of cutting to a closer shot, moving the camera to the character (and ring), or moving the actor closer to the camera to get this important image across to the audience. Likewise, "Maggie hides her cash under her belt while she goes to answer the door" gives specificity to the action and yet allows the director the choice of dollying with the move, panning with it, letting Maggie's image shrink as she goes away from the camera, or letting her image grow as she approaches the camera.

Besides indicating some aspects of how individual moments and actions can be shot for maximum effectiveness, the description of visuals in a screenplay can do a great deal to establish the style of story (realism, fantasy, Gothic romance). In addition, it helps establish the world of the story and gives indications of the many kinds of contrasts between scenes or even changes within scenes (from nearly black and white to very colorful, from loud to quiet, from fast to slow, from talky to non-dialogue, from lyrical to earthy). On top of all this, the scene description in a script should give indications of changes in pace and rhythm throughout the story.

In summary, scene description should include detailed information concerning one or more of the following areas:

1. The physical location of the scene.

2. Indications about the world of the story.

3. Which characters are present, and indications of their physical condition or appearance.

4. The specific actions of the various characters.

5. An indication of the image size, motion of the camera or the character, and/or a hint at the composition of visuals within the frame, without dictating exact particulars to the director, who clearly makes the final decisions.

6. Clues about the style of story being told and about the style of the individual scenes when there are changes (from the present to a flashback, from reality to fantasy, from surreal to lucid).

7. Contrasts between scenes or between various moments within scenes.

8. Indications about changes in pace and rhythm.

9. Indications of light, texture, and color.

10. Indications of sounds, both objective (generated by sources on screen) and subjective (used for dramatic effect, as in a character's heartbeat during a dangerous moment).

11. Clues to the costume designer, the production designer, the hairdresser, the landscapers, and all the other professionals who contribute to what the audience actually sees and hears on screen.

THE DRAMATIC SCENE

You always attack a movie scene as late as you possibly can. You always come into the scene at the last possible moment.

—WILLIAM GOLDMAN

Most scenes are rarely about what the subject matter is. Most people rarely confront things head-on. They're afraid to. I think that most people try to be accommodating in life, but in back of their accommodation is suppressed fear or anger or both. What happens in a dramatic situation is that it surfaces. And it shouldn't surface too easily or it's not realistic.

—ROBERT TOWNE

Scenes really don't work when characters are being distorted to serve plot.

—TOM RICKMAN

What makes a good scene is that it becomes part of the whole without showing its edges . . . it's inevitable.

—BILL WITTLIFF

*T*he scene is, in a sense, a one-act play in itself, but one that dovetails with the preceding and subsequent scenes to form part of the longer screenplay. Conventionally constructed (as many of the best scenes are), the scene has a protagonist, just as the full story does. In addition, the best scenes have an objective, obstacles, a culmination, and a resolution. It should be emphasized that the scene's protagonist isn't necessarily the same as the story's. Rather than complicate matters by thinking in terms of the protagonist for each scene, the screenwriter is be better advised to ask "Whose scene is it?"—yet another of Frank Daniel's contributions to storytelling theory. It can be phrased this way:

"Whose want (or pursuit of an objective) makes a given scene happen?" Even in scenes where the protagonist of the overall story is present, it is not necessarily his or her want that makes the scene happen.

In *North by Northwest* the initial meeting of the protagonist, Roger Thornhill, and the antagonist, Phillip Vandamm, happens after Roger has been kidnapped by Vandamm's men. The scene "belongs" to Vandamm as he tries to unmask what he believes is a secret agent pretending to be an impatient and offended advertising man. In *Bringing Up Baby*, the grand finale, the scene in which all of the principals and both of the leopards wind up in the town jailhouse, the scene is created by the sheriff. He is a minor—though memorable—character, and his desire to get to the bottom of all the goings-on is what drives the scene, what forces the scene to happen. Therefore it is his scene.

The dramatic scene gives one aspect of the larger conflict, but at the end it leaves the larger conflict still unresolved. If a scene comes to a full and complete resolution, it stops the forward momentum of the story, which then takes precious screen time to get rolling again. The story's protagonist is either closer to or farther from his goal; or he started the scene by moving closer to that goal, but ended it even farther from it (or vice versa). The subsequent scene will be another development in the encompassing story, and will again alter the position of the protagonist in relation to his objective. In general, as the story progresses, these swings from hope to fear and back again intensify, become stronger and more pronounced.

In *Shane*, after Shane and Starrett have had a brawl with Ryker's men in the town general store and have been patched back together by Mrs. Starrett, the action of the story shifts for a few scenes. We follow Ryker's dirty work in clearing the homesteaders off their land, and establish Torrey's desire to get revenge on Ryker. Though these scenes don't include Shane, they still intensify his quest to keep from strapping his guns back on, because they increase the pressure on him to take up guns to solve the problems of the peaceful settlers with whom he is aligned. The scenes work on the audience's hope versus fear, in this case promoting its fear on behalf of Shane. Later, when Torrey is killed by Ryker's men, there is even more intensity to the pressure on Shane, and our consequent feelings of hope and fear increase.

Often the separation of scenes is much less distinct. Instead of completely separate scenes, tiny bits of information that urge on our hope or fear are delivered in and around scenes that have other purposes as well. Sometimes we will see that a character overhears something or sees something that the other characters don't suspect he knows. Sometimes we see a gun hidden inside a coat, which has not been revealed to another character, or an engagement ring or the necessary money to complete some objective. The accomplished screenwriter attempts to make these moments flow together seamlessly, to obscure the stitches that hold together what are, in fact, parallel story lines. These various lines of action are woven together into one continuum, which is the way we experience them.

The dramatic scene (which includes comedy as well) is the basic building block of a screenplay. A screenwriter who cannot create an effective and convincing dramatic scene will not be able to hold an audience, no matter how compelling the story might be when summarized. Just as with the overall story, a scene at its simplest is *Somebody wants something badly and is having difficulty getting it.* The somebody is the person who owns the scene, the want is the objective, and the difficulty is the obstacle (there are often more than one). A scene must at the very least answer who, where, when, and what happens, but scenes often carry much more than that. Sometimes *why* is dealt with; sometimes a significant new character is first seen and must be given a revealing and memorable introduction; sometimes a scene will help create a dramatic irony or will have a moment of recognition; sometimes time is ellipsed between scenes (or, much more rarely, within a scene); sometimes advertising or elements of the future are employed to point the audience forward in the story; and sometimes one line of action is resolved only to help create the next.

When sitting down to write a first draft of a scene, it is critical to have in mind whose scene it is, what he or she wants within the scene (not the overriding objective of the story as a whole), what obstacle(s) could be in that character's way, when and where the scene takes place, and what principal characters are present. It is not a good idea to put any more pressure on the writing of the first draft than that. First get the scene down on paper, have it make sense and approximate what it was intended to do; then, when it is time to rewrite, analyze the scene by asking a number of questions about it. Not all of the following questions apply to all scenes:

1. Is it clear whose scene it is, and what he or she wants?
2. What is the conflict of the scene? Is it with one or more of the characters, with the circumstances or the surroundings of the scene, or is the conflict within the character?
3. Where and when does the scene take place? Could another time or location serve to heighten the impact?
4. What characters are present at the beginning, which ones enter during the scene, and who is there at the end?

5. Is any new character introduced? If so, does the introduction give the audience a glimpse into the nature of the character and make the character memorable enough?

6. Where were the characters before the scene started, and where are they going after it ends?

7. Has time been ellipsed since the last scene? If so, is it clear to the audience that time has passed and how much time has passed? Are any minor ellipses of time within the scene clear and believable?

8. Has there been a transition from the previous scene, and is there a transition to the next scene?

9. Is there a scene of preparation or a scene of aftermath? Is one necessary? Not all scenes require them.

10. Does the scene contrast in some way with the preceding scene or the scene to follow? Again, not all scenes will contrast.

11. Do the actions of the characters fit their "through lines"? That is, do the characters stay true to who they are and what they want?

12. Are the actions of the characters clear and motivated? Do they reveal character and move the story forward?

13. Is there any use of dramatic irony?

14. Is there unity of action?

15. Is the scene thematically related to the rest of the story?

16. Are the obstacles difficult enough? Are they too difficult?

17. Are the events plausible? Must disbelief be suspended? Do these events obey the "rules" of previously suspended disbelief?

18. Does the audience know what might go right or wrong within the scene? When in the scene do they know? When does one or more of the characters know?

19. Does the dialogue reflect character?

20. Are the inner lives of the characters revealed through action, dialogue, and reaction?

21. Are any elements of the future used? Should they be used? Does the scene bring the action of the story too much to a standstill, or does it propel the story forward?

22. Are there visual and audio clues, suggestions, and plans for the other professionals who will make the film?

23. Does the scene belong in the story being told?

REWRITING

I really believe in rewriting, but it isn't just rewriting, it's rethinking, reconceptualizing, approaching things anew.

—TOM RICKMAN

When you're rewriting, very often you're doing the scenes that don't work. The toughest scenes in a piece of material may not only have been the toughest for the writer who worked ahead of you, but may also be the most difficult scenes to solve, period. So they are the ones you have to keep redoing.

—ROBERT TOWNE

Writing is rewriting. Sometimes even when a picture is done, you say, "I wish I could get my hands on it again."

—WALTER BERNSTEIN

*N*o discussion of screenwriting would be complete without dealing with rewriting. Whether or not it includes the screenwriter per se, the rewriting of a screen story is not complete until the film is in the theaters. Even then, there are reissues of films with material included that was cut from the initial release. But for all practical purposes the revising and fine-tuning of a screenplay's story continues throughout the shooting and the editing process, and ends with the release print the first audiences see.

Most of the time, the screenwriter's involvement in rewriting ends when the shooting begins. Sometimes a writer must rewrite tomorrow's pages while today's are being shot, but this is a less than desirable circumstance. And sometimes the writer is brought in at the editing phase to create new dialogue that can be looped in, or to write a voice-over, or, if the budget allows, to write new pages for a few days of reshooting to improve the film. Whenever the screenwriter's involvement ends, one thing is clear, there has been a great deal of rewriting. Anyone who shoots the first draft of a script is either a fool or has a genuine genius for a screenwriter.

The highly respected novelist Pat Conroy, whose novels have often been made into films (*The Great Santini, The Lords of Discipline,* and *Conrack*), tried his hand at screenwriting by adapting his novel *Prince of Tides* (with Becky Johnston). This is what he had to say about the experience:

> *Writing scripts is simply one of the most difficult things a human being can do. There's something so naked about screenwriting. I can fake you out with a paragraph in a book. I can throw verbiage and I can throw narratives where they make a weak scene look better. You can't do that with movie writing. It's got to be visual. It's like they hand you musical notes and then give you a* haiku *and say "Put this together."*

One cannot expect to do something as complicated and difficult as writing a screenplay without mistakes on the first try. The beginning screenwriter who expects to do little or no rewriting is setting himself up for serious disappointment and failure. It is a far better idea to embrace the notion of rewriting as an opportunity for improving a project that already exists. There is a real sense of discovery in the writing of a first draft, no matter how detailed the step outline may be. By the time one writes the FADE OUT at the bottom of the last page, the pages near the initial FADE IN no longer fit quite so neatly together with the story. The writer has discovered a great deal about the characters, about the story, and about his or her own intentions while writing that first draft.

Just like the characters, the screenwriter doesn't always consciously know what she wants or what she is after, but that doesn't mean she's not after something. One hopes that, by the end of the first draft, it has become clear. So, at the very least, the early part of the first draft must be rewritten to match the end. And there are all manner of plantings and payoffs that need to be woven into the story. Then there are the scenes that never really worked, which must be redone. (The list on pages 93–94 of questions to ask about scenes should give you an idea of how many ways a scene can go wrong.)

But this is only the tip of the iceberg of rewriting. Once that first draft is touched up and made to match, and the necessary items have been planted and elements of the future have been woven in, it is time for one of the screenwriter's most dreaded moments: giving the script to someone to read. The nakedness Conroy talks about is never more palpable than at this moment. Knowing and experiencing that moment, when someone else reads what you have been slaving over, is a time when a sensible screen-writer thinks quite positively about rewriting, saying, "I can make it better. Just give it back and let me work on it a little longer." Don't succumb to the temptation to put off the inevitable outside feedback; it doesn't get easier. Rather, accept the reactions of your first readers, then go back to work.

This doesn't mean you have to change everything that anyone objected to or didn't understand or didn't buy into. The feedback has identified a potential problem, but you must determine for yourself whether it truly is a problem that needs to be fixed. If all or most of your early readers have the same problem, then the answer is clear that you must rework it. Some-times rewriting is merely patching and repairing, like fixing a hole in the wall. Other times—and these are the rewrites that are most necessary and most difficult to face—the entire story or a large portion of it must be rethought from the ground up. Don't throw your hands up and start building another house because this one needs repair. That's the same as throwing away all the work, thought, and heartache you have put into developing the story and writing the first draft.

It is a far better idea to go back and look at the structure of the house, see where the foundation is sound and where it is weak, where the framing (read *skeleton*) is solid, and where it is indistinct or missing. Go back through the entire tool chest we have been discussing, find the element or elements that are missing, incomplete, or unclear, and go right back to work on them just as you did when you were developing the story the first time through. Once the superstructure has been bolstered and fixed, study the scenes to discover which ones no longer fit and what new ones must be created. Sometimes this process must be repeated more than once, but one hopes that with each successive draft, the script is improving.

At the same time, keep in mind that it is also possible to rewrite a story to death, to damage beyond all recognition the spontaneity and life that found their way onto the page when the story was newer, when the writer was fresher, and when enthusiasm still existed. So it is necessary to strike a balance: rewrite as much as the script demands, but no more. When a producer, a director, and several actors start putting their money, ideas, and hearts into the project, another whole round of rewriting will begin, but that is the subject of another discussion. The purpose of this book is to help you find ways to satisfy yourself with your efforts, to get to the point where your third or fourth or fifth draft gives you the same sense of com-pletion (read *resolution*) you have been attempting to give to your audience.

THE
ANALYSES

ABOUT THE ANALYSES

*W*hat follows are detailed discussions of the various tools introduced in this book as they are put into practice in each of sixteen widely disparate films. These essays are not meant to be definitive analyses of the films; rather, they are intended as demonstrations of the way screenwriting tools have been employed in successful and well-made films. The tools have not been used equally in all films, as the reader will quickly grasp. It is essential to be very familiar with each of the films before reading its analysis, in order to learn most effectively from this section, even if that means reviewing an old favorite. Watch the film with an eye to picking out the tools discussed here, then use the analysis as a study guide.

The films analyzed were chosen with great care. It would be natural for you to suppose that I see these as the sixteen best films or screenplays of all time. Surely each of the films dealt with here is superbly made, with as much care given to the craft of filmmaking as to art, style, stars, and all the other elements that make up a first rate film. Yet my list of "best" films was not the criterion for selection, however much I admire the films contained here.

I wanted films that would demonstrate not only the basic principles dealt with in the book, but also many of the variations and distortions that the storytelling form can withstand. So I have chosen films with simple, straightforward by-the-numbers storytelling, and I have chosen films that so thoroughly mask their underlying structural elements that they seem to the novice to have no structure and to defy all theories of drama. There are films that seem to have two central characters instead of one, and films that seem to have four or five characters all elbowing each other off center stage. There are films that are adaptations of superb plays, and many that are original to the screen. There are old Hollywood classics, new Hollywood classics, and European and Japanese films.

There are dozens if not hundreds of films that I would gladly have included if only there were space, time, and energy. Unfortunately, I could not. I have not included a token representation of every nation with a once or presently thriving film industry, nor have I attempted to represent every "school" of what is artistically or politically correct, nor have I sought out the socially, politically, spiritually, or artistically inflammatory. Rather, the basis of deciding upon which films to include was a composite of these criteria: (1) masterfully crafted storytelling; (2) clear and effective demonstration of one or more of the dramatic theories dealt with in the book; (3) wide enough distribution to expect that most prospective readers would be familiar with the film; (4) broadening of the spectrum of types, styles, genres, story patterns, and storytelling approaches delineated in the book; and (5) availability of the film on videotape for intensive study and analysis by the reader.

So I offer my unrestrained apologies to all the great filmmakers whose films are not included here and all the nations whose filmmakers are not represented. No slight of any kind is intended.

Regarding the order of the following analyses, I decided to avoid simple chronology and opted instead for an approach that would lend itself to study by the reader. I have begun with films that utilize more easily grasped dramaturgy and have attempted to put the films in an order that, if followed by the reader, will build knowledge of the basics of storytelling and screenwriting, will expose some of the innumerable variations and explore the incredible range of storytelling techniques available, and will in the end lead to some kind of comprehensive understanding of what can and cannot be used as effective tools of screenwriting.

E.T.

(1982)
Written by Melissa Mathison
Directed by Steven Spielberg

One of the highest grossing films of all time, a landmark in the use of special effects and, in particular, mechanical puppetry, *E.T.* is one of those films that touched an emotional chord for young and old alike and "made them believe." Although it is a certified Hollywood blockbuster, it has few if any of the usual trappings; there is no kind of warfare, there is no charismatic rogue male lead doing superheroic deeds at every turn, and there is no sex, swearing, or sadism. Instead, we have a simple story, one verging on a fable or fairy tale, one with universal appeal—a child with a special secret that he must keep from adults who would destroy it. The story is well told at every level, and this, more than the impressive wizardry, is what made audiences flock to the theaters and bring friends for return visits.

SYNOPSIS

A spaceship lands in a desolate forest and a little creature with a glowing red midriff wanders about in the night. It is scared by the hooting of owls and the barking of dogs, it marvels at tall trees, and it runs for its life from men in pickup trucks with rings of keys on their belts and threatening flashlights playing over the underbrush. The men scare the ship into taking off, leaving the creature to fend for himself. Meanwhile, nearby, Eliot Taylor tries to join a game with his older brother and his buddies, but he's an outsider, unaccepted.

Eliot hears the creature in the family shed and gets scared off by it, but when he tells everyone, he isn't believed. In the middle of the night he goes in search and comes face to face with the little troll-like creature. They run in opposite directions, fearing for their lives, but Eliot sees which way it headed. The next day he makes a trail of candy, trying to lure it, then sits up all night to see it again. They meet, both get over their mutual fear, and Eliot lures the creature into his bedroom. He pretends to be sick the next day and spends the day with it, dubbing him E.T. (his own initials). He tries to communicate and finds that E. T. is curious; soon the creature is imitating Eliot's every move.

After his brother Mike comes home from school, Eliot swears him to secrecy, then shows him E.T., but at the same moment his little sister, Gertie, walks in, gets one look at E.T., and screams her head off. E.T. does the same, and everyone is in a fright and a panic that Mom will find out. The three kids try to find out where he's from, and when they show him the solar system he puts balls in orbit like the planets and lets them know he's from outer space—"home." The next day, when Eliot is at school, E.T. is home alone and gets into mischief, drinking beer and rewiring numerous electrical gadgets while learning about earth from TV and newspaper comics. He sees a television ad for long distance and wants to phone home himself. But Eliot, at school, gets "drunk" in sync with E.T., liberates an army of frogs that are about to be dissected, and lands in trouble for being drunk.

Gertie discovers E.T. has learned to talk and now wants to phone home. The kids help him gather anything that looks like it might work, and E.T. sets about creating a phone for himself. But Mike notices that E.T. is not looking very healthy. Eliot declares that "we're fine," clearly reacting to this link between the two of them. When Eliot cuts his finger, E.T. heals the wound with one touch of his finger. The phone is ready, but they need to go back up to the clearing in the forest to use it. It is Halloween night and the three kids conspire to sneak E.T. out of the house dressed as a ghost and get him up there to do the calling. When the house is empty, the men with keys on their belts, who have been hovering all around the family with high-tech equipment, enter the house and inspect it. The kids get away, and on the way, E.T. makes Eliot's bike fly and drop them in the forest. But E.T.'s phone doesn't seem to work, and Eliot falls asleep. When he wakes up in the morning, E.T. is nowhere to be seen and Eliot is feeling totally miserable.

When he gets home, he sends Mike out to find E.T. He is found facedown in a river, all white and in serious physical trouble. At home, when E.T. and Eliot are together, it is clear that they are both suffering from the same malady. Mom is finally told about E.T. and quickly removes her kids from this "monster," but when she tries to lead them from the house, "Keys" and his men take over, turning the house into an otherworldly nightmare. The technicians and doctors examining E.T. and Eliot find they are completely linked and fear they are losing both of them. Eliot begs them not to hurt E.T. and tells them from his own feelings that they are scaring him or hurting him.

But E.T. separates himself from Eliot, and as Eliot recovers, E.T. slips into some kind of coma that all the doctors can't seem to arrest. Once they finally pronounce E.T. dead and "put him on ice," Eliot is distraught, knowing that they will dissect his friend. Keys allows him a few minutes alone with the body, and Eliot discovers the refrigerated compartment is exactly what E.T. needed; he is very much alive, and Eliot learns that the phone has worked, and a ship is coming for E.T. Eliot gets Mike to help him, then sends a note to Mom through Gertie. With Mike driving, they manage to steal E.T. from the men and arrange a rendezvous with their other young friends to escape on bikes. They lead a hellish chase over the hills of suburbia, with hundreds of police and Keys's men after them. Just when it seems they are trapped, E.T. has all five bikes in the air and flying up to meet the ship. Mom, Gertie, and eventually Keys all arrive in time to see E.T. off. There are sad good-byes, E.T. tells Eliot he will be alive in his mind, and then boards the space ship, finally going home.

PROTAGONIST AND OBJECTIVE

This would seem to be a story with dual protagonists, the two E.T.s. They have a special link that connects them physically, which bolsters this feeling. But upon closer consideration it becomes clear that what they want is not the same thing. Eliot wants to keep his special relationship/friendship with E.T., but E.T. wants to get home, to return to his own kind. The obstacles they both face, while linked, are not the same, and the predicament around which this story is told belongs squarely to Eliot.

So it is Eliot's story, and his objective is to keep something that we have seen him establish, a special mystical bond with E.T. Because this objective is not an especially aggressive and active one (though the execution of it becomes very active), the telling of this story depends on establishing circumstances that actively impinge on the objective and make it difficult.

OBSTACLES

There are two basic sources of obstacles to Eliot's attempt to keep his special relationship with E.T.—those from Eliot's world and those from E.T.'s. From Eliot's world come the obstacles that no adults can be trusted, even Mom, and that Keys and his men are actively trying to find—and presumably take away—E.T. From E.T. himself come the other two obstacles—he can't survive for long in our world and he desperately wants to go home. Each of these four sources plays directly against Eliot's objective.

PREMISE AND OPENING

The premise in this story doesn't predate the telling of the story, but is established with the opening—which does slightly predate the introduction of the protagonist. A harmless and loving alien, who finds our world frightening, is accidentally abandoned in a forest by his spaceship, which must flee human trackers. This premise is quickly established in the opening scene and then we go immediately to Eliot in the midst of his world. Before they even meet each other, we begin to see parallels between these two little outsiders—both are underestimated and misunderstood.

MAIN TENSION, CULMINATION, AND RESOLUTION

The main tension is established when all the parameters are in place: E.T. and Eliot have formed a special bond; Eliot wants to keep him and communicate with him and he has sworn his brother and sister to absolute secrecy, thus clearly identifying adults as the enemy. So the main tension could be stated as simply as this: "Will Eliot be able to keep his special bond with his unusual little friend, E.T.?"

The culmination comes when that bond is broken. When they are both under adult medical care and seem to be dying together, E.T. separates himself from Eliot, physically but not emotionally. This comes shortly before E.T. is pronounced dead by the adults.

The resolution comes when Eliot says good-bye to E.T. and is told that he will be alive in his mind, in his memory and imagination. Then E.T. boards his ship for home.

THEME

The thematic link in this story becomes clear in the very last scene, when E.T. touches his lighted finger to Eliot's head and says that he will be alive in his mind. Implicit in this moment is that this is true because Eliot *believes* in him. This is brought up overtly earlier, when Eliot thinks he is talking to E.T.'s corpse and says that he will always believe in him. But the subject of believing and not believing has been there from the very beginning. When Eliot tries to tell everyone about the monster in the shed, he isn't believed. When he tells them about the creature he has found, he isn't believed. When he finally shows E.T. to Mike and Gertie, they believe, but they swear secrecy from Mom, who they don't expect to believe. When Gertie tells Mom about E.T., she isn't believed. The same goes for Eliot when he tells Mike's friends about the spaceman at their house.

But it isn't simply a matter of being believed or not believed in the real-world sense. There is magic in the air with this story, the stuff of fantasy. It is no accident that Mom reads Gertie the section of *Peter Pan* about believing in fairies—it goes right to the thematic core of the story. It is not just for the sight gags that critical parts of this story take place on Halloween, a festival devoted to belief in the supernatural. And there is a note of irony, in a thematic sense, with the character Keys, who has been perceived as the ringleader of the bad guys, but who turns out to believe in just the same way Eliot does. This is why Keys is allowed, and justifiably so, at the final good-bye scene—he is the adult with a ten-year-old Eliot still alive and well inside of him. So this story is an exploration of believing in the childlike sense, the same believing that makes Peter Pan fly.

UNITY

Since Eliot's objective is to maintain his special bond with E.T., and it is his pursuit of this goal that is actively opposed by the numerous obstacles, the unity of action is at work here, even though the action is largely of a defensive nature. Maintaining a status quo is a viable dramatic objective if that status quo is actively threatened.

EXPOSITION

The earliest exposition, the premise of the story—E.T.'s abandonment on earth—is delivered directly and simply to the audience. With a masterful use of sound and visual design and no dialogue, we are shown all we need to know about how E.T. came to be stranded on earth. The sounds that scare the creatures that we know to be harmless are an effective way of making us feel sympathetic toward them. The early exposition of Eliot is handled similarly. Though there is dialogue, none of it really pertains to the important things we learn. Instead, it is Eliot's estrangement from the group and his efforts to join it that come through; it is his being alone and lonely that we see. And when he goes to explore the sounds in the shed, we see the same kind of curiosity and innocent courage that E.T. showed when exploring our scary world at the very beginning.

Elsewhere the exposition is delivered with both conflict and humor. When the children try to find out where E.T. is from, the difficulty of communicating lends conflict to the scene. When we discover the strength and depth of the physical link between E.T. and Eliot, we have the humor and the conflict of his getting drunk in school and freeing the frogs.

CHARACTERIZATION

The most important characterizations are obviously E.T. and Eliot. Unlike a protagonist and an antagonist, here we have two kindred spirits who would at first seem to be just the same, but as the story evolves we discover their differences. First we are given their similarities: they are outsiders, scarable, curious, and more than a little clever; Eliot's thermometer trick has no doubt become a standard for all truants since this film's release.

But whereas Eliot wants to keep his special friend and the love relationship he has formed, E.T. wants to go home; he wants to return to his own kind, despite the love relationship. Neither is an outright rejection of the other, but these two peas in a pod carry within them all the seeds of conflict necessary to make this story work.

The characterizations of the adults are especially interesting. Until the end, the only adult we see is Mom. Though she is nice, she is generally in a hurry, coming or going in some direction and setting down some kind of rules on which we will learn she is actually quite lax. All the other adults are seen from waist level, characterized by their keys, their flashlights, their equipment, and the urgency of their pursuit. This anonymity makes them that much more frightening, and shooting them from low angles helps to put us into the shoes of our protagonist, a boy against the adult world, outgunned at every turn.

DEVELOPMENT OF THE STORY

Once the bond is established between Eliot and E.T., it is the conflicts inherent in their two worlds that force this story into being and make it continue to develop. E.T.'s inability to adapt to our world and his desire to go home force much of the action, while the hovering presence of Keys and his men seems to justify Eliot's lack of trust in adults and at the same time gives an ominous foreboding to every moment in which E.T.'s presence might be revealed.

DRAMATIC IRONY

Dramatic irony is used extensively in the telling of this story. From the moment when Eliot first goes to explore the shed and we know more or less what is in there, we are dealing with irony. Once he has befriended E.T. the irony shifts to the rest of the household, as one by one they each find out about his existence. Another irony at play here is that we know about Keys and his men hovering around the house, but the family and E.T. are all oblivious to them.

Much of the humor in this film stems from the ironies: when Gertie is telling Mom about E.T. and isn't believed even as E.T. is in the scene; when Eliot tells Mike's friends that he has a spaceman at his house and is laughed at; when Eliot gets "drunk" in class and collapses under his desk; when Mom takes a picture of Eliot, Mike, and E.T. as a goblin; when Eliot fakes a fever using a light bulb on the thermometer; when Mom reads the scene from *Peter Pan* to Gertie while Eliot and E.T. listen in. Each of these moments is funny in part because we know something that one or more of the characters don't know.

PREPARATION AND AFTERMATH

There is a nice scene of preparation for the first meeting of Eliot and E.T. Eliot is camped out with the flashlight and a cover. He is sound asleep, having failed at his guard duty, and the whole lighthearted mood of their first meeting—frightening to Eliot, but we know it is safe—is set before he wakes up and the scene begins. After Eliot has introduced E.T. to Mike and Gertie, there is an aftermath with the siblings and E.T. hiding in the closet staring at each other, while through the door louvers we see Eliot being read the riot act by Mom. The details of the scene in the other room aren't important, but the reactions of the trio in the closet, and their continued amazement with each other, are focused by the sense of danger that Mom's presence brings.

There is a series of fine aftermaths to major scenes in the third act. The first comes at the end of the escape in the van when Mike's buddies first see E.T. while Eliot and Mike come down from their success at stage one of the escape. After they have pedaled like mad all over suburbia and E.T. has finally flown them all up to the woods, there is another nice aftermath when all five boys and E.T. watch the spaceship land and are filled with awe. And then, after all of the good-byes, there is E.T.'s protracted exit, which enables all the emotional aftermath that Eliot, the boys, Gertie, Mom, and Keys can deliver watching him board the ship and then watching it take off while the music swells.

PLANTING AND PAYOFF

Both functional plants and metaphorical plants are used in this story. The trail of candy Eliot uses to lure E.T. is established and paid off in their first meeting, first when Eliot lures him into his room and back in the woods, and later when Keys finds a stash and even eats a piece. The closetful of stuffed animals is also a nice plant with a very effective payoff when E.T.

hides from Mom by pretending to be one of them. In fact, Keys himself is a plant, and his name comes from the plant. Since we only see him and his men from the waist down, the loop of keys is an effective way of distinguishing one of the group for us to focus on. Later, when he becomes a visible character for us, we are shown our familiarity with him through the payoff on the keys.

When Eliot cuts himself and says "Ouch," E.T. picks up on the meaning of the word and repeats it. Later, when he is telling him how much he wants to go home, there is a payoff on the use of the word. At the end, when E.T. says "Ouch" right before the spaceship lands, the word has reached the metaphorical level. For Eliot and E.T., the word has come to mean emotional pain more than physical pain. And the flowering plant in particular takes on a metaphorical role in this story. The first time E.T. resurrects the dying plant, it draws our attention to it. When the plant wilts with his "dying," and then rejuvenates when he is alive again, it has become a metaphor for his resurrection.

ELEMENTS OF THE FUTURE AND ADVERTISING

When Eliot states, shortly after bringing E.T. home, that adults would "give him a lobotomy or experiment on it," he is making a kind of prediction that is an element of the future. When Mom sends the kids off for trick-or-treating and demands that they be back one hour after dark, she is establishing the kind of deadline that is also an element of the future; we wonder if they will all get back in time. And when Mike asserts to Eliot that E.T. isn't looking too good, that he seems to be getting sick, it is also an element of the future, containing as it does the germ of a prediction of future deterioration.

Halloween night, which is such a crucial time in this story, is advertised early, when the kids discuss what costumes they'll wear for trick-or-treat. When E.T. tells Eliot that the phone machine has really worked and that the spaceship is returning for him, it is also advertising.

PLAUSIBILITY

All stories that contain supernatural elements need to create the circumstances that lead the audience to suspend their disbelief willingly. In most supernatural stories we begin in our own recognizable world, then the supernatural element intrudes, and as the protagonist comes to believe in it, the audience is convinced as well.

Here, however, Mathison and Spielberg have used a different tactic. They have opened the story with the supernatural being and have quite effectively put us into its shoes—or at least its feet. We quickly learn of its fear of our harmless sounds, its terror at the sight of pickup trucks and bobbing flashlights; we see people from low angles and only up to the waist—in other words, we have been forced cinematically to be inside the alien, to inhabit its point of view. After that, how can we not believe in it? We have already identified with it before we've even gotten a good look at it. And these storytellers know that the audience will go along with almost anything at the outset of a film in hopes of finding a story they can sink their emotions and desires into. With an opening like this, we have suspended our disbelief before we meet our human charcters.

ACTION AND ACTIVITY

When Mike backs Mom's car out of the garage, it is planting for the van escape, but it is also an activity. There is nothing more to it than a kid who is dying to learn to drive. But when he drives the van, he is not dying to learn to drive, he is afraid of dying because of not knowing how to drive. The activity of driving has become an action, and there is a very real purpose behind it.

When Eliot scratches his face thoughtfully soon after getting E.T. into his room, it is merely an activity. But when he discovers E.T. mimicking him, he tries a number of movements that have now become actions because he is attempting to find a way to communicate with E.T.

When Eliot has discovered that E.T. is still alive and he doesn't want the adults to find out, all of his actions are clear and have a discernible purpose. He covers the glowing heart with his blanket, he zips up the body bag, he closes the cover, he cries over the window, he distracts Keys. All of these are actions with purpose behind them.

DIALOGUE

This is a story told from the child's point of view, though obviously, from its enormous and wide appeal, it isn't merely for children. The dialogue is generally quite natural "kidspeak." The way they talk, their conceptions and misconceptions, come through in dialogue, and each of the three primary children is given a distinctive voice. Eliot's voice first comes through when he's showing E.T. his toy soldiers, his shark, and his fish tank. Mike's is introduced in the moments right before he first sees E.T., when he is teasing his little brother. And Gertie's voice comes through after she first meets E.T. and she asks if it's a boy or a girl and tells Mike to "give me a break."

A film that created a line that has become part of the American argot, *E.T.* gave us the line "phone home."

VISUALS

A significant element of the visual design has already been alluded to—shooting the adults from the waist down until the last section of the story. This is the essence of how the camera interprets a story for the audience; it leads them to see only what it (and the person behind it) wants. In this case, the storytellers don't want the adults other than Mom to be real human beings yet, and so we are given them only from the child's point of view.

Another way in which the visuals are used to accentuate a significant element in the story is by helping us into the magic of the story. After E.T. and Eliot first meet and flee for their lives, we see the wake of E.T. still descending the steps up toward the forest. When E.T. takes the balls and makes them orbit like our solar system, we see some of the magic in his hands. And especially with the two bike-riding scenes, we are given the magical juxtaposed with the earthly. Though the boys ride with incredible skill, their feats on the bikes up and down the hills and over the cars are all things that can happen in our world. Daring and spectacular, but possible. Right on the heels of this dazzling display, we fly with E.T. on the bikes and a whole different mood sets in—using the music, of course—but also in large part because of the visuals, first flying over forests, then flying in front of the moon (or, in the final escape, the setting sun).

DRAMATIC SCENES

A particularly effective dramatic scene is the one when Mike and Gertie first meet E.T. There is a scene of preparation of Mike coming home from school and being in a good mood. He teases Eliot and reluctantly makes the big promise his brother insists on. This is preparation by contrast; he is cocky and joking and, because of the irony of what we know that he doesn't, we wait excitedly for his reaction. Then the scene we have been anticipating suddenly changes: there is a twist when Gertie abruptly steps into the room, sees E.T., and screams like mad. There are verbal and physical reactions from all four characters in the scene, and then another twist when Mom starts coming close. And then there is the aftermath in the closet.

Another effective dramatic scene is the one in which Eliot discovers that

E.T. is still alive. There is a brief preparation of Eliot standing on the outside looking through plastic at the group around the now "dead" E.T. Keys intercedes and gives Eliot some time alone with E.T. Here our fears and dread of E.T.'s death are elaborated upon, and while this is the heart of the scene, it is also preparation by contrast for the twist that is about to come. Eliot concludes what he thinks will be his last moments with E.T. without discovering any change. We are clued in to the fact that E.T. is alive by the red glow of his heart, but Eliot doesn't see it, creating a new irony. But as he is dragging himself off, he sees the flower coming to life (the metaphor has been created), and goes back to find his friend alive. From here it changes into a totally different scene, one of hope and fear rather than dread. Hope that he will be able to cover up this resurgent life and fear that the adults will find out and go back to torturing E.T. After Eliot has successfully masked the fact that E.T. is alive and he is led away, there is a moment of aftermath with the fully alive flower and then his delivering the news to Mike that E.T. is alive.

SPECIAL NOTES

One school of thought states that there are two basic kinds of stories: ordinary people in extraordinary circumstances and extraordinary people in ordinary circumstances. While these two kinds account for a great percentage of all the well-told stories, ordinary people in ordinary circumstances can create very compelling and well-told stories if the wants and the obstacles are sufficiently strong and evenly pitted against each other. Still, as this film shows, the first of these story types works quite well.

We are encouraged to believe that Eliot is an ordinary boy in an ordinary family. The extraordinary circumstance of being visited by a stranded alien is what creates this story. The fact that Eliot is just like millions of other young boys makes it easy for us to identify with him, even if we can't identify so readily with his circumstance. The interesting thing about this dynamic is that it seems to require that the ordinary protagonist eventually attempt some extraordinary feat to fit the nature of the circumstance. In this case, Eliot's engineering a daring escape from hundreds of trained men constitutes an extraordinary feat.

Some Like It Hot

(1959)
Written by Billy Wilder and I. A. L. Diamond,
based on an unpublished story by R. Thoeren and M. Logan
Directed by Billy Wilder

No book of film analyses would be complete without at least one Billy Wilder film; the only difficulty is choosing from among so many worthy films. Wilder usually co-wrote his scripts, for the first half of his career with Charles Brackett and then with I. A. L. Diamond, who often co-produced. For this film he and Diamond were nominated for an Academy Award for the script and Wilder for directing. We have chosen this Wilder film because it allows for a discussion of what would seem to be dual lead characters, since this is a very early example of the now prevalent "buddy picture."

SYNOPSIS

In the gangster-ridden Chicago of 1929, Spats Colombo runs a speakeasy with free-flowing booze and a lively band. But he is fingered to federal agents by Toothpick Charlie. Joe and Jerry play sax and bass in the band at the speakeasy, and are anxiously awaiting their first paycheck in four months. When the feds bust the joint, Joe and Jerry manage to escape into the cold night with their instruments and coats, but no paychecks. Joe wonders if their bookie would take the overcoats to cover a bet. The next day, without overcoats, they visit music agencies, looking for but not finding a job.

Sweet Sue and her manager Beinstock visit an agent looking for a bass and a sax player for her "all-girl band." Later Joe sweet-talks his way in to see the same agent to try to get the job with Sweet Sue in Florida. When they find out it's for women musicians only, Jerry's ready to don a wig, but Joe nixes the idea and instead gets a one-night stand for Valentine's Day and talks the secretary into loaning them her car. When they go to pick up the car, they stumble into Spats Colombo's revenge on Toothpick Charlie for fingering him. Unseen at the back, Joe and Jerry witness the famous St. Valentine's Day Massacre, but then are discovered. They narrowly escape with only the bass fiddle being "wounded."

In a panic to disappear, Joe calls the agent and, speaking in falsetto, becomes Josephine wanting to take the Florida job. Josephine and Daphne, as Jerry names himself, now in dresses and wigs, try to learn about walking like women by watching Sugar Kane board the train. The pair join Sweet Sue and the band on board the train for Florida. They meet Sugar stealing an illicit sip from her flask in the ladies' room, and Jerry is really taken with her. The band has a rehearsal on the train, and during it, Sugar drops her flask, which could get her fired. Jerry takes the blame and forms a bond with Sugar. The train trip turns into a slumber party in Daphne's berth, and Joe has to caution Jerry to control himself—no mean feat with Sugar snuggling close and being very friendly in the tight berth. In a moment alone, away from the party, Sugar tells Josephine about her chronic attraction to male sax players and tells of her plan for a change—to meet and marry a Florida millionaire.

When the band arrives at the Florida hotel, ancient Osgood Fielding III takes an instant liking to Daphne, who has to fend off his boyish advances while learning that he's filthy rich. Joe and Jerry share a room right across from Sugar and are visited by Beinstock looking for his lost suitcase. While Daphne and Sugar go for a swim, Joe takes out Beinstock's stolen resort clothes and his extra pair of glasses. He goes to the beach and contrives to meet Sugar as "Junior," the heir to Shell Oil. Jerry is livid and tries to show him up in his masquerade by rushing Sugar back to the room to check on Josephine. He is quite surprised to find her there in the bath, and when they've gone, Joe steps from the bubble bath fully dressed and ready to kill Jerry. But just then Osgood calls for Daphne and invites him/her to his yacht for the evening. Joe forms a plan—Jerry will get Osgood ashore so that he, Joe/Junior, can entertain Sugar on the yacht.

While the band plays and Sugar looks in vain for Junior to come see the show as he promised, flowers come for Daphne from Osgood. Joe changes the card and sends them to Sugar from Junior and invites her to the yacht. After the show, Joe makes a frantic dash, changing clothes, then racing to the dock on a bicycle, and manages somehow to escort Sugar out to the yacht he's never been on before. While Daphne keeps Osgood out all night dancing, Joe/Junior has Sugar trying passionately to make up for his lost love, who died. At dawn, Junior motors Sugar ashore just in time for Osgood to stumble drunkenly into the launch and head back to the yacht.

Jerry is still wound up from his night of dancing with Osgood, and tangos about, telling Joe "I'm engaged." After the wedding, he'll tell Osgood the truth, annul the marriage, and live on the alimony the rest of his life. Joe doesn't think the plan will work, but then he sees the diamond bracelet

Osgood gave him and suggests they not send it back. Meanwhile, Spats and his thugs have arrived at the hotel to meet with the mob leader, Little Bonaparte. One of the thugs seems to recognize Josephine and Daphne, and notes their room number.

At the same time, Junior is busily sending the diamond bracelet to Sugar as a present, which makes Jerry angry. But they feel trapped by Spats's men and, to avoid being seen, climb out the window as Joe did earlier. They land right in the middle of the battle between Bonaparte and Spats. They are recognized and barely manage to escape, but hear that all the exits out of town are being watched. Joe persuades Daphne to call Osgood and suggest eloping tonight. Josephine races to tell Sugar she'll get over Junior, but he gets spotted by one of the gangsters. Daphne and Josephine escape by hiding in the gurney that is carrying out Spats's body, and race down to the dock where Osgood waits. Just then, Sugar bicycles up and the four of them head out to the yacht. Joe takes off his wig and confesses the truth to Sugar and she kisses him. When Jerry finally blurts out to Osgood that he's a man, the reply is "Nobody's perfect."

PROTAGONIST AND OBJECTIVE

At first look, one would be tempted to say that this is Joe *and* Jerry's story. They are both on the lam from the gangsters, they both dress up like women, they both have star-crossed romances that depend on masquerades. But it must be remembered that drama rotates around decision. Without some degree of free will, without two choices, there is no drama; the dramatic nature of a moment stems in large part from the decisions made and the difficulty of those decisions. Thus, the person who makes the decisions that create the major changes in a story is the protagonist, even if another character is in similar circumstances and has just as much screen time—which means that this is Joe's story. Right from the beginning, Joe makes the decisions that both characters follow through on. Jerry may protest—and usually does—but what Joe decides is what they end up doing. From an early moment, when they give their overcoats to the bookie, to a later one, when Joe decides they should take the jobs as women musicians, and still later when Joe persuades Jerry/Daphne, over great protests, to entertain Osgood for the night, in each case it is Joe who decides what they both will do.

So Joe is the protagonist around whom the story is built, though clearly it could not be told without Joe and Jerry together. Joe's objective is to escape from the gangsters who want to kill the two of them for having witnessed the massacre. The objective is not to seduce Sugar; that is a secondary story line, a subplot that arises after the story is fully under way.

OBSTACLES

The obstacles to Joe's objective of escaping the gangsters are many. Both he and Jerry are recognizable, they are broke, they can't find a job, and are stuck in Chicago. Once they hit on the idea of masquerading as women musicians and going to Florida, their first obstacles seem to be replaced by a new, major obstacle—the difficulty of two healthy and heterosexual men passing as women for an extended period of time. This single obstacle of passing for women is compounded by Joe's overwhelming attraction to Sugar and by Osgood's overwhelming attraction to Daphne. And by the end, both sets of obstacles come into play at the same time: the gangsters find out about Joe and Jerry just as the masquerade has about run its course.

PREMISE AND OPENING

The premise here involves three different groups of people who are forced into conflicting situations with each other. Joe and Jerry are barely employed and down-on-their-luck musicians. Spats Colombo owns a speakeasy and has a grudge against Toothpick Charlie. Sweet Sue is missing two women musicians and is due to leave for a big job in Florida. The collision of these three elements creates the story.

For their opening, Wilder and Diamond chose to introduce us to the underworld of 1929 Chicago with a hearse delivering booze to a speakeasy. Once the circumstances and locale are introduced, we immediately meet Joe and Jerry.

MAIN TENSION, CULMINATION, AND RESOLUTION

The main tension asks if Joe (along with Jerry) will be able to escape from the gangsters by masquerading as a woman. This tension begins fully when Joe phones the musical agent as Josephine and sets up their job with Sweet Sue.

The culmination comes right after the two most important subplots have reached their most intense moments: when Joe/Junior spends the night with Sugar and when Jerry/Daphne spends the night with Osgood. Immediately following the aftermath of that night, Spats and his men enter the hotel, and one of them seems to recognize "the two broads." Joe and Jerry realize their new danger.

The resolution is when the "girls" elude the gangsters by hiding under a corpse and manage to escape with both of the "love interests"—Sugar and Osgood.

THEME

Even when a well-made film is a romp—when its intention is to be fun, exciting, and funny—it still has a thematic thread that links the disparate story elements into a cohesive whole. In *Some Like It Hot*, the thematic link deals with masquerades. The masquerades of Joe and Jerry are obvious from the moment they dress up as women. But Sugar pretends to come from money when she's with Junior. Spats's men pretend to be Harvard lawyers, and his enemy Bonaparte pretends to good intentions. Osgood is a marvelous variation on this theme because he pretends to nothing; he joyfully and boastfully admits to all his intentions, foibles, and failures. In a way, Osgood acts as the exception that proves the rule.

UNITY

As discussed in the "Protagonist and Objective" section above, this is Joe's story, even though he seems to be joined firmly to Jerry. The unity stems from his effort to keep both of them safely away from Colombo and his men. Even though he seems to get totally sidetracked into the subplot with Sugar, he never goes so far as to give up their masquerade as Josephine and Daphne. So, even though this defensive line of action fades for a while, it doesn't disappear completely.

EXPOSITION

The early exposition is delivered with humor and conflict. The shootout between police and the "pallbearers" in the hearse not only sets some of the tone for the picture, but introduces the notion that not everything is as it is presented. At the same time, we learn the nature of the gangster world, which will drive our protagonist to create the rest of this story.

A scene in which a character voluntarily delivers exposition that doesn't seem too easy or straightforward occurs when Sugar tells Josephine about her weakness for sax players. This scene is given a feeling of conflict because we know that she is revealing this secret not only to a man, but to a sax player, no less. There isn't a conflict between the characters, yet the scene generates a feeling of conflict through this irony.

CHARACTERIZATION

Joe and Jerry want to escape the gangsters, but their characterizations begin much earlier and come more from what they want prior to that predicament. Joe is a womanizer, a man who uses charm before work, a smile before talent. This tendency is clear long before they witness the massacre, and it comes into play in his attempt to seduce Sugar falsely rather than honestly.

Jerry is capable of enjoying just about anything that happens, and this plays into his being dominated by Joe. He likes playing in the club in the opening, he rather likes playing Daphne, he even eventually likes all the attention he gets from Osgood.

Sugar is someone who sees her lot in life as "getting the fuzzy end of the lollipop." She deserves better, she deserves life's sweetness, but it isn't her fate to have it come her way. That, of course is why we worry about her through much of the second act.

Because this is a story about two men who dress up like women, and their stories involve "love affairs" of starkly contrasting nature, it is essential that the storytellers deal with their sexuality early and effectively. From the first moment we meet them, they are robust and very heterosexual, displaying interest in the showgirls at the speakeasy. With Jerry, who will have a romance with a man, it is especially critical to make it clear that this is not his orientation, which is why he is the one first turned on by Sugar, and he is the one driven crazy in the train berth with her. If we had any doubt about his sexuality, his night of dancing and "engagement" to Osgood would work in a far different way, if at all. Because Joe actively pursues Sugar through most of the second act, it is less critical to confirm his sexuality, but still his charm with the agent's secretary and his history of womanizing are well established.

DEVELOPMENT OF THE STORY

For a story in which much of the major driving force comes from outside the protagonist—gangsters want to kill him and his friend—this film has a number of complications stemming from the nature of the characters. In fact, the outside force of Spats and his men is used to establish the major circumstance—Joe and Jerry pretending to be women—and then left on the back burner until it is time to resolve the story. This leaves the second act mostly to be developed by the characters acting out their own driving passions.

Joe is in pursuit of the incredibly desirable Sugar. Sugar is out to find a "rich millionaire" to marry. Jerry is out to have fun and, if possible, make Joe's life a little more miserable. And Osgood is out to find wife number eight or nine. Each of these characters is acting out his or her inner desire; this creates the complications of the second act and keeps the story rollicking swiftly along.

DRAMATIC IRONY

This film depends heavily on dramatic irony. We know that Josephine and Daphne are Joe and Jerry. Nearly everything that happens to them, with Sugar or Osgood or the people in the band, is tinged with the irony of our knowing that the other characters don't know what we do. There is also irony in our watching Sugar lie to Junior about who she is, when we know not only that what she says isn't true, but that *he* knows it isn't true. And there's irony in our watching Osgood's passionate pursuit of Daphne, and humor when it is marvelously thrown back in our faces with the last line of the film, "Well, nobody's perfect."

A scene that especially capitalizes on the use of irony is the long slumber party scene on the train, where Jerry is relegated to telling himself, "I'm a girl, I'm a girl. . . . " Every move that Sugar and the other women make, every reaction from Josephine in the berth below, is given double meaning by the irony of what we know that others don't.

PREPARATION AND AFTERMATH

A marvelous example of preparation and aftermath comes with the scenes of the night-long romances of Junior with Sugar and Daphne with Osgood. It all begins in the ballroom, with the band playing and Osgood flirting with Daphne. The music and atmosphere of the scene set the mood for the evening of an enjoyable romp. This feeling is kept up through the night in both of the parallel actions. The aftermath comes when both of them are back in their hotel room. Daphne is still dancing, while Joe is in a happy afterglow of his night with Sugar. Joe's success is accentuated when Sugar comes in to tell them all about her wonderful evening with Junior.

On a smaller scale, there is effective preparation and aftermath to the scene where Joe and Jerry first pass themselves off as women. They watch with amazement as a real woman sashays up to the train and enters. Their inexperience and bad instincts are accentuated in just a few short beats. Then they meet Sweet Sue and Beinstock and succeed in being received as women. As they enter the car, Joe berates Jerry for taking the name Daphne, emotionally closing off the scene.

PLANTING AND PAYOFF

There are many examples of planting and payoff, ranging from lines of dialogue to minor characters to objects. In particular, lines of dialogue (see the "Dialogue" section below) are brought back with great effectiveness. For instance, when Junior and Sugar are kissing on the yacht, he says he should send money to the milk fund. Later, when they are saying good-bye the next morning, the milk fund comes up again, only the figure is now ten times higher; this little gag is used as a measure of his satisfaction with and desire for Sugar.

Another marvelous use of dialogue that constitutes planting and payoff starts on the train when Jerry is so smitten with Sugar and Joe tells him to keep reminding himself "I'm a girl, I'm a girl. . . . " It comes up again when Sugar is snuggling with him in the berth, then much later in the third act when Daphne has gotten engaged to Osgood and Jerry now has to remind himself, "I'm a boy, I'm a boy. . . . " This not only pays off on the setup but creates a nice gag at the same time. Yet another nice use of dialogue with planting comes when Sugar says her father was "a conductor . . . the Baltimore and Ohio." Later on, when she is trying to impress Junior with her debutante background, she says her father was in railroads, "the Baltimore and Ohio."

A planting and payoff that stems from a prop and helps create a major plot turn comes when Jerry's bass is shot by the gangsters in the Chicago garage. We are reminded of the holes twice on the trip, and then, when Spats's men show up in Florida, they confirm who these two "broads" are by spying the holes in the bass.

ELEMENTS OF THE FUTURE AND ADVERTISING

There is an effective use of elements of the future when the agent's secretary spells out the entire trip to Florida with Sweet Sue, omitting only that it is two women musicians who are needed. Immediately following that scene, when Joe and Jerry find out the job is for women, Jerry explains everything that they will later actually do in order to take the job—borrow dresses, get wigs, and so on. At the time the plan is ruled out by Joe, and thus it doesn't quite seem like a prediction, but later they change their minds and it comes true. Although neither scene truly advertises something we know will happen, each paints a picture of a possible scenario that finally does come about.

A good example of advertising appears when Sugar invites Joe/Junior to come and see her show that night. The impossibility of that happening with Joe/Josephine playing in the same show with Sugar is accentuated by Daphne, but it is advertising because we know Sugar's expectation is going to be dealt with, and we are trying to anticipate how this problem will be handled. Another effective use of advertising comes when Osgood tells

Josephine all about his invitation out to the yacht for the cold pheasant, champagne, and Rudy Vallee records. Again, though the event doesn't happen as expected, the yacht and the grand seduction implicit in the setup do become events.

PLAUSIBILITY

This film is hardly meant to be taken as literal realism, as something that would happen in the real world. Rather, it portrays a version of the world that is stylized for the fun of it. We are introduced to this notion from the very beginning. When we go inside the hearse and we see the mugs on the pallbearers, we are already suspicious. When this "funeral" becomes a shootout and a chase with the cops, we are starting to be let in on the gag, and by the time the booze is leaking out of the shot-up coffin, we are attuned to the story's skewed version of reality. Once this is set, the film stays within the "rules" of the universe it establishes.

This is a comic story designed to be a rollicking good time, yet early on, seven people are gunned down in cold blood. Of them, only Toothpick Charlie has been established as a character and he hasn't been made into anyone we really care about, so we are encouraged to keep our aesthetic distance from the killings. This distance is increased when the two characters we do care about are put in imminent danger, which distracts us from the otherwise horrifying notion of this multiple homicide. We come away feeling that the danger Jerry and Joe face is real, yet at the same time we aren't distracted from the comic side of the story. When Spats is gunned down in the end, he is a major source of danger to Joe and Jerry, so the emotional impact of his murder is diminished.

ACTION AND ACTIVITY

In the scene where Joe and Jerry are introduced in the band at the speakeasy, their instrument-playing is merely activity; there is nothing more to it than what is on the surface, no intentions are behind it. When they are playing with the band on the train, and Sweet Sue wants them to "goose it up," their playing becomes action because they are trying to solidify their positions on the band, to win acceptance.

On the train, when Daphne invites Sugar up to his/her berth for a drink and a "surprise party," the drinking and invitation are clear-cut actions. Later, when the party grows, the drinking and partying are activities for all the other women—and an impediment for Daphne.

Even riding in an elevator can be made into an action rather than an activity. When Osgood joins Daphne on the elevator upon first meeting her, he tells the operator to take it "once around the block and keep your eyes on the road." He is using the ride as a means of being alone with, and making a pass at, this woman of his affections. This intention behind his riding the elevator makes it an action.

DIALOGUE

Wonderfully playful and expressive dialogue abounds. Some of it can be very simple characterization. Osgood's "Zowie!" reveals a great deal about him. Another effective use of dialogue delivering a clear subtext, expressing a far different meaning from what it says on the surface, comes when Osgood asks Daphne how she plays the "bull fiddle . . . do you use a bow or do you pluck it?" And Daphne retorts, "Mostly I just slap it."

There is a whole area of this story in which food is used as a synonym for sex and sexual attraction. When Jerry is excited about being on this train with all the women, he tells about his love of pastry shops. But Joe insists there will "be no pastry and no butter." Later he tells Jerry to stay clear of Sugar (the ultimate in sexual attraction), that "the honey stays in the hive . . . there will be no buzzing around tonight."

And dialogue is also used to suggest levels of irony in a playful and humorous way. When Josephine and Daphne show up at the train, Beinstock tells them, "You girls really saved our lives," and Daphne responds, "Likewise, I'm sure." This exchange is merely a figure of speech for Beinstock, but it is literal reality for Joe and Jerry.

VISUALS

The visuals in this film are consistently kept in support of the story and the humor. In comedy, it often works best to keep the camera out of the way of the performers; the old rule of thumb in comedy is "shoot wide." Though this general advice is not always correct or applicable, it is put to effective use here.

After the speakeasy has been busted and all the patrons and employees are being loaded into paddy wagons, we stay wide and watch the action being brought to us. The flow is accentuated by the drunk with the coffee cup wandering counter to the stream of people, then being herded along. All the while we are searching for Joe and Jerry, and only when the whole circumstance is set do we move close to them.

Another fine use of "shooting wide" occurs in the big chase in the third act through the hotel lobby, when the gangsters are after Josephine and

Daphne. We pan though the crowd with the action, wait outside the door, and watch the two "women" go in different directions and the gangsters get lost, only to have the action come back to us again. This is a perfect example of a director knowing where to put the camera to capture all the essentials, and then letting them play out. It would have diminished this chase seriously to chop it up with cuts.

An example of a fine shot and composition that are used to underline a point is on the porch at the hotel in Florida, where we see a long row of interchangable "millionaires" in rocking chairs, taking their glasses off in unison at the arrival of all the women, and tipping their hats to them as well. Only Osgood becomes a real character, but this visual accentuates that he is one of many of his ilk.

DRAMATIC SCENES

The scene between Sugar and Daphne alone in the train berth is an example of a first-rate dramatic scene that utilizes characters, props, and location to great effect. There is a brief scene of preparation where Daphne admires Sugar and is called "honey." Then Sugar is forced to jump into Daphne's berth, and the crowding has a profound effect on Daphne, to the point where Sugar comments on her shivering. The escalation of this predicament, when Daphne gets the idea of having a drink and a "surprise party," grows from the basic irony that Daphne is Jerry and is very attracted to Sugar. The immediate aftermath of the scene, when other women climb into the berth and end Daphne's hopes, turns into another scene all its own.

Another effective dramatic scene occurs when Daphne returns from a night of dancing with Osgood. A brief preparation to set the mood comes with Daphne still "dancing" in the bed and singing away. Then Junior climbs into the room and Jerry explains his engagement to a mystified Joe, who then says the plan won't work. But when Jerry shows the diamond bracelet to him, Joe changes his tune immediately and encourages him to stay engaged. We don't know what Joe's planning, but we know he's up to something. The scene is interrupted by the arrival of Sugar and it evolves into a three-sided scene, but one that continues the old conflict between the two men over Joe's seduction of Sugar. And there is a brief but effective aftermath with the arrival of the bellboy.

SPECIAL NOTES

There is a tendency among many novices to think of so-called "serious" movies as a different—and higher—level of filmmaking, as if a quality "serious" film took more skill to write and direct than a quality genre picture or a comedy or an "entertainment."

One of the greatest filmmakers of all time, Billy Wilder would not restrict himself to just one kind of film. He applied his formidable talents to everything: manic comedies like this one, "issue" pictures (*Lost Weekend*), suspense and film noir (*Double Indemnity*), romantic comedy (*Love in the Afternoon*), war/comedy (*Stalag 17*), and even a purely character-driven story (*Sunset Boulevard*). The list goes on much longer, varied and impressively laden with Academy Awards and every other film accolade. There can be no denying the eminence of Wilder as both a screenwriter and a director—he is the consummate filmmaker.

In each of his films, he has applied all of his skills and resources, has made no distinction in his work between the serious and the funny, the disturbing and the delightful. His interest throughout his career has been in telling great stories in the best possible way, for the greatest possible impact on the audience. The principles of storytelling and filmmaking detailed in this book apply to all kinds of well-made films and are neither more nor less applicable to one film than another. This truth is perfectly illustrated in the long and successful career of Billy Wilder.

North by Northwest

(1959)
Written by Ernest Lehman
Directed by Alfred Hitchcock

A film that finds Hitchcock at the top of his directorial form, working from an Academy Award–nominated script by Lehman, *North by Northwest* contains, among other things, two of the most famous and memorable sequences in all of Hitchcock's work—the cropduster sequence and the chase across the face of Mount Rushmore.

SYNOPSIS

Roger Thornhill, a self-confident and successful New York advertising executive, is mistaken for someone named George Kaplan and is kidnapped. He is brought to meet the urbane and controlling Lester Townsend and accused of being a secret agent. Roger's denials are disbelieved, and Townsend's men attempt to kill him. Roger manages to escape, but the police and even his mother don't believe his crazy story. Roger decides to find Kaplan at his hotel and clear up the misunderstanding, but again the same men nearly entrap him and he narrowly escapes.

Roger goes to the UN Building in hopes of clearing things up with Lester Townsend, but finds that this is not the man he met after his kidnapping. Townsend is murdered, and Roger is photographed holding the knife. He flees, now on the run from the police, and takes a train for Chicago in hopes of tracking down Kaplan. The Professor and his associates, who run some kind of secret U.S. government agency, reveal that Kaplan is a fictitious agent, but that there is a real agent as well. On the train, Roger meets and gets saved from the police by Eve Kendall, who hides him out in her stateroom. Through the night, Roger and Eve begin to fall in love, but she sends a note to Vandamm, who masqueraded as Townsend, elsewhere on the train, revealing that she is allied with him. When they arrive in Chicago safely, Eve calls "Kaplan" and arranges a meeting. When Roger goes out to the middle of nowhere for the meeting, he is attacked by a cropduster plane equipped with a machine gun. He escapes by flagging down a gasoline truck, and goes back to Chicago.

He discovers Eve's connection with Vandamm and follows her to an auction, where Vandamm bids on a primitive statue. Vandamm's men try to kidnap Roger from the auction, but he makes a scene and gets himself arrested. Now rescued by the police, he is taken not to the station but the airport, where the Professor reveals that Eve is the real agent and is now in danger of being discovered and killed because she fell in love with Roger. Roger decides to take on the role of Kaplan and play out a vignette that will make her safer. Below Mount Rushmore, Eve "shoots" Roger and he seems to be killed, convincing Vandamm of his safety. But when Roger finds out Eve will be staying with Vandamm, he escapes from the Professor and hurries out alone to the spy's estate to rescue her. There he discovers Vandamm's men have found out about Eve, and manages to warn her. Together they escape and lead a harrowing chase across the face of Mount Rushmore with the primitive statue Vandamm bought at the auction. Vandamm's men die in trying to stop them, the statue breaks, revealing crucial microfilm, and finally Roger manages to haul Eve to safety. Soon after, they are married.

PROTAGONIST AND OBJECTIVE
Roger Thornhill is the protagonist of the film, a sympathetic and wronged man who is blameless in his predicament. His objective is to clear up this misunderstanding, to prove that he is not the agent in question. He is opposed by a clear-cut outside antagonist, which makes this a primarily external conflict.

OBSTACLES
The first obstacle Roger encounters is that of being mistaken for a man who apparently uses many names and who disguises himself so that Roger's every protest of innocence and his assertions of his true identity are thought to be a very good, if overplayed, act. While he really isn't a secret agent and really doesn't know what's going on, Roger acts as the antagonist would expect the agent to act, and almost accidentally is very good at this business—which simply strengthens his opponent's conviction that he is the agent.

In addition, Roger faces obstacles not simply from the antagonist and his men, but from his supposed allies as well. The Professor knows of Roger's plight, but rather than rescue him, he uses Roger to divert attention from the real agent. Eve, who is the real agent, first must act against Roger to safeguard herself, and only much later becomes his ally.

PREMISE AND OPENING
The premise of *North by Northwest* deals with events and situations that predate the moment when Roger stumbles into the story. Vandamm and

his people are in the business of selling state secrets; the Professor and his men are trying to stop them and have sent a succession of agents who have been discovered and killed. Finally they have created a fictitious agent to keep their real agent above suspicion.

For the opening, Lehman has chosen to establish Roger's real identity and name quickly and forcefully while at the same time giving us an idea of his self-confident, pay-his-own-way demeanor. The moment we have firmly been introduced to his attitude to life and have been reminded repeatedly of his real name, he is mistaken for another man and kidnapped.

MAIN TENSION, CULMINATION, AND RESOLUTION

The main tension asks if Roger will be able to find the real George Kaplan, clear up the misunderstanding, and extract himself from the consequences of the mistaken identity.

The culmination is the moment when the mystery is solved—that is, when Roger finds out about Kaplan and about Eve. This establishes the new third act tension, which asks if Roger will be able to save Eve.

The resolution comes on the face of Mount Rushmore, when Eve falls, Roger holds her, and they manage to outlast Vandamm's man, who is trying to send them plummeting to their deaths. The twist in the third act comes when Roger discovers that his first attempt to save Eve when colluding with the Professor has enabled her to go on with Vandamm, leaving Roger to attempt her rescue all on his own.

THEME

The theme has to do with lying and deception. Right from the beginning, Roger says, "There is no such thing as a lie, just the expedient exaggeration." When he tells the truth it's thought to be a lie; when he lies it's thought to be the truth; when he finds out the truth about Kaplan, it has all been a lie.

The subplots are all variations on the theme of lying and deception. Vandamm's whole life and career are based on deception. Eve lies first to Roger, then to Vandamm, then disbelieves the truth from Roger and finally believes it. The Professor is the master of the "expedient exaggeration," and one who proves to himself the effectiveness of lying. Even between Vandamm and Leonard, his chief assistant, what begins as a totally trusting relationship has a moment when deception and lying test it on the way to the truth.

UNITY

Action is the unifying element in this story. Roger's pursuit of his objective is the continuing focus of the story. Though there are some scenes in which he does not appear, in those he is still the source of the scene, its subject, and his objective is heightened in one way or another.

EXPOSITION

The early exposition is dealt with by using Roger's secretary as the sounding board for letting us know who he is, what he does, and what he expects in the near future. Once he is kidnapped, his protests and explanations of himself are an effective example of exposition through conflict. Only in the scene where the action shifts away from Roger to introduce the Professor and reveal the fact that Kaplan doesn't exist is the exposition handled in too straightforward and overt a manner.

CHARACTERIZATION

From the very beginning, Roger is clearly a man accustomed to getting what he wants and having his way, and who doesn't mind paying for what he seeks. When his circumstances become dire, these traits come fully into play and see him through the ordeal of the mistaken identity. His unflappability, the self-confidence and assurance he demonstrates with his secretary and business associates, remains steady throughout the story, even when he is in danger.

Vandamm is like a mirror image of his opponent: dapper, confident, smooth, and bright. But where Roger is outraged, Vandamm is amused; he seems to feel he is above the petty travails of other men. But by the end he has succumbed to his own vanity, his own disbelieving amusement, and has been forced down from his lofty perch.

Eve is a distinct contrast to the two men. While outwardly she shares their sense of self-confidence, hers is much more easily shaken, she more readily feels that she is in over her head. But it is especially in her relationship to the truth that she departs from them. Her witty seduction of Roger over dinner seems to be utterly truthful, while his mouth seems to be full of lies. When she is forced to betray him by setting up the false meeting with Kaplan, she is devastated by the falsehoods and their consequences. Although at times she is dishonest in words, her emotions are consistently honest.

DEVELOPMENT OF THE STORY

What begins as a simple mistaken identity snowballs into ever more dire circumstances for Roger. His every effort to extract himself from this dilemma convinces his opponents that he is who they think he is. Vandamm's objective, to rid himself of an agent who is trying to stop him, creates escalating obstacles to the continued survival of Roger. Eve's objective is first to protect herself; then, when she falls in love with Roger, she tries to protect him without revealing the truth about herself to him.

For all of these primary characters, their obstacles are the direct outgrowth of the pursuit of their objectives.

DRAMATIC IRONY

To its core, this story is based on a dramatic irony: the fact that Roger is mistaken for an agent who doesn't exist. From the moment we learn this information, which he will not discover for some time, we see Roger's increasingly desperate actions through the lens of irony, which increases both humor and suspense.

He travels to Chicago to find Kaplan, when we know there is no one to find. We know that Eve has sent him to a meeting planned by Vandamm's men, and while he waits at the side of the road, the dramatic irony of our knowing the setup and his ignorance of it increases the scene's tension.

Once Roger figures out that Eve and not Kaplan set him up, he confronts her in her hotel room. She doesn't know that he figured it out and he doesn't know that she really does love him and is genuinely glad he survived. Only the audience knows the full truth and thus enjoys the compounding ironies.

PREPARATION AND AFTERMATH

A textbook example of preparation and aftermath occurs in the famous cropduster sequence. Hitchcock was the grand master of preparing an audience for an upcoming shock or dramatic twist. Here he reverses the normal use of music in a scene of preparation and leaves an eerie silence as part of our emotional setup for the attack that we know is coming, but we have no idea from which direction. He uses wide-open spaces, silence, and the interruptions of traffic as buildup for the inevitable attack. At the end of the scene, when the plane crashes into the gasoline truck, there are a number of onlookers who view the event as a tragedy rather than a triumph, tinging the aftermath with a note of irony.

PLANTING AND PAYOFF

A very clear case of planting and payoff is Roger's book of matches with his initials on them, *R.O.T.* The book of matches is emphasized when Eve asks what the *O* stands for when they are dining on the train. Later, at Vandamm's house, when he has to warn her of imminent danger, he uses the matches and she knows right away that Roger is nearby.

Another planting and payoff is Roger's mother's attitude toward his drinking. Very early on, Roger tells his secretary his mother will smell his breath and that he fully intends to have two drinks in him. When he has been arrested for drunk driving and is facing the judge, he tells a preposterous story about men forcing him to drink liquor. This true but doubtful-seeming assertion is finally countered when even his own mother disbelieves him.

ELEMENTS OF THE FUTURE
AND ADVERTISING

In the scene where Roger and Vandamm meet for the first time, Vandamm recites George Kaplan's hotel itinerary, where he was before, where he is staying in New York, where he will stay in Chicago and then in Rapid City, South Dakota. While the overt conflict of the scene masks it and makes this information seem simply like fodder in Vandamm's attempt to convince Roger/Kaplan that he has been caught, it is in fact advertising for the major shifts in location that the story will take.

Elements of the future abound. When Vandamm tells his men to "entertain Mr. Kaplan," we are made to wonder exactly what they have in mind. When Roger explains to his mother his plan of taking the train to New York, again we are pushed forward into the story: Will his plan work, will it work as he expects it to? At the auction, when Roger plants a very real suspicion in Vandamm about Eve, we are made to hope and fear about her future. When we learn of Roger's expectation that his little scene below Mount Rushmore will set Eve free, again we are encouraged to have hopes and fears.

PLAUSIBILITY

This is not a gritty, real-world story, but it achieves plausibility within its own rules and within its own world. The story begins with a fairly realistic version of New York and Roger's world. By the time Vandamm's men attempt to kill him with alcohol and a Mercedes, the story has led us into a make-believe world that we accept readily. Our disbelief has been overcome, and we have been seduced into the story by the storytellers.

Once we have suspended our disbelief and signed on for the ride of this story, each turn of events seems a natural and inevitable outgrowth of what has come before. The cleverness of Roger's escapes from imminent danger, which in turn simply lead him toward other dangers, are such a logical extension of the wit and brightness we have already seen in the man that we revel in his cleverness at the same time we accept the events as inevitable.

ACTION AND ACTIVITY

An excellent example of both action and activity in the same scene is the auction scene. Roger's approach to Vandamm and Eve and his pointed barbs at her are actions; they have a specific purpose behind them, to get revenge and a reaction out of her. Meanwhile the auction is taking place around them, solely as an activity. Later in the scene, when Roger begins his crazy bidding, thus participating in the auction, he is again making a purposeful action, attempting to make enough of a ruckus to be rescued by the police.

Other examples of activities are the eating of the meal on the train, looking at Mount Rushmore through the telescope, Vandamm wanting champagne as they await the approaching plane at the end. Other examples of actions are searching Kaplan's New York hotel room, getting all the ladies to leave the elevator first when he is escaping from Vandamm's men, and Eve persuading Roger to take a shower in her Chicago hotel room so that she can escape and go to her meeting with Vandamm.

DIALOGUE

The dialogue, particularly Roger's and Eve's, is too witty and sharp to be taken as exactly realistic, as everyday speech. This quality of their speech adds to the general air of this film: it's not quite our real world, but it almost could be. It is close to reality, but just far away enough for us to be able to thrill at it—we are encouraged to maintain our aesthetic distance.

The dialogue given to Vandamm is consistently very droll and delivered with a tone of haughty superiority. One of his men, Valerian, has the most stylized language of any character in the film. This helps to allay our fears that the death and mayhem in this film will become too real, more difficult to bear (as it did the following year with the shower scene in *Psycho*).

VISUALS

From the claustrophobia of train compartments and bathrooms to the open vistas of the cropduster sequence, this film delivers a wide variety of visual stimuli for the audience. Incredibly evocative shots abound in all of Hitchcock's work, and this film is no exception—from the shot high above the UN building to the dolly along the row of phone booths when Leonard is giving Eve instructions for sending Roger out to meet the cropduster, to many of the shots in the cropduster sequence itself.

Beautiful small images also can be very effective, such as the way Eve touches Roger's hand when he lights her cigarette in the dining car and the way his hands are held off her even as the two embrace in her hotel room after the plane attacked him. Also, Vandamm's proprietary hand on Eve's neck at the beginning of the auction scene is a simple but telling gesture—just as the moment when he removes the hand is a much clearer depiction of his inner world than any words could convey.

DRAMATIC SCENES

For all the action and thrills of this film, there are still some very effectively staged dramatic scenes. When Roger and his mother investigate Kaplan's hotel room, both characters have clearly defined wants. He wants to find out about Kaplan and she wants to persuade him to quit this nonsense. While he is actively searching, questioning, and even trying on Kaplan's suit (trying on his life?), she is physically and figuratively trying to drag him to the door.

When Roger confronts Eve in her hotel room with the question, "How does a girl like you get to be a girl like you?" the hurt and anger of his feelings and her genuine relief at his survival, coupled with her anxiety about his presence, are visible in the interaction of the two characters. The dialogue, while effective and sharp, is only a small part of what makes the scene work.

When Vandamm first enters the study in Glen Cove to meet "George Kaplan," it immediately becomes a game of cat-and-mouse between these two rivals. Vandamm sets the stage by closing the drapes and turning on various lights, while he and Roger circle about each other, sizing each other up. The certainty with which each character takes his position strengthens the conflict between these two men with opposing wants. (Again, Roger wants to clear up the mistake and Vandamm wants to reveal the truth about this "agent.")

SPECIAL NOTES

This film is a fine example of the interplay between mystery and suspense. A mystery is a story that has a detective, or an equivalent, who is actively trying to find out what is happening and/or what has happened. As such, a mystery is a function of the past tense and the present tense. A mystery, whether it is the overall structure of the story or an element in the early part of another kind of story, is a very effective tool for initially engaging an audience, because it appeals immediately to our sense of curiosity. We can quickly become intrigued by a mystery.

Mystery cannot, however, sustain audience interest and participation for an entire story, because it is a function of past and present tenses. To get an audience emotionally involved, hoping and fearing, participating in the story, we have to exercise the future tense, make the audience look ahead. Suspense is pure future: What will happen? is the foremost question in the audience's mind. Some element of suspense, then, is necessary in every kind of film, not just in mysteries. It is necessary to make the audience feel that hope versus fear, that anticipation, which is the essence of involvement in a story.

Ideally, mystery and suspense are woven together; this film is a masterful example of how the two coexist, supporting and strengthening each other. When Roger is kidnapped, both he and the audience are mystified, wanting to know what is going on. When the interview with Vandamm reveals a small portion of what has happened—the mistaken identity—it ends with the order to kill Roger. Immediately we shift into suspense: What will happen, how will he get away? We are looking to the future. When Roger goes to Kaplan's hotel room, he is actively taking on the role of the detective and trying to figure out the mystery of who this person is and how this mistake came about. When Vandamm's henchmen are on their way up to the room, we shift back into suspense, no longer thinking about the past or present, but about what will happen in the immediate future: How will he escape?

A good mystery will shift back and forth between mystery and suspense for much of the story. But by the end of the second act it is advisable to have solved the major mystery and to move on to nearly pure suspense. In this film, the end of the second act occurs when the Professor reveals the last threads of the main mystery, that Eve is the agent, and Roger learns what we already know, that Kaplan is a fiction. From the moment Roger signs on to help save Eve, we are primarily in a suspense mode. There can still be minor mysteries—the nature of the Professor's plan in the restaurant, for instance—but our feelings are largely given over to suspense.

Beginning screenwriters will often try to sustain the mystery until the last minute of the film, like a whodunit murder mystery novel, but this is antithetical to drama. Drama depends for its very existence on the audience participating, anticipating, hoping, and fearing—being in a state of suspense. Without this, we become mere witnesses to the story, outside and uninvolved, and the story doesn't seem dramatic. At best, unduly sustained mystery can pique our curiosity, but it can't touch our feelings.

The 400 Blows

(1959)
Written by François Truffaut and Marcel Moussy
Directed by François Truffaut

Though this was not the first film of the *Nouvelle Vague*, *The 400 Blows* was surely among the earliest films that introduced the French New Wave to the world, along with the works of Claude Chabrol, Jean-Luc Godard, Eric Rohmer, and Jacques Rivette. Openly autobiographical and lacking a pat, happy ending, this film established Truffaut as a true *auteur*, a film-maker of strong feelings and psychological depth. *The 400 Blows* won the Grand Prize at the Cannes Film Festival in 1959, and the script by Truffaut and Moussy was nominated for an Academy Award for Best Screenplay written directly for the screen.

SYNOPSIS

In the middle of a classroom examination of thirteen-year-old boys, a cal-endar-girl picture is being circulated. When it gets to Antoine Doinel, he is caught by the schoolmaster and made to stand behind the blackboard in the corner. Denied recess, Antoine scribbles his complaint on the wall and this gets him in further trouble, leading to a take-home assignment of con-jugations and a vow of revenge against Mauricet, who told on him. After school he commiserates with his best friend, René, then hurries home.

Antoine swipes a little hidden cash, then does his chores in the family's small, empty apartment. He snoops in his parents' bedroom before sitting down to do his conjugations. But before long his mother, Gilberte, returns home and is angry with him for having forgotten to buy the flour she re-quested. He runs out on the errand and returns with his affable father, Julien, who has a new fog light for his beloved automobile. Gilberte de-mands the change from Antoine's purchase, but he turns around and gets money from his father. After dinner, he hears his parents discussing send-ing him to camp next summer. Then Julien asks his wife to join him on the auto-club trip on Sunday but she begs off. He jokes about her "touch system" typing, and she lambasts him for his constant jokes and his seem-ing failure at work.

Worried about how to face the schoolmaster without having completed his assignment, Antoine rushes off toward school, only to find René urging him to play hooky. The boys hide their briefcases and run off for a day of fun—going to a movie, playing pinball, and taking rides at a carnival. On their way home, they spot Gilberte kissing another man. They decide she won't tell about Antoine's truancy because of her own circumstances. But when the boys retrieve their briefcases, they are spied on by goody-goody Mauricet. René offers his absence note to Antoine to copy in his mother's handwriting, but before Antoine gets it copied, his father returns home.

Julien announces that Gilberte has to work late and that the two of them will be bacheloring tonight. They cook eggs together, and Julien asks Antoine about school. Later, in his cramped little bed in the apartment vestibule, Antoine pretends to be asleep when his mother comes home. He listens as his parents fight about her late night with her boss, about Antoine's lying, and about the fact that he isn't actually Julien's son.

While Antoine hurries off to school in the morning, Mauricet goes to the Doinel's to squeal on Antoine for having skipped school yesterday. René and Antoine discuss what excuse to give the schoolmaster and conclude "the bigger the better." Antoine says his mother died and finds sympathy from the teacher. But when Antoine's parents show up at his class, he is slapped and told he will be punished tonight. Sure that he can't go home anymore, Antoine plans to spend the night on the street, but René has a better place, his uncle's printing plant. Julien reads a note from Antoine about his not coming home while Gilberte wonders why it was she that he killed off in his excuse. She also admits that the boy irritates her.

Alone on the street late at night, Antoine passes Christmas decorations, narrowly escapes being caught in the printing plant, and finally steals a bottle of milk, which he devours hungrily. In the morning Antoine returns to school and is summoned from class to the principal's office. There his mother hugs him and asks where he spent the night. Gilberte bathes him and puts him into her bed to nap while she tries to get him to open up to her. But her real concern is what he meant in his note about explaining everything. When he says only his own behavior, she relaxes and makes a deal with him: if he gets a high mark in French, she will give him some cash, but they won't tell his father.

When the gym teacher leads a parade of the boys out for a jog, they desert the line in droves until only two boys are left. Alone at home, Antoine reads Balzac and puts up a picture of him in his wall shelf. In school the teacher assigns the boys to write about an important event in their lives, and Antoine choses to write about the death of his grandfather. Antoine lights a candle in his little shrine to Balzac, then over dinner the family smells smoke and finds his whole wall unit is on fire. Gilberte defends

Antoine, and they decide to go out together for a movie. They have a good time together and come home happy.

But in school the next day, Antoine is accused of plagiarizing Balzac for his essay and is thrown out of school. René gets himself expelled as well. Antoine is sure he will be sentenced to a military academy if he returns home. He admits the navy wouldn't be so bad, because he's always wanted to see the sea. René invites him to stay at his house. Antoine is astounded by the huge, strange apartment, then watches in awe as René steals some hidden cash and the boys run out for some fun. René eats alone with his father, sets a clock ahead, then takes the remaining food when his father makes a hasty exit. Antoine also takes the food as the boys rush off to the cinema. After the movie, they steal a movie still, swipe change from a rest room, and steal a clock.

The next day, with a little girl in tow, the two boys go to a puppet show. As the little kids are enthralled, the older boys plot how they will get the money they need for Antoine to survive in hiding. They decide to steal a typewriter from Julien's office and pawn it. Antoine gets into the office and out with the typewriter without a problem, though carrying the heavy instrument down streets and into the subway is a burden. Finally they find a shady man who will hock it for them, but he takes off with it. They get it back only when a cop appears and they conclude they won't be able to sell it. Fearing his father will figure out he took it, Antoine decides that he will return the typewriter to the office and wear a hat so he won't be recognized.

But the night watchman catches him returning with the typewriter and calls Julien. His father takes Antoine to the police and says that they have tried everything; he gives up. Antoine is arrested, photographed, fingerprinted, and locked in a cell with a man. After he is put into a prisoner van with adults, Antoine watches Paris recede through the bars of the van. Gilberte tells a judge about Antoine's home life, and it is decided that he will go to an observation center for a while. At the center, Antoine is punished for eating his bread first. Later he is interviewed by a female psychologist and explains why he brought the typewriter back and how he stole money from his grandmother.

When visiting day comes, Antoine is excited to see René, but they are not allowed to visit. He does see his mother, and she chides him for the "personal" letter he sent his father and tells him that Julien has no further interest in him. She predicts he will go to reform school. During a soccer game, Antoine makes a run for it and manages to elude the guard racing after him. He runs and runs and finally reaches the seashore. He races up to the waves, then turns back inland and looks to be lost, hollow.

PROTAGONIST AND OBJECTIVE

This is Antoine's story. He is the one who is always caught, he is the one neglected and misunderstood by his parents, and he is the one who continually must pay the price. Here we have an example of an objective that the character himself is not fully aware of: he wants to find a place in the world. He wants to belong somewhere, to be wanted somewhere, and to be appreciated somewhere. Though he can't articulate these desires, they are nonetheless his motivating factors.

OBSTACLES

Antoine's obstacles can be summed up in one word: adults. He has a selfish, deceitful, and resentful mother who is decidedly ambivalent about him. He has a weak, cowardly father who loves him, yet cannot stand up to his wife. His teacher already has him pegged as a troublemaker, and all other adults equally distrust and misunderstand him. Additional obstacles come from inside him; Antoine is consistently his own worst enemy. By not thinking things through very well, he sets his shrine to Balzac on fire and steals from his own father's company. He is like a terrible cardplayer who takes a bad hand and plays it poorly.

PREMISE AND OPENING

An unwanted and only nominally loved thirteen-year-old Parisian boy tries to make do and find his way in the world, but finds that the deck is always stacked against him. For their opening, Truffaut and Moussy chose an elegant little example of Antoine's lot in life. His "sin" with the calendar-girl photo is no greater than any of the other boys', yet he is the one singled out for punishment. When he is left on his own to stew in the injustice of it, he compounds his own troubles and gets himself into even more hot water.

MAIN TENSION, CULMINATION, AND RESOLUTION

The telling of this story does not depend on the creation of an intensely driving central dilemma. Instead this film is rather anecdotal and seemingly casual in pace and narrative structure. Yet there is still a clear narrative thread that holds together the telling of the story. It has to do with Antoine's well-being, his ability to find a way to get through life with a minimum of trouble, though we continually foresee, more clearly than he does, what may go wrong. The main tension might be, "Will

Antoine be able to make life work with his parents?" Will he be able to catch up, get into good graces, get past his "bad" behavior, be himself and still be appreciated, to have a place in the world? Here the main tension isn't a tangible, hard and fast thing; it is the state of his being that we hope and fear about.

The culmination comes when he is caught returning the typewriter and his father gives up trying with him. When he is taken to the police and made a part of the "system," Antoine is now beyond finding a place to be in this world with his family—after the failure of many different attempts. And the resolution comes when he escapes from the observation center and is truly on his own, alone in the world. We hardly feel that his troubles are over, but at least he has his freedom, a chance to make his life work on his own terms.

THEME

This story is about the basic human struggle between belonging and freedom. Each of the four principal characters struggles with the desire to belong somewhere, with someone, and the desire to be free. Antoine would really prefer to be happily ensconced with his family, if only he could also be himself and still be accepted. René has this combination, though at the price of incredible distance from the parents to whom he actually only nominally "belongs." Julien married Gilberte and gave her son a name so that he could belong to a family, but largely gave up his freedom to get it, except for his beloved auto-club tours. And Gilberte gave up her freedom as well so that her son wouldn't be illegitimate. Yet she rebels by exercising a forbidden freedom, when she sees other men and lies to her husband. Each of them is torn by these seemingly irreconcilable wants, but it is only Antoine, through force of circumstance more than his own compelling desire, who comes to grips with them and opts for freedom at the complete sacrifice of the desire to belong.

UNITY

Because there is a clear-cut central character, this story has the unity of action even though the protagonist is not always conscious of his actions or their underlying motivations. For the most part, Antoine thinks he is merely trying to muddle through, to cover up his latest mistake, or to keep something from going out of control. In fact, he is always trying to make his life work, to find a place where he is wanted, accepted, and loved. He is willing to lie, cheat, and steal to make it happen, and it is his natural rambunctiousness that usually defeats his attempts, along with the misperceptions and intolerance of the adults in his world.

EXPOSITION

The exposition in this story is delivered through both conflict and routine. When we see the automatic way in which Antoine performs his chores around the house, we begin to understand the nature of his position in the family. When he forgets to buy flour, the curtness of his mother and her insistence on the return of the change show us about their uneasy relationship. And when he asks his father for money, the father's exploration of both sides of the conflict and his eventual acquiescence show us the nature of their relationship.

Examples of back-story exposition through conflict can be found throughout the film. We learn through the parents' fighting that Antoine was illegitimate and not Julien's son. We learn his fear of going home when he is in trouble at school. We discover through Julien's jokes that he knows more than he's letting on about his wife's affairs, and we find out how little respect she has for him through her intolerance of his jokes. In a nice little bit of exposition in an offhand moment, we learn about the family's financial woes when an unexpected knock on the door makes the parents fear it is the gas man.

CHARACTERIZATION

Antoine is characterized as the ultimate thirteen-year-old boy, one prone to mild defiance and petty resistance to authority, possessing a sense of wilfullness—in other words, a boy who turns his every effort into more trouble for himself. Even a simple thing like a shrine to Balzac turns into disaster, to say nothing of trying to lie away a day of truancy.

Gilberte is characterized as vain, selfish, and very short-tempered. She wears a fur coat, but they are behind with the gas man. She takes the money for Antoine's sheets, and lays the blame on him. She is concerned with the lines in her face, but sees Antoine's bed in the tiny vestibule only as an inconvenience to her, not a hardship on him. And Julien is affable, always trying to put a good face on things with a joke, yet he is really a coward. He continually tells Antoine how to keep the peace with his mother by giving in. René is a spoiled rich boy who seems to lead a charmed life. He gets away with everything that Antoine gets caught for. Even when he is kicked out of school, it is because he knowingly asks for it. There are no repercussions for René's actions.

DEVELOPMENT OF THE STORY

Each new problem of Antoine's grows out of the rest of the story with an unerring and distressing logic. He is caught with the calendar-girl picture, so he is punished. He laments the injustice, so he is punished more. Because he is unable to complete the extra homework assignment, he is susceptible to René's suggestion that they skip school. But unlike his friend, he has no note and must lie. Even Mauricet, who snitches on Antoine to his parents, does so as a result of Antoine's threat of revenge against him— he just beats his rival to the punch.

After some kind of familial peace seems to have been made and Antoine is building his shrine to Balzac in hopes of winning his mother's good graces and the promised money, his very nature leads him right back to trouble, when he is accused of plagiarism. Kicked out of school, he is desperate for money. He decides to steal from his father's office, and he gets caught trying to return the stolen typewriter. Each of these steps on his descent toward the penal system and permanent separation from his family is logically built on the shoulders of the preceding events.

DRAMATIC IRONY

When the boys decide to play hooky, their nemesis, Mauricet, spies on them and then goes to tattle on Antoine, creating a dramatic irony that further compounds Antoine's troubles, because he lies to his teacher shortly before his parents come to check on him. A marvelous example of the use of an irony that is not revealed, but adds a subtext to a scene, comes after Antoine spots his mother kissing another man. That night Julien tells Antoine his mother has to work late and expresses a great deal of sympathy for her plight, saying that offices always take advantage of women.

There is an effective use of irony in the scene where René manipulates his father by setting the clock forward. And there is a special irony in the fact that Antoine is finally caught not when he steals, but when he returns the thing that he successfully stole earlier. This moment is a dramatization of what he says later, in the interview with the psychologist, that even when he tells the truth he isn't believed.

PREPARATION AND AFTERMATH

An effective scene of preparation comes when Antoine sits down to copy René's absence note for himself, but is interrupted by his father's return. It sets up his attempt to conceal his truancy and demonstrates his fear of revealing his actions to his parents. When his father asks about school and what he studied, this preparation adds a certain poignancy to the moment.

Later that night, when Antoine lies in bed and pretends to both parents that he is asleep, it is a statement of the essential dishonesty in their relationships, but also a preparation for the scene to come where he listens to them fight about him, his lying, his mother's lying, and the fact that he was illegitimate.

A very effective use of preparation by contrast comes in the scenes where Antoine and both parents go out for an evening together—to a movie and for a drive in the car. They are all happy and laughing together. Immediately following this happiest moment that the family shares comes the accusation that Antoine plagiarized, and he is kicked out of school. That horrible moment is made all the worse because it comes right on the heels of a good time. And an effective scene of aftermath comes right after he is kicked out of school. Antoine is sure he will be sent to military school and allows that a naval school wouldn't be so bad because he has always wanted to see the sea.

PLANTING AND PAYOFF

This desire of Antoine's to see the sea is also a planting for the final moments of the story. The sea achieves a metaphorical level in this story, because it represents for Antoine the ultimate freedom, escape. The initial plant is supported by Gilberte with the judge, when she reiterates that Antoine has a fascination for the sea.

Balzac is also a planting and payoff. First we see Antoine reading Balzac, then putting up his picture in the wall unit and covering it with a curtain. The first payoff comes after he has lit the candle in his little shrine and nearly burns the apartment down. The second payoff comes when Antoine is accused of having plagiarized from the story we first saw him reading.

ELEMENTS OF THE FUTURE
AND ADVERTISING

There are numerous occasions when one or both of his parents, or Antoine himself, talk about his not living with the family anymore. Each time is an element of the future—not a guaranteed turn of events, but something of a prediction. He alludes to being sent to military school, his father talks of sending him off to camp, his mother talks of boarding him out, and then the observation center is brought up. We are regularly being reminded that his staying with his own parents is tenuous at best. Another element of the future that involves a prediction comes when Julien confronts Antoine after the theft of the typewriter and tells René that he won't be seeing his friend for a long time.

And a nice bit of advertising comes when René brings up the fact that Antoine will need an excuse for his day of hooky. The first solution is that Antoine will copy René's note, then that he will tell a lie—the bigger the better. This is a moment that we know will have to be delivered—whatever his excuse, we expect to see it.

PLAUSIBILITY

There is absolutely no need for suspension of disbelief in this story, in that all the events are believable, plausible, and realistic. We have known kids in similar circumstances, and have felt similar injustices ourselves. Nothing he does is unbelievable on the face of it, and because all of the events grow with such relentless logic out of what has preceded them, we are fully prepared to accept the whole sequence of events as realistic and painfully true.

ACTION AND ACTIVITY

Most of Antoine's chores around the house are activities—setting the table, taking out the trash, fetching flour for his mother. Yet when Gilberte and Julien are arguing and she sends Antoine out with the garbage, it is an action on her part—to get the boy out of the way for a few minutes while they fight. When father and son cook eggs together, it is an activity, as is Antoine's building of his shrine to Balzac.

But when Gilberte is nice to Antoine after his night out alone and his note about "explaining everything," it is not the mere activity of a mother taking care of her son. While there may be an element of that in her actions, behind them is also her concern about what she perceives as a threat—his revealing that he saw her with another man. When she is assured that his explanations were only about his own actions, her mood changes and she makes a deal with him to get better grades in French. Near the end, when Antoine is playing soccer and he insists on going after the out-of-bounds ball, it is a clear-cut action because he is intending to try to escape.

DIALOGUE

This story is told primarily visually, and thus it has a diminished necessity for rich and telling dialogue. There is nothing wrong with the dialogue here—it fills its function and helps to tell the story—yet the overwhelming load of the storytelling is in the visuals.

In such a circumstance the dialogue is most effective in terms of helping with the characterizations. Julien's use of the word *apropos* is an affectation that reveals his intellectual pretensions. The schoolmaster's love of and insistence on the flowery language of the poem is also revealing. The guarded way that Gilberte couches her terms reflects her secretiveness, and the defensive way in which both parents describe Antoine's home life to authorities tells of their insecurities as well as their rationalizations.

VISUALS

From the visual design to the individual shots, the way this story is shown to the audience is the strength of the storytelling. The early part of the story puts Antoine into tight, inhospitable spaces—behind the blackboard, cramped into a tiny bed in the vestibule, at a table pushed up against the sideboard. When he and René go out for fun, the spaces open up; a telling detail is that one of Antoine's happy adventures involves going around in circles and getting nowhere. Later, when he is on his own, Antoine is in open space; after his arrest, he is led down endless narrow corridors, through a labyrinth, and into tiny cells. By the time he escapes he is in open fields, running down roads and then onto a huge expanse of seashore with nothing but space around him.

During his long night alone on the street, the visuals and the actions the boy takes help to underline his desperation and his loneliness. His cramped hideout in the printing plant quickly becomes dangerous, and he has to go out. His hunger is established in the shot of him staring into a café—nicely designed to be shot from inside the restaurant. Once he steals the bottle of milk, there is a long single take of him slurping down nearly the whole bottle that says more than words could about his hunger. And after that long night, he goes to a shut-down public fountain and has to chip the ice on the surface of the remaining water to wash his face. What a strong and effective way of demonstrating his hardship, much more telling than hours of shivering.

Another marvelous image comes when Antoine is put into the prisoner van and cries as he watches his last glimpses of Paris recede behind him. We see him with adults who presumably belong there. We see him through bars and we feel his longing for the city he is leaving and intuit, perhaps, his sadness over the family he is also leaving, probably forever.

And the closing scene and the final shot of the film deserve attention. While his reaching the sea at last is meaningful as his own private little triumph, it does nothing for his real predicament in life, and we are painfully aware of that. When we see the lost look on his face juxtaposed with the happy antics of his body, and that look is emphasized for us by the zoom in on the frozen image of his face, our sense of foreboding for his future overpowers our joy in his escape. This shot makes this the classic bittersweet ending—we are happy he is free at last, and yet we are filled with fear and dread for his future and we see the first inklings of those mixed emotions crossing his face. (A similarly effective closing shot comes in *The Graduate,* when Benjamin and Elaine escape on the bus with her still in her wedding dress. Their triumph is tainted by an awesome dawning of all that undoubtedly lies ahead of them.)

DRAMATIC SCENES
There is a marvelous example of a dramatic scene after Antoine has returned to school after spending the whole night out alone. His mother has come to pick him up at school, and it seems that she has finally seen the error of her ways as she washes him and then ushers him into her bed to rest. But we quickly pick up on her real intention, which comes from the note he left about "explaining everything." Her worry that he will tell his father about seeing her with the other man has prompted her to do everything she thinks her son wants from her. She confesses to her own girlhood peccadilloes in hopes of opening him up, and then, when she finds out he meant to explain only his own troubles, her relief comes in the guise of making a deal with him to get him to make better grades. The subtext is clear to us, if not to Antoine, and his own difficulty even in owning up to what he had meant to explain in the letter is quite effectively rendered.

SPECIAL NOTES
One of the more distinctive features of the films of the *Nouvelle Vague* is that they don't lightly resolve complex and real dilemmas with pat solutions. This would be an utterly different drama if Antoine's parents saw the error of their ways, missed their son, and brought him home for another try—no doubt in a spacious new apartment. Rather, this film, like so many of the early and formative films out of this movement, ends with an ambiguous "open" resolution. Life will go on, the problems won't quickly go away, perhaps at most the character is one step closer to (or, in some films, farther away from) grasping the real complexities of his or her life.

When well done, this kind of film is utterly thought-provoking. It leaves the audience with much to mull over, a great deal to discuss and argue about, and, in the end, conclude for ourselves. Some films by the lesser imitators of the movement can leave one with a sense of copping out, of not resolving a story because of "artsiness," rather than the resolution coming from a truthful immersion in a real-life dilemma that refuses a simple solution.

Since Truffaut and his mentor at *Cahiers du Cinéma*, André Bazin, were two of the earliest proponents of the *auteur* theory, this film offers a good opportunity to discuss this much disputed idea of who is the "author" of a film. In the case of a film such as *The 400 Blows*—which is autobiographical and was co-written and directed by one person—there can be no disputing that Truffaut is the author of the film and its story. While there will always be films that fit this description, some superb and others self-indulgent, there will always be a larger number of well-made films that don't have such clear-cut and singular authorship.

The danger then in the *auteur* theory—and the source of its controversy—really stems from attempting to make what is specific to some films and a handful of filmmakers into a universal designation. Not all directors are *auteurs*. Not all films, even among the best and most heartfelt, are wrenched from the soul of one person. More often than not, the wrenching begins with the writer, is augmented by the director, and receives considerable assistance from the actors and others who help to make the film come alive. In fact, the same person could be the *auteur* of some of his or her films but not all of them. It really comes down to the individual project, how it comes into being, who creates the story, and who really does the primary shaping of how it is told.

The artist's place is not to declare himself an artist, but rather to do the painting, sculpting, weaving, dancing, or whatever art form he practices. It is the place of the viewer to declare one person an artist and another a craftsman or a want-to-be or a dilettante. The true *auteur* should be content to let the film viewer decide, and meanwhile do his job and let the others on his team do theirs.

Citizen Kane

(1941)
Written by Herman J. Mankiewicz and Orson Welles
Directed by Orson Welles

Often considered the greatest film ever made, and always considered among the best of all time, *Citizen Kane* is a tour de force performance by twenty-six-year-old first-time director and screenwriter Orson Welles, who also plays the title character. While perhaps not as emotionally charged as other films, which leaves it somewhat shy of profound, this film has nonetheless had enormous influence on American and international filmmakers, modes of cinematic expression, and the use of all the tools available to the filmmaker.

SYNOPSIS

Charles Foster Kane, an enormously wealthy and powerful man, head of a chain of newspapers, dies holding a little snowflake globe and whispering the word "Rosebud." A newsreel of the 1940s gives the bare-bones outline of his life, but fails to capture the essence of the man. A reporter for the newsreel company named Thompson is sent on a quest to find out what the last word meant, in hopes it will shed light on this enigma. He goes about interviewing those who knew Kane and investigating his past.

In a cheap nightclub, Thompson tries to interview Kane's widow, Susan Alexander Kane, but she refuses. Next he goes to the Thatcher library to read the memoirs of the banker who was Kane's guardian from early in his life, when his mother inherited a gold mine. Though both of Kane's parents were alive, he was sent to live with Thatcher, over his great objections, "for his own good."

Thompson interviews Bernstein, Kane's business partner, and learns more. When Kane actually comes into possession of his inheritance, he decides to put his time into a newspaper he has holdings in. Along with his friend Jed Leland and partner Bernstein, Kane runs the paper like a crusade for the poor against the rich, a money-losing crusade to Thatcher's way of thinking. Once the newspaper is a thriving success, Kane loses interest, goes traveling, and comes back with a wife, Emily, the niece of the President of the United States.

Jed Leland also doesn't know what "Rosebud" means, but he sheds some light on Kane's personal life. We see nine years of marriage pass at the breakfast table, then go immediately into Kane's first meeting with his second wife, Susan, a would-be singer. Meanwhile, Kane has decided to run for governor and seems the odds-on favorite until his opponent exposes his affair with Susan. Emily divorces him and he marries Susan, though the "love of the people of this state" has been robbed from him in the process. Kane builds an opera house and goes about orchestrating a singing career for Susan, despite her own objections. When Jed passes out, drunk, while writing a scathing review of her opening night, Kane fires him and finishes the review as Jed began it, hatefully caustic to the last line.

Susan finally agrees to tell Thompson her story. More performances and many bad notices later, Susan tries to end the singing career, but Kane won't listen until she takes an overdose of sleeping pills. Finally he relents and they move to Florida, where he is building a huge castle that he is stocking with art from around the world. Lonely and frustrated, Susan rebels against him. When she is packed and ready to go, Kane is reduced to begging her to stay, but she leaves and he trashes her room in anger.

At the castle, after Kane's death, Thompson interviews the butler, Raymond, who says the only other time he heard Kane say "Rosebud" was right after Kane destroyed Susan's room. It was when he had just picked up the snowflake globe with a little cabin inside, pocketed it in front of all the household, and gone off to be alone. The castle's incredible collection of art and stuff—Kane "never threw anything away"—is being catalogued as Thompson concludes that he hasn't found out much about the man, just the many parts of a jigsaw puzzle. As he leaves, a workman throws a sled into the furnace, the sled Kane had played on as a boy, before he was taken from his family. As it burns, we see that the brand name on the sled is Rosebud.

PROTAGONIST AND OBJECTIVE

Because the story of Kane's life is contained within a framing story, that framework has its own structure. The protagonist of the framing story is Thompson, whose objective is to find out what "Rosebud" means. But there is no confusing the real protagonist of this film, for Thompson is barely allowed to become a character; he is nearly always off screen or filmed in heavy shadow. We are not made curious about Thompson; he is merely the personification of our curiosity about Kane.

Kane, the real protagonist, firmly holds center stage. His objective is to use his wealth and power to make himself loved, though his approach is imperious and unbending.

OBSTACLES

Kane's first obstacle to being loved comes when he is suddenly wrenched from his family home when his mother decides that he will have a better life if he goes to live in the city with Mr. Thatcher. Although she has her son's best interests in mind, this seems to be a horrendous event to the young child, one that separates him from all that he knows and loves in the world. This banker is an unloving man, and Kane grows to adulthood with little in the way of a sustaining family life. His newspaper becomes his family, but then he grasps for the love of the state by running for governor. When he is soundly defeated in scandal, he becomes hardened and cynical. When his quest to make Susan into a singer prompts Jed's horrible review, he rejects his best friend and focuses his whole quest for love on Susan. When she rejects him, he has nowhere else to turn but memory.

PREMISE AND OPENING

A powerful and wealthy newspaper publisher dies in seclusion in a castle that is overflowing with his art acquisitions, yet his final moments are as difficult to fathom as his lonely life. As their opening, Mankiewicz and Welles chose an ominous and foreboding view of the castle, coming ever closer to a window behind which we find first the snowflake globe raining snow on the little cabin, then the lips of the man whispering "Rosebud," which begins the mystery.

MAIN TENSION, CULMINATION, AND RESOLUTION

The main tension has to do with Kane's quest for love: "Will Kane be able to force or seduce the world into granting him love?" or something similar. The culmination comes when Kane's last hope for love tries to kill herself rather than be bullied and badgered by him any longer. Though he and Susan continue to live together, the chance at love has passed. The resolution is that Kane, now alone and unloved, lives out his days immersed in memory of a time when love was a part of his life, as evidenced by the sled and the globe, which contains a little cabin much like his childhood home.

THEME

The theme of this story has to revolve around love; that is Kane's quest, and that is the central issue of the story. Four of the five storytellers within the film—Thatcher, Bernstein, Leland, and Susan—are the people in a position in Kane's life to love him, and each demonstrates in his story how (or if) that love developed and ended.

UNITY

Even though this film has a framing story with its own main character, and the rest of the story is told through five other characters, the unity of the story still stems from the unity of action, from Kane's quest to make the world give him love. Unlike *Rashomon*, in which we get conflicting views of the same incident, here the five narrators tell interwoven but complementary stories, each dealing with that person's interaction with Kane.

EXPOSITION

The device of the newsreel account of Kane's life and accomplishments is used early to set out the objective facts, in part because the storytelling, moving back and forth through time, needs a simple base on which to build. While rather inelegant and too much on the surface for truly effective exposition, this is acceptable because, as Robert Towne says, "an audience will forgive you almost anything in the beginning of a picture." Other exposition within the various stories about Kane is handled in a much more cinematic way, such as when Kane moves into the offices of the editor of the newspaper he has just taken over.

CHARACTERIZATION

Kane is a complex character, one that does not easily fit into simplistic psychology. In fact the very way this film story is told arises from the filmmaker's desire to show us a rounded and complex psyche with its many facets. The key to his characterization is his objective, his quest to wrench love from a world that he thinks must be bullied to relent. Susan rather clearly throws this back in his face when she says, "You don't love me. You want me to love you. Sure! 'I'm Charles Foster Kane. Whatever you want, just name it and it's yours, but you gotta love me.' "

The other characters are not presented with as much complexity. Thatcher is depicted as a haughty and conscientious man, doing what he believes is his duty to his young charge. The shrewd and charming Jed has an integrity that destroys their friendship once Kane becomes dishonest.

Susan is a small masterpiece—an attractive but common young woman foundering in an artistic and social milieu she is incapable of understanding.

DEVELOPMENT OF THE STORY

This story is told with an interesting mode of development. Since it is told by the various characters who knew the central character at times in his life, each of their stories has its own progression, its own three acts and completeness or mini-resolution. Because each of these stories is a recollection, we have a great deal of latitude with time. In fact, we go into old age, back to youth, back to old age, and so on, depending on where we are in these interlocking stories. This allows the storytellers to create the moments of Kane's life, not for historical accuracy, but for the creation of a complex psychology complete with ambivalences, contradictions, and all the other paradoxes of real human behavior.

DRAMATIC IRONY

An early use of dramatic irony comes in the first meeting of young Kane with Thatcher, when everyone but the boy knows he is being taken away to live with the banker. Another superb example of irony comes when Jed has passed out drunk over his review of Susan's opening night, and Kane decides to finish it as begun. Another example is when the music teacher is trying in vain to get Susan to hit her notes, and we see Kane enter the room long before the others do.

PREPARATION AND AFTERMATH

An effective scene of preparation occurs when Kane and Leland drive up to the newspaper office right before taking over. And a good example of aftermath comes when the editor of that paper leaves, never to return. Another effective aftermath comes after the confrontation scene in which Kane, Susan, Emily, and Kane's opponent for governor confront each other. Emily and the opponent leave together, with Kane shouting after them.

PLANTING AND PAYOFF

Perhaps the most famous planting and payoff in all of cinema is in this picture—"Rosebud." We are made curious about it from the very beginning, reminded of it, our curiosity expanded until we have nearly given up on finding out, only to have the payoff in the closing shot of the story. This is the sort of planting and payoff that achieves the level of metaphor.

Another good planting and payoff comes with Kane's handwritten "declaration of principles," which Jed keeps. When Kane is at his lowest and most dishonest, Jed sends it back to him—again the creation of a metaphor.

ELEMENTS OF THE FUTURE AND ADVERTISING

That same "declaration of principles" is also an effective element of the future when it is presented. Kane has predicted his future behavior, and we look forward to finding out how well he follows his own prediction. The wedding announcement delivered to the newspaper office is a simple form of advertising, not of the wedding, but of the marriage, which we see encapsulated in nine years of breakfasts and the changes those years bring. When we first meet Susan, she lets on that she would like to be a singer, which is an element of the future.

PLAUSIBILITY

This is a study of a highly controversial figure. The events of his life and his actions seem ultimately logical and inevitable to the extent that we accept the "theory" that "Rosebud" is a primal force in his life. If we believe in that, then we can buy into the story without reservation.

ACTION AND ACTIVITY

A meaningful action comes early, when the boy attacks Thatcher with his sled, showing both his rejection of the banker and emphasizing the sled. Another comes when Kane's bedroom furnishings are brought to the newspaper office even as he is first meeting his staff. This shows that he is planning to make the newspaper his life, his home and his co-workers his "family." Of course, his furious destruction of Susan's room after she has left him is a marvelous example of how action can be a window into the inner life of a character. Examples of activities are when the young Kane is sledding and throwing snowballs at the sign on his cabin home. Also, Susan's crossword puzzles are activities; they are not actions intended to bring about some effect in Kane.

DIALOGUE

Although the story is structured around interviews and recollections, this is not an overly talky film. Dialogue is used sparingly and well. An example of a fine, short exchange comes when Kane is finishing up Jed's review of Susan's opening. *Jed:* "I thought we weren't talking." *Kane:* "We are. You're fired." Another comes in the scene where Kane is signing away control of his newspaper industry and says, "If I hadn't been very rich, I might have been a really great man."

This was remarkably realistic dialogue for its day, a mature use of language and a skillful tailoring of the language to the characters, as a comparison of Emily's and Susan's dialogue reveals.

VISUALS

This was a breakthrough film in its use of visuals and in expanding the visual repertoire of the filmmaker, at least in mainstream American films. Some interesting uses of visuals are the series of increasingly distant breakfast vignettes between Kane and Emily; the pan up from the opera opening to two workmen high above in the catwalks with their visual comment about the work; and the camera moving through the nightclub sign, down through the skylight, and into Susan's current world.

DRAMATIC SCENES

Effective dramatic scenes abound: when Mrs. Kane is signing away the boy and his father can't stop it; when Kane moves into the newspaper offices to live; when Kane is confronted by his political rival and his wife over his affair with Susan; and many more. The scene in which Susan moves out of Xanadu repays close scrutiny. There is a brief scene of preparation when Kane is summoned to her room. Their exchange is well staged and her moving is effectively shown with the suitcases and the interruption of a servant. When Kane has been brought to his knees—the great man finds himself begging her to stay—he is practically straight into the camera and framed, nearly isolated in the doorway. His wrecking of the room afterward is an elaborated scene of aftermath.

SPECIAL NOTES

Whole books have been written about the unique qualities of *Citizen Kane*, but one area related to the discussion of this book is this film's use of time. Because the storytellers chose to tell this story through the recollections of several people involved in Kane's life, it freed them from any time constraints, allowing us to experience the story backward and forward in time, as the various characters' reminiscences would be. This is an especially effective tool in a story that covers a very large time frame—in this case, something like sixty years.

Also, because the mystery of this story is not what happened in Kane's life, but rather what it meant, this ability to go anywhere in time, and to any location, with the ease of a recollection, helps the storytellers build up the sense of mystery: What did the events mean to Kane? We can be tantalized with one character's version of the opera opening and have another, but complementary, view of it from another character. We see Thatcher's view of Kane's business affairs and newspaper management, and get a very different view from Bernstein. The contrasts, comparisons, and juxtapositions allow the storytellers to focus our attention on the underlying reasons, motivations, fears, and obsessions of Kane.

Witness

(1985)
Screenplay by Earl W. Wallace and William Kelley
Story by William Kelley, Pamela Wallace, Earl W. Wallace
Directed by Peter Weir

Nominated for eight Academy Awards, including Best original Screenplay and Best Director, *Witness* is a first-rate example of the melding of solid storytelling with the verve of modern filmmaking techniques. A story that revolves around one of the central issues of modern society, the use and misuse of force, and that dares to find drama in the peaceful world of the Amish, this film proves that with solid command of the craft of storytelling, a compelling film can be created out of even the least likely material.

SYNOPSIS

An Amish boy and his widowed mother, Samuel and Rachel Lapp, traveling by train, stop in Philadelphia for a three-hour layover. Samuel witnesses a brutal murder in the railroad station men's room. The policeman called to investigate is John Book. Rachel is appalled by Book's violence, but the boy is wide-eyed in his first view of the outside world. Samuel got a good look at one of the killers, and while he is at the police station going over mug shots, he makes a positive identification of the man—an honored police lieutenant named McFee.

Book quickly gets the boy safely hidden at his sister's house before he goes to report this news to his superior and former partner, Captain Schaeffer. Book thinks McFee is mixed up in a drug-supply operation and has gone bad. Schaeffer asks who else knows about the boy's identification, and Book says just the two of them, and they decide to keep it that way. Book goes home and finds McFee waiting for him; a gun battle ensues, and McFee flees after wounding Book. Now knowing that Schaeffer must also be dirty, Book has his current partner permanently "lose" the file containing the names and addresses of Samuel and Rachel, then, without telling them of his wound or their danger, he drives them back to their Amish home, where he thinks they will be safe.

He intends to drive away, leaving them there, but he passes out at the wheel and only then do they discover his wound. He is nursed by Rachel with help from one of the Amish elders and, after nearly dying, recovers.

But all three of them must stay in hiding in the Amish community while he tries to figure out how to solve this dilemma. He finds out that he is wanted in connection with the murder in the railroad station, and that the dirty cops are putting on a lot of pressure to find him.

So Book has to try to assimilate, or at least to appear Amish. He dresses in Rachel's dead husband's clothes and tries to fit into the household, which includes Rachel's crusty but good-hearted father-in-law, Eli. When the boy gets hold of his gun, Book tries to instruct Samuel about safe use of the weapon, but Eli gives him a lecture on the Amish views on the use of violent force; then the gun is hidden away, unloaded, in the cupboard. Book wears "plain" clothes, milks a cow, helps out around the house, and becomes a member of the family while he and Rachel grow increasingly attracted to each other. He meets Rachel's Amish suitor, Daniel, and the two become working partners during a one-day barn-raising, where they find common ground in the hard work of carpentry. Having proven himself to his unspoken rival for Rachel, Book finds a growing admiration for the ways and choices of the Amish. But when Rachel offers herself to him, he can't accept her offer, knowing the chasm between them.

When he finds out that his partner has been killed, clearly by Schaeffer and McFee, Book's mask of Amishness melts away and he takes out his anger on a young man who is taunting the Amish, especially Daniel, preying on their nonviolence. When Book beats up the man, his action brings enough attention for Schaeffer to find out exactly where Book and the boy are. Book makes his final preparations to leave. Despite the community pressure on Rachel to stay clear of "the English," she can't help herself and they finally express their passion for each other.

Schaeffer, McFee, and the other killer, Fergie, approach the farm at dawn, heavily armed. Book is doing his farm chores when the men take Rachel and Eli. Book finds Samuel and sends him running to Daniel's farm, but the boy has only gone a short way when he hears shooting. Book uses his knowledge of the farm to kill Fergie in a corn silo and get his gun. With that he kills McFee while Samuel rings the family dinner bell repeatedly until it attracts all the Amish neighbors, who come running. Schaeffer has his gun to Rachel's head and disarms Book, but when he tries to take Book and the boy away, Book uses the power of a whole community of witnesses to show Schaeffer that it's over, and Schaeffer gives up. As the local police clear out of the crime scene, Book says good-bye to Samuel, then has a knowing parting from Rachel. Eli warns him to be careful "out among them English," and as Book drives back to the city and the life he must lead, Daniel walks by on his way to see Rachel.

PROTAGONIST AND OBJECTIVE

Despite the title, which refers to the boy, this is clearly John Book's story. A tough, flawed, and violence-prone man in a violent world, Book is nonetheless a sympathetic character. His respect for Rachel and Samuel saying grace, his desire to do what is right over what is expedient, and his overwhelming effort to protect these innocents from his world all help him be sympathetic. His objective is equally clear: to protect his witness from the crooked cops who are out to kill the boy and himself.

OBSTACLES

The first and foremost of his obstacles is that his enemies, the killers, are all policemen with credibility and all the tools of the police force at their disposal. But also Book is badly wounded and, for a time, completely incapacitated. In addition, he is an unwanted and untrusted intruder in the Amish community, which wants nothing to do with his troubles and only gets involved because of the danger to Samuel. On top of all that, one of his major obstacles is that he can't change his nature as easily as he changes his clothes. He might look Amish to the tourists, and he might be a respected carpenter who learns to be quiet during grace, but to his core he is still the man of action—sometimes violent action—and it surfaces when he is cornered, when his emotions run high. And in the end, his obstacle is that three heavily armed men are out to kill him, and he has no gun or other weapon from his urban and "English" police world.

PREMISE AND OPENING

The premise of this film is divided equally between social and personal circumstances that predate the beginning of the story. On the social side is the very fact that the nonviolent Amish community lives essentially in another time while surrounded by the ever more violent and fast-moving world of modern America. On the personal side, Book is a tough, right-minded cop who depends too much on his sister and her two children for his sense of family.

For their opening, the Wallaces and Mr. Kelley chose to introduce the audience to something of the Amish culture, while at the same time revealing to us the personal situation of Rachel, by showing the funeral of her husband. Because this is a story built around the clash of two cultures—one culture altogether too familiar to the audience, while the other is practically unknown—it was a smart decision to begin in this way. If they had gone for a flashy action opening, the murder in the men's room for instance, it would have severely undermined the impact, because we would have no clear idea of who these Amish people are or anything of the nature of their lives. That information would then all have to be delivered when the story returns to the farm, where it would be too late.

MAIN TENSION, CULMINATION, AND RESOLUTION

The main tension asks, "Will Book be able to keep Samuel and himself safely hidden from the crooked police?" At the end of the first act, the audience is not asking itself whether Book will be able to defeat Schaeffer and McFee, but rather whether he will be able to keep from being found by them.

The culmination comes when Book's true nature emerges and he beats up the young man and blows his Amish cover. This leads Schaeffer to Book's hiding place.

The resolution of the main story line comes when Book finally gets Schaeffer to back down and give up in front of all the Amish witnesses—to face the inability of his violence to overcome the nonviolence of this community.

THEME

The theme here comes more from the social sphere than from the personal one. The theme explores the place of force in society by contrasting two cultures, one accustomed to violence and the other forbidding it. While there is no use of violent force within the Amish community, there is a very real use of force. The prospect of Rachel's being shunned by the community is as powerful and threatening to her as the more overtly violent danger that Book faces. In the end, when Schaeffer's gun comes up against a unified community, the latter force is the winner.

UNITY

The unity here is the unity of action, following John Book's attempts to protect his witness. Although not every moment of the story focuses intensely on whether or not Book will be able to keep Samuel hidden and protected, that objective is always in the background of shorter-term goals. When he is being nursed back to health, when he is trying to win acceptance in the Amish community, when he is trying to resist his attraction to Rachel—always behind it is his ultimate desire to protect Samuel. And the scenes involving Schaeffer's efforts to locate Book and identify the boy and his mother all escalate the obstacles to Book's primary goal.

EXPOSITION

Different approaches to exposition are effectively used here. Because much of the world in which this story takes place is so new and foreign to the majority of the audience, this increases the demands on exposition. The introduction to the Amish world uses the funeral as a means of showing how this community interacts. It also gives us an introduction to the major setting for the story, the Lapp family farm. There are small moments of conflict (Daniel giving his sympathy to Rachel in front of the other women), and a few moments of humor (a joke about horse testicles, Daniel racing his wagon to keep up with Samuel and Rachel riding the train). But for the most part, these first few minutes of exposition are presented without conflict. This will work in the opening of a film when the audience will tolerate almost anything, regardless of conflict or tension. It would be ill-advised to do this later in a story.

A good example of streamlined and humorously delivered exposition comes when Book buys hot dogs for Rachel and Samuel, and she recounts the sister's analysis of Book's shortcomings. We not only learn some of the truth about Book's personal life, but see how he reacts to this potentially embarrassing moment.

A good example of economy in delivering exposition is how Book's long-standing and close relationship with Schaeffer and his family is shown simply getting him from the front door to the study. Book's familiarity with the house, his relationship with the wife and the daughter, all come through to make us conclude he has been here many times before and is an honored and welcome friend and guest.

Exposition delivered through conflict is well demonstrated by the scene where the wounded Book is in bed and the Amish elders have gathered to decide how to deal with him. Their conflicting feelings about what to do and how to handle this unwanted intrusion of "the English" into their safe and protected world speaks volumes, not only about the structure of their leadership heirarchy and their social/religious views, but also about Eli's stature in the community and the potential social danger Rachel is putting herself in.

And an effective use of exposition through a "lecture" to an onscreen character is the scene with Eli, Samuel, and Book's gun. While Eli lectures Samuel on the evils of killing and the nonviolence of the Amish people— a scene fraught with a strong, subtextual conflict as well—we learn a critical part of the teachings of the Amish.

CHARACTERIZATION

John Book is introduced as a man comfortable with being in charge, one who won't shrink from what needs to be done, both pragmatic and a little bit insensitive. Most of these traits remain pretty consistent through the story with the exception of the insensitivity, which changes with his rising awareness of the Amish world. His characterization centers around his objective: to do his job fairly, honestly, and effectively.

Rachel shares a few characteristics with Book; she has the same pragmatism and the same forthright way of tackling a job without equivocation. She differs considerably in the areas of control and sensitivity, but her biggest change is in her desire to take charge of her destiny and her willingness to pay the consequences. She won't shy away from her passion for Book, even in the face of the threat of being shunned in her world. Her characterization is also focused on what she wants, which is to do what is right according to her own heart as opposed to what someone else says is right—be it the police in the city or the elders in her world.

Samuel is presented as a normal boy, no different from his counterparts in the mainstream culture—curious, excited and excitable, amazed by the world outside his own sphere.

Eli is an interesting contrast to Rachel. He thoroughly believes the teachings of his Amish culture, and what motivates many of his actions in the story is to do what is right in the eyes of his society. Where Rachel is willing to do what is right, regardless of whether it looks proper, Eli puts a premium on the appearance. His dealings with the elders, his fear of Book's arrival, his fear that Rachel will find herself shunned—and his fear of the consequent social isolation he would also suffer—all stem from pressures outside himself.

Schaeffer presents a solid contrast with Book. Two men who were once partners, mentor and student, men cut from the same mold but who clearly went off in separate directions, Book and Schaeffer have much in common. Both are smart, cunning, know the game that they are playing together, and will do anything it takes to achieve their aims. And that is where they diverge. Book wants to protect his witness, whereas Schaeffer wants to protect himself and his partners and to keep his corruption from being discovered.

DEVELOPMENT OF THE STORY

This entire story evolves from one mistake Book makes out of ignorance: he reveals to Schaeffer that he has an eyewitness and positive identification of McFee as the murderer. Without this inadvertent slipup, the story would be vastly different. Though neither Book nor the audience is aware of it at the time, this moment of revelation is what triggers the rest of the story.

The direct result of Book's revelation to Schaeffer is that Book is shot and McFee and Fergie go after him and the boy. This forces Book to find a place to hide them from the police/killers. As a result of Book's decision to try to hide Rachel and Samuel back at their home, a choice complicated by his wound, he is forced to stay with them. Despite their reluctance, the Amish decide to help Book, and he masquerades as an Amish man in an effort to keep from revealing Samuel's whereabouts, which for a time seems to work. But this unprecedented pressure on Book to behave like an Amish man, which is directly counter to his instincts, leads to his second mistake: he gets in a fistfight that ultimately reveals his hiding place. The direct result of that revelation is that the peaceful Lapp farm is visited by three armed killers, and because of his attempt to accommodate to the Amish way of life, Book is unarmed at the time they appear.

DRAMATIC IRONY

Though the central revelation that creates this story is not delivered with the use of irony—we learn that Schaeffer is one of the murderous group at the same time that Book does—there are other effective uses of dramatic irony here.

When Book summarily hauls Rachel and Samuel out of his sister's house and drives them to the farm, we know that he is wounded and that they are in danger, and we know that they are unaware. The entire effort to pass Book off as an Amish man, and make him sufficiently plain, is tinged with irony as the tourists and townspeople are unaware of the masquerade. This irony is brought to a particularly dramatic moment when Book, looking like an Amish, approaches the swaggering young tough who has been taunting Daniel. We are well aware how good Book is at "whacking," but his young opponent is expecting a nonviolent Amish man.

PREPARATION AND AFTERMATH

The fact that Samuel is *the* witness is well prepared by showing him as a wide-eyed, curious boy exploring the train station and ogling everything in sight with a voracious interest. When he witnesses the murder, it is with the same wide-eyed amazement. When Book finds the wrong suspect and "whacks" him up against the car to show him to the boy, there is a moment of preparation in the car, the display of the suspect, and then a particularly effective scene of aftermath where Rachel registers her fear and distrust of Book, his methods and his world. This is especially necessary in a story in which this clash of ideas and approaches is central.

Another important moment in the story features effective preparation and aftermath. Samuel finds Book's gun and is curious, drawn to it in an innocent yet irresistible way. When Book catches him with it, we have two contrasting scenes for which this was a preparation. First, Book lectures him on the danger of the gun and lets him touch it, indulging the curiosity. Then Eli lectures him on the implications of the gun and the Amish way of thinking on violence and killing. And a very effective aftermath follows in which Book gives the gun to Rachel to hide, separate from the bullets.

PLANTING AND PAYOFF

Here we have an interesting example of how the same moment or scene can fulfill more than one function. The aftermath of Samuel's discovery of the gun, discussed above, comes when Book gives the gun to Rachel to hide. But this is also planting for a later moment when he wants it and gets the bullets from the flour bin, and still later when he needs a gun and we are all too aware of how impossible it is to get.

Another use of planting and payoff occurs when Samuel shows Book about the silo and then Book uses it to kill Fergie. The kitchen bell calling them for breakfast is planted and paid off at the end, when Samuel's ringing brings the neighbors. When we see Book working with wood tools, fixing the birdhouse, it is planting for his "initiation" into the Amish community at the barn-raising. A use of a line of dialogue for planting and payoff is Eli's catch phrase, "You be careful out there among them English," which takes on a nice irony by the time he says it to Book at the very end of the story.

A fine example of planting and payoff that create a metaphor is the use of Rachel's bonnet. Most of the time, she wears the bonnet like all the other Amish women, and at these times she is behaving in the expected and traditional manner. But when she and Book dance in the barn, she is not wearing it and she is indulging in the forbidden. The same goes for the scene where she offers herself to him. When she sees Book putting up the repaired birdhouse and realizes that he is preparing himself to go, she deliberately takes the bonnet off, and that action is emphasized for us; the wearing and removing of that bonnet has become a metaphor. She is bareheaded for their passionate kiss when their forbidden attraction comes out in full force, and the absence of the bonnet has taken on new meaning for us.

ELEMENTS OF THE FUTURE
AND ADVERTISING

A few examples of elements of the future occur when Book declares to Rachel that there won't be a trial of the murder; when he calls his partner and asks how "hot" he is and what they are going to do; when Eli and Rachel discuss the fact that Book will be leaving the next day; and when Eli warns Rachel that she might be shunned for bringing "the English" into their world. Each of these moments pushes us to anticipate what may or may not be coming up later; it isn't guaranteed to happen, but we can anticipate that it might.

A good example of advertising comes when Rachel invites Book to the barn-raising during the dance scene in the barn.

PLAUSIBILITY

There is no particular need for a suspension of disbelief in this story. Although we might entertain tiny doubts about how hard it would be to find a "foreigner" in the Amish community, the primary elements in this story could happen. There is nothing inherently implausible in a city cop, city crime, and the nonviolent Amish community coming together and creating a story.

And in the area of inevitability, this story excels. Because so much of the story develops when solutions to short-term problems create the next problem, the audience comes away with the feeling that this story couldn't really have happened any other way.

ACTION AND ACTIVITY

Examples of activities are the serving of food at the funeral and the preparation of food at the barn-raising; Book fixing his car in the barn; the barn-raising itself; and the ringing of the bell for breakfast.

But when Book pulls Rachel into a dance in the barn, it is an action; he is trying to get through to her, to bridge the distance. When she turns to face him when bathing, it is an action because she is offering herself. When Daniel makes a point of sharing his lemonade with Book during the barn-raising, it is an action, for he is demonstrating that he welcomes Book and that no one should make anything of their subtextual rivalry. When Book unloads his gun and hands it to Samuel, it is an action, as is Samuel's ringing of the bell to bring the neighbors running.

DIALOGUE

One of the primary uses of dialogue in this film is in distinguishing between the two worlds being depicted. The old-fashioned language of the Amish contrasts with the slang and profanity-riddled language of the city and especially Book. Many uses are made of this contrast, from Rachel's old-fashioned use of "whacking," to Book's profanity in his sleep while Rachel nurses him, to his threat to a tourist lady in city language while he appears to be Amish, to Samuel's description of McFee as not *stumpig*.

In addition, dialogue can take on a prophetic quality, as when Daniel at the train station tells Samuel that he "will see so many things" on this trip. And a fine example of an oft-repeated line of dialogue and the many different readings an actor can give it is Eli's "You be careful out there among them English."

VISUALS

This film is visually stunning, almost painterly at times, but the beauty of the compositions is never allowed to dominate the storytelling. From the opening images of fields of waving grain, to the emphasis on the statue of an angel holding a dying person in the train station, we are given visual images that reach beyond simply what they show to give an emotional context or even a very subtle pointer in the direction this story will go. The image of the statue in the station is repeated when Rachel discovers that Book has been wounded. She and Eli must drag him from the car, and in that action the image and composition are repeated.

When Schaeffer, McFee, and Fergie first find the Lapp farm in the third act, their car comes a short way over the ridge, then its headlights are turned off and it is backed down off the crest to be out of sight. In the glorious country morning, this simple image is evocative and disturbing, giving the audience a subtextual feeling of foreboding.

When Book and Rachel are saying good-bye at the door at the very end of the story, stretched out behind him is the road that will lead him back to his world. Behind her is the house and her world, which she cannot leave. The elegant simplicity of this design makes words unnecessary; when she turns inside to her world and he turns outside to his, there is nothing more to say. The visual design lends a great deal to the impact of the moment.

DRAMATIC SCENES

There are a great many effective and illustrative dramatic scenes in this film. When the Amish elders gather around Book's bedside, they have their own wants—to be rid of this English intruder. Against them is Rachel, who wants to protect her son and therefore must keep Book away from a doctor. Then there is Eli, who wants to support his daughter-in-law, but wishes to maintain his position in the community that this intrusion jeopardizes. These active and conflicting wants focus the moments and make the scene effective.

When Eli warns Rachel about the potential of being shunned for bringing Book into the community, there are sound conflicting wants. Eli is still worried about his social standing and the power of their community, while

Rachel wants to continue as she has been and wants it known that she has done nothing wrong.

The major showdown between Schaeffer and Book in front of all the Amish witnesses at the end is a strong dramatic scene with a complete preparation and aftermath. Schaeffer has stayed clear of the violence until McFee is killed, but he drags Rachel and Eli toward the barn, then holds a gun to Rachel's head to disarm Book. While dramatic on the surface, all of this is really preparation for the major scene, the showdown over the boy and Book. Schaeffer didn't come to kill Rachel, though he's saying he's willing to do it to get his way. This preparation promotes a feeling of urgency that leads into the scene where both Rachel and Schaeffer become hysterical while Book, though excited, is able to take charge. When he has convinced Schaeffer of the impossibility of winning and Schaeffer gives up, there is a brief aftermath where we are allowed to digest all this and even, in a sense, feel some degree of sympathy for Schaeffer.

SPECIAL NOTES

One of the most interesting aspects of *Witness* is the fact that the societal elements dominate the personal side of the story. This is a story about the clash of two cultures. Book, Rachel, Samuel, Eli, and Schaeffer all become specific human beings, but the driving force behind their conflicts has to do with their different cultures. The collision of the violent urban life of city cops with the tranquil and aggressively nonviolent world of the Amish creates and sustains this story.

As discussed in the "Theme" section above, this film is an exploration of the uses of force in our world. The storytellers are wise enough not to attempt to coerce an answer out of the material, to make this an indictment or a thesis instead of an exploration. If they had the definitive answer to force and violence in society, they shouldn't make a film but should go directly to the United Nations with it. What they have created is an exploration of a complex and troubling issue. Modern urban society isn't depicted as all bad and the Amish aren't all good; there are forms of force in both societies, just as there are admirable things about them both. While, in the end, one use of force triumphs over another, that can hardly be a universally applicable solution. Rather, what the filmmakers have done is to make the audience confront its own feelings about violence and the use of force, to see that it is complicated and there are no pat answers, but, most important, to explore how each of us feels about the various faces of force we come to know in the story.

A Streetcar Named Desire

(1951)
Written by Tennessee Williams from his play,
with an adaptation by Oscar Saul
Directed by Elia Kazan

Produced when Williams was still in his early thirties, this play has enjoyed enormous success on stages the world over, and had a superb translation to the screen under the same title. The play won Williams the first of his two Pulitzer Prizes, while the film version was nominated for nine Academy Awards in all the major creative categories. It won three acting awards; only Marlon Brando as Stanley, of the four principal characters, did not receive top honors for his work.

(Note: The following synopsis and analysis are based on the film version of the story, since it was brought to the screen with Williams's extensive collaboration and it is readily available on videocassette for study.)

SYNOPSIS

Blanche DuBois arrives in the New Orleans train station looking a little lost and seeking directions to find a streetcar to Elysian Fields. When she arrives, the rowdy bar and street life scares her, but she finds her way into the courtyard of her sister's apartment building—a place she can't believe her sister lives in. She is sent to find her sister at a bowling alley. She and Stella hug while Stella's husband has a fight over lane assignments. The sisters retire to the alley bar, where Blanche downs two quick drinks and tries to explain why she left home before the end of the semester. They talk about their family home, Belle Reve.

Blanche is surprised at how small and plain Stella's home is, and wonders how Stanley will react to her coming to stay with them. Stella reveals her deep, passionate yearning for Stanley when he's on the road, while Blanche brings up the sacrifices she made trying to keep Belle Reve, and says she is not to blame for it being lost. While Blanche always seems on the edge of hysteria, when she first meets Stanley, she just seems prim and a little skittish. But a cat screech makes her lose her control and go into memory.

Stella asks Stanley not to tell Blanche that she's pregnant, but reveals to him that Belle Reve has been lost. Suspicious that Blanche has cheated her sister of the family estate, and citing the Napoleonic Code, Stanley goes through the flashy and seemingly expensive things in Blanche's trunk. Bathed, perfumed, and affected, Blanche puts her case back together while Stanley accuses her of cheating them. Blanche shows him tons of papers on the family estate, but closely guards a packet of love letters from her late husband. Stanley looks through the papers, saying that a man has to look out for his wife's affairs, especially with a baby coming.

While the sisters go out for the evening, Stanley has his buddies over for poker, including the man who lives upstairs and his best friend, Mitch. When the game goes on later than it should, the wife of the man from upstairs makes threats, and Mitch wants to go home to take care of his sick mother. Stella tries to break up the game, while Mitch and Blanche meet and find each other interesting. They discover a shared "sensitivity" and love of the poetry of Browning. Blanche turns on the radio and makes a gushy show for Mitch while Stanley loses a hand and angrily throws the radio out the window, then hits Stella. The sisters end up upstairs with the neighbor's wife, while the men restrain Stanley and sober him up in the shower. He is overcome with remorse and calls for Stella, and, to Blanche's horror and surprise, she goes downstairs to him.

In the morning, Blanche is astounded to find Stella looking contented. Without knowing that Stanley can overhear them, Blanche tries to persuade Stella to leave Stanley, calling him common and a brute. Stanley returns without betraying what he has heard, and charms Stella. But later he asks Blanche if she knows a Mr. Shaw and the Flamingo Hotel. She denies it, but later asks Stella if she's heard any gossip about her. Blanche admits how badly she wants Mitch and that she wants to leave and she'll no longer be trouble to anyone. Alone in the house, Blanche meets a handsome young man who reminds her of her dead husband, and she kisses him right before Mitch comes to take her out for the evening.

Mitch is clearly smitten with Blanche, impressed with her wit and knowledge and taken in by her ladylike decorum. Still, he would like more physical affection, but she holds him at bay with her "old-fashioned ideas." They talk about their loneliness and Blanche reveals that she feels she is responsible for her husband's death; he was weak, she lost respect for him, and he killed himself.

Later, Mitch fights with Stanley over what the latter has said about Blanche. Then, at home, Stanley tells Stella what everyone in Blanche's hometown is saying about her, even that she was fired after getting involved with a teenaged boy. He also reveals that Mitch has been wised up. That night Mitch doesn't show up for Blanche's birthday dinner. Stella lashes out in anger at Stanley; he destroys his dishes and says he is "king around here." Blanche calls Mitch while Stella reminds Stanley of how things used to be between them. While Stella lights the candles on Blanche's birthday cake, Stanley gives her a bus ticket home.

Stella goes into labor, and Stanley takes her to the hospital, leaving Blanche home alone. Mitch finds her groggy and drunk. He wants to see her face, and he confronts her with what he has heard, making her admit that she had "meetings with strangers," including a teenaged boy. Mitch tries to embrace her, but is only interested in sex with her now. She screams and sends him running, then hides from the neighbors and police who come to check.

All dressed up in her mock-expensive clothes, including a tiara, Blanche dances about when Stanley comes home high and joyful over his impending fatherhood. She tells him she has received a cable from an old beau and is invited on a cruise. After believing her at first, Stanley throws her fantasies and lies back at her. When she attempts to leave, he blocks her way and then rapes her. Later, with the baby at home and the men playing poker, Stella tries to prepare Blanche for going away, though she doesn't reveal to Blanche that she is to be taken to a sanitarium in the country. Blanche has clearly lost all touch with reality, and is still waiting for the beau with the yacht. When she is confronted with the doctor and matron who have come to take her, Blanche is afraid at first, but then, in the end, she goes, depending, as always, on "the kindness of strangers." Meanwhile, Stanley has been denying that he touched her, but Mitch has to be stopped from punching him, and Stella walks out of the house with their baby, vowing never to return.

PROTAGONIST AND OBJECTIVE

Blanche is clearly the protagonist; it is her story, not Stanley's, that we follow. The protagonist and the objective go hand in hand; if the protagonist is strong, assertive, and capable, the objective must be something difficult for that person to achieve. In this case, Blanche is weak; she needs shelter, sympathy, and understanding. She asks more than life, especially hers, can deliver. She is a woman on the ragged edge, near desperation, someone who is trying to save herself, but she has very few effective resources to make it happen. So her objective could be to make life give her what she needs for her emotional survival, but her tools are weak and her efforts are mostly fantasy.

OBSTACLES

While Blanche's own weakness contributes to her downfall, Stanley is the principal obstacle that she faces. Were it not for him, she might possibly find a place in society; she might even marry Mitch and live happily. But her airs and pretensions to refinement, her attempts to draw Stella away from him, and even her presence in the little flat all lead Stanley to regard her as a threat to his marriage and his way of life. Also, her past is a major obstacle for her. Not only the past in the Flamingo Hotel that catches up with her, but the death of her young husband and the guilt she carries from it, as well as the relentless diminishment and ultimate loss of the family estate, Belle Reve. These ghosts—all this baggage she carries—make her weak and susceptible to Stanley's opposition.

PREMISE AND OPENING

Blanche, a sensitive and refined schoolteacher who has lost a husband to suicide and lost the family estate to financial reverses, has taken up a life of having "meetings with strangers" in a small-town hotel, including one with a teenaged boy. When she is fired from the school and driven out of town, she goes to stay with her sister in New Orleans. But her sister is married to a coarse, sometimes brutish man, and they live in a flat far too small to contain the three of them peacefully.

For his opening, Williams chose to show Blanche's arrival in New Orleans. The first thing she does upon leaving the train is to ask the help of a stranger, a young sailor. When she arrives in her sister's neighborhood, she is frightened by the rowdy nature of the place and distressed by the conditions her sister apparently lives in.

MAIN TENSION, CULMINATION, AND RESOLUTION

Once the conflict between Blanche and Stanley over Belle Reve has been established and she is fully moved into the apartment, the main tension is established. Will Blanche be able to make a world—or a place for herself in the world—that fulfills her desperate needs?

The culmination comes when Stanley gives Blanche a ticket home, summarily ending her shaky welcome there, and she loses Stella, her protector, who goes to the hospital to have her baby. Right on the heels of this, Mitch comes, nailing shut the coffin that has already been closed.

The resolution occurs when Blanche is about to be taken away, and she has completely retreated from the world into fantasy and remembrance.

THEME

Thematically, this story revolves around self-deception. Blanche is a grand master at making herself believe what she wants to believe, if only for brief moments. Stanley is the polar opposite, yet of the same material. He doesn't go in for make-believe, yet somehow convinces himself that he is king of his castle. Stella, though firmly rooted in reality, tries valiantly to believe that things will be okay, that she can keep the peace between husband and sister. And Mitch is Blanche's kindred spirit, though hardly so extreme. He is taken in by her airs and swallows her pretenses because he wants them to be true.

The resolution firmly cements this thematic design. Blanche has retreated totally into self-deception. Stella has finally had her eyes opened to her husband, Stanley, who now deceives himself when he thinks his denials are plausible.

UNITY

The unity of action is the prevailing element here, though the unity of place is also important, owing to the theatrical origins of the story. All elements in the telling of this story relate to Blanche and the circumstance of her downfall.

EXPOSITION

Blanche is a woman with a great deal of baggage, literally and figuratively. The earliest exposition comes out in the scene with Stella where Blanche is defensive about leaving school in mid-semester—Blanche perceives a conflict, even if Stella doesn't intend it. But much of the early exposition is accomplished by the story of her trunk. The loss of Belle Reve, the style of life Blanche's clothes imply, the love letters from her dead husband—all are revealed with the trunk.

Some of the exposition of Blanche's past becomes a weapon in Stanley's war on her, and thus its revelation is done completely through conflict. This conflict is not immediately evident when Blanche tells Mitch about her husband. Yet even here, where she volunteers the information, her internal conflict is so palpable, and Mitch's reaction to the information so visceral, that a subtext of conflict is conveyed.

CHARACTERIZATION

It would be hard to find four more sharply drawn and contrasting characters than the principals here. Blanche is shown to be jittery, flighty, and skittish, putting on airs and trying to distance herself from earthy and earthly matters. Stanley is of the earth, dirty and coarse and reveling in his contact with everything she abhors. Stella, though she is Blanche's sister, is more like Stanley. More refined, perhaps, but she clearly loves the sensual, the earthly pleasures, the plebeian manliness of Stanley. And Mitch is depicted as a man torn between the sensitivity of a mama's boy and the rough-and-tumble world of his friends.

Telling moments in the characterizations of these four include when Blanche buys a paper lantern to make a shade for the bare bulb in her room, to dress reality in a better glow. In the same scene where she asks Mitch to put the lantern up, he reveals his cigarette case, which is inside a protective sleeve, a revealing detail. Stella shows some of her nature when she hugs the picture of Stanley and talks about how she can't stand it when he is away. Stanley is introduced creating a fight in the bowling alley, and then shows up at home in a sweat-soaked shirt that he summarily strips off in front of Blanche.

DEVELOPMENT OF THE STORY

This story develops out of a simple paradigm. Blanche moves into the house wanting to find a home, some protection and solace from the world. But Blanche's very presence in the home, to say nothing of her efforts to draw her sister away from her husband, threatens Stanley's marriage and his way of life. From this elemental and irresolvable conflict stems the rest of the story.

When Blanche tries to gain a foothold in the house, it is an effort toward achieving her goal; so are her attempts to show Stella the coarseness of Stanley. Stanley's attempts to find a lever to pry Blanche out of his life are based on his goal of defending his marriage and home. When Mitch begins to fall for Blanche, she rightly sees his interest as an opportunity to get what she needs without having to fight Stanley for it. But by the time Stanley has his ultimate weapon against her, his knowledge of her past, he is so vindictive that he uses it and destroys the one opportunity for both of them to get what they want.

DRAMATIC IRONY

Dramatic irony is used to strong effect in this story. We already know about Stanley's suspicions concerning the loss of Belle Reve, when an unwitting Blanche comes out of the bathroom and is flirtatious. Later we know that he has overheard Blanche's attack on him—and Stella's defense of him—

and neither woman knows he has. Particularly during the birthday dinner scene, dramatic irony has a great deal of impact. We know why Mitch hasn't come, and we know that Stella is broken up about it, but Blanche knows none of it. When Blanche tells Stanley that she's been invited on a yacht, we know it isn't true, just as we know that Mitch didn't come and apologize, but Stanley doesn't, and we wait for him to figure it out. And at the end we know that Blanche is being taken away, but she doesn't. At the same time, we know that Blanche's story of the rape, which Stella disbelieves, is actually true.

PREPARATION AND AFTERMATH

Preparation and aftermath, particularly as they have been discussed in this book, are peculiarly cinematic devices, depending as they do on the ability of the storyteller to break up the action into smaller increments than the stage generally allows. In a play the scenes are usually quite long, and one course of action segues naturally out of the last, without separate scenes between to help the audience digest the latest events, or prepare for what is to come. Nowhere is the theatrical past of this film more evident than in this area.

While many plays are made into films, and some, such as *Amadeus*, successfully manage to mask their theatrical backgrounds and become fully cinematic, this film shows its origins as a play in every scene. It rarely has separate and distinct scenes of preparation and aftermath in the cinematic sense. However, some comparable moments appear within the flow of much longer scenes: Blanche peeks around the curtain when Stanley enters the house before their first meeting. The sisters giggle as Mitch walks away, then comes back and hands Stella the towel after getting flustered on first meeting Blanche. Blanche reacts when she hears that Stella is pregnant, then rushes to embrace her.

PLANTING AND PAYOFF

The paper lantern is an effective use of planting and payoff. When Blanche buys it, it is Mitch who puts it up, and at the time it means refinement. Later, when he is distrustful of everything about her, he is the one who tears it back down, wanting to see her in the light to check her age.

Stanley plants a potential bomb on Blanche when he mentions his friend, Mr. Shaw, who travels regularly to the town she lived in. This is paid off later, when he reveals all that he has found out from his friend about

Blanche, and then again when Mitch reveals that he also checked with the man before he believed the stories. Another plant occurs when Blanche reveals that her husband died as "just a boy." When the truth of her past comes out about the teenager she became entangled with, we know the source of that affection, just as we know what is going on inside her when she kisses the young man who comes to collect for the newspaper.

ELEMENTS OF THE FUTURE AND ADVERTISING

A clear instance of advertising occurs when the card game is discussed and Stella intends to keep Blanche out until the game is over. And one circumstance is both advertising and an element of the future—Stella's pregnancy. We know that a birth will happen, that labor will take her away and that a fourth member of the household will arrive, yet at the same time we don't really know what part the pregnancy and birth will play in the later story.

A moment of foreshadowing comes in the bowling alley bar when Blanche says Stella's put on some weight, especially around the hips. Another element of the future comes when Stanley asks Blanche how long she'll be staying and she says she doesn't know. When Stella makes the outright prediction that Blanche and Stanley will get along just fine, it is an effective element of the future, as is the moment when Stanley asserts that Blanche's future is cut out for her.

PLAUSIBILITY

As with any story that is well written and tightly constructed, the characterizations and motivations of the principals are so balanced and locked together, so believable and intrinsic to each of the people, that the course of events seems utterly logical and inevitable. Blanche is doomed from the moment she sets foot in Stanley's home. Who they are, how they live, and what they want are so antithetical to each other that one must inevitably destroy the other. Stanley, being the stronger of the two, is the ultimate winner, which just lends credence to what we have believed all along.

ACTION AND ACTIVITY

Even though this is largely a well-filmed play and thus is quite dialogue-dependent, there is still a great deal of telling action. After the big poker-party fight, when Stella returns to Stanley and they go inside, Mitch comes back to Blanche to prove to her that he is not like Stanley. After Stanley overhears Blanche's diatribe against him, he comes in acting sweet and charming to prove to Stella that her sister is wrong. And when Stella runs into his arms in front of her sister, she proves her feelings. When Blanche resists Mitch's kisses at the pavilion, it is not because she has no interest in him, but rather because she is trying to convince him that she is really worthy of his attentions. When Stanley "clears his place" at the birthday party, he is demonstrating his power and position in the household.

Activities abound as well, particularly with Blanche, whose nervous energy demands that she always be on the move—putting her things back into the trunk, spritzing perfume or covering her face or checking her reflection. Though at times these mannerisms are actions, often they are merely what she does with her energy. At the same time, this is a part of what drives Stanley crazy about her. And he has his own activities, changing his T-shirt or checking its fit, pouring a drink or picking at his cold supper.

DIALOGUE

Dialogue is used as an effective tool of characterization. Although the mood of the play is poetic, the dialogue throughout is realistic. Even with Blanche's high-flown speeches, it is believable that those words would come of the mouth of a woman like her; we believe it is natural speech for Blanche. When Stanley talks with great authority about the Napoleonic Code and his many "acquaintances," his clumsy stumbling through this intellectual territory is just as telling of his character as his crudest, coarsest utterances.

Marvelous and memorable lines abound, including Blanche's often quoted last line, "I have always depended on the kindness of strangers." Another telling line of hers, which plays right into the heart and soul of this story, comes when she tells Mitch, "Deliberate cruelty is not forgivable." As cruel as we have seen Stanley behaving early in the story, it is always when he loses control and often when he has been drinking. He is not coldly, premeditatedly cruel to Stella, or even to Blanche for a while. But when he ruins her chance with Mitch, even though it would solve his own pressing problem of getting rid of Blanche, he has engaged in the one thing Blanche—and the play—show to be unforgivable, deliberate cruelty.

VISUALS

Visual design is important here, particularly when it comes to the treatment of Blanche. When she first appears, she walks out of the mist in the train station. When she tells Mitch about her husband, mist swirls about her. There is mist outside when she is trying to escape from Stanley near the end. And there are innumerable instances of steam rising off her hot baths and swirling out of the bathroom. When she is not shrouded in mist, Blanche is seeking shadows or checking her appearance in a mirror. When she is assaulted by Stanley at the end, a mirror is shattered at the same time as her last shred of sanity is destroyed.

DRAMATIC SCENES

The scene in which Mitch offers Blanche a cigarette from his silver case is especially effective. While on the surface there seems to be no conflict—they both want to talk with each other—there are really two conflicts going on, one inside each of them. Both are anxious to find ways to impress each other, to connect. They use the case and its inscription to tell about themselves, show their interest, and demonstrate their own worthiness.

After Stanley has beaten Stella and wakes up alone in the shower, dripping wet, there is both preparation and aftermath. He wanders through the little flat alone, looking for her and seeming to be a lost little boy. When he comes out into the courtyard and pleads for her, we have a full and action-driven scene. His carrying her inside over his shoulder is an apt demonstration of their lives and love. And we have an aftermath with Blanche and Mitch that helps focus for us the impact of the scene.

A marvelous scene that shows the power of subtext is the birthday-party scene. Stanley has dropped a bomb on Stella about her sister, and is just biding his time to find an opportunity to use it on Blanche. Stella is devastated with anticipation and dread while Blanche is mystified by, and trying to explain away, Mitch's absence.

A particularly effective scene that uses a variety of dramatic tools occurs when Mitch comes to have it out with Blanche after Stanley has told him about her past. The full set is used, the change in lighting from her preferred darkness to his shedding light on her age, the preparation of her groggy wakefulness and the interruption of the lady selling flowers for the dead, the aftermath with the crowd outside—all of these elements are used to bolster the scene, to emphasize the complete nature of Blanche's downfall, and particularly to make our reaction gut-wrenching.

SPECIAL NOTES

An aspect of this film (and play) that is well worth additional discussion is the subjective use of sound. Details that help to externalize Blanche's memories and unstable state of mind include trains, cat screeches, a blues piano, inhuman voices, jungle cries, the song that plays when she's thinking of her dead husband, and the gunshot that only she hears. These effects, which are used in the theater and well designed in the film, help to put us into the shoes of our central character.

Though Blanche is sympathetic, we don't easily identify with her; we prefer not to think of ourselves as having her insecurities and affectations. But as she enters a new home and tries to find her place in it, we are drawn into her life and her mind in part because we are made to be intimately privy to it. We hear what only she hears, we are lured into imagining the scene she torments herself with again and again by getting tantalizing tidbits of it on the soundtrack. This freedom from the strictly realistic that Williams and Kazan have allowed themselves shows a firm control of the storytelling craft, where emotional involvement is far more important than factual accuracy.

Chinatown

(1974)
Written by Robert Towne
Directed by Roman Polanski

Chinatown, a favorite of film buffs the world over, won Towne an Academy Award for Best Screenplay and was nominated in six other categories including Best Picture, Best Director, and Best Actor. A film that quickly immerses the audience in its world as it lures us into a very complicated plot, this story is vividly written and directed with a flair that brings out the essense of the story without subjecting it or the audience to unnecessary flash. For both writer and director, this film is perhaps their greatest achievement and at the very least, represents a tour de force for them both.

SYNOPSIS

Private detective Jake Gittes shows photographs to a man named Curly of his wife making love in the woods with another man. After he gets rid of the distraught Curly, Jake takes his next client, Mrs. Mulwray, who thinks her husband is cheating on her. Gittes and his two associates, Duffy and Walsh, are impressed that the man in question is the head of water and power for all of Los Angeles. As Jake follows Mulwray, we are introduced to the city and the politics of water in the 1939 drought. Finally Jake spots the man with a lovely young woman and takes pictures of them in a little tête-à-tête.

Unfortunately, this photo ends up in the newspaper, which creates a scandal about Mulwray. When Jake gets to his office, he is visited by another woman claiming to be the real Evelyn Mulwray, who clearly never hired him and now threatens him with a lawsuit. Burned by this embarrassment, Jake goes to see Mulwray at his office, but is diverted by his assistant, Yelburton. Leaving the building, Jake meets Mulvihill, another ex-cop private detective with a checkered past. Jake goes to visit Mrs. Mulwray and sees the grounds of her palatial home. She abruptly drops the lawsuit against him and wants to hire him to find the employer behind the woman who pretended to be her. She also tells Jake to look for her husband at a reservoir.

But when Jake gets to the reservoir, he finds a police investigation led by his old friend from the district attorney's office, Lieutenant Escobar. They are just pulling Mulwray's body out of the reservoir. Jake guides Evelyn through the police and coroner's inquiries and she promises him a check to make her hiring of him official. Jake finds out from the coroner that a local derelict drowned in the Los Angeles River, even though the riverbed is dry. When he finds out that every night water is discharged into the river, he goes back to the reservoir, climbs inside the fences, and almost gets drowned by gushing water. But no sooner has he saved himself from the torrent than he is accosted by Mulvihill and a little man who tells him to keep his nose out of it, and then slits his nose open with a knife.

Back with his associates, Jake says he wants to nail the big guys, the ones making the payoffs. He gets a call from a woman named Ida Sessions, who claims she was hired to play Mrs. Mulwray, but had nothing to do with the murder. She gives him a clue to look for a name in the obituaries. When Jake questions Evelyn and she seems to be lying, he finds out that Cross is her maiden name and that Noah Cross was the man who built the water-supply system for L.A. with Mulwray. Jake declares she's hiding something and goes back to Yelburton, whom he accuses of being part of the murder and the dumping of water. Through the man's denials, Jake finds out that some water is being diverted to the northwest valley orange groves.

Evelyn now hires Jake to find out who killed her husband. She admits that her husband and her father had a major falling-out, but says that it was about a dam that burst. Jake goes to see Noah Cross and is promptly offered twice what Evelyn is paying to find the girl that Mulwray was with. In the hall of records, he finds out that land ownership in the valley has changed hands a lot lately. He goes to the valley to check it out, and has a run-in with an orange grower and his sons. They knock him out, but only after telling him that someone has been destroying their water supply, not sending them water. Evelyn is called to fetch Jake, and on the drive back they figure out the clue about the obituaries, which leads them to a retirement home. There they meet the new "land barons" of the valley, and find them to be sweet old ladies, ignorant of any of it. Upon trying to leave the home, Jake is accosted by Mulvihill, but beats him up and manages to escape from the little man with the knife when Evelyn roars up in her car and drives off with him.

Evelyn cleans up the wound in Jake's nose and then the pair fall into bed together. She finds out about his past with Chinatown and the DA's office, but then she gets an urgent phone call. She rushes off, and he follows her to a house where he sees the girl Mulwray had been with, seemingly being held captive. Jake confronts Evelyn and tells her what he thinks, but she says the girl is her sister and that she wouldn't kill her husband. Jake goes home alone and gets a call saying that Ida Sessions wants to see him. When he goes, he finds her dead and Escobar hiding, hoping he will incriminate himself. He tells Escobar about the water-dumping, but isn't believed.

He goes back to Evelyn's house, where he finds the servants closing up the house and discovers a pair of broken glasses in the pond there. He catches up with Evelyn back at the house where the girl was kept and accuses her of murder and says the glasses were Mulwray's. He calls the police and gives Escobar the address before she reveals that the girl was her sister *and* her daughter, and that she is trying to keep her away from her evil father. Jake sends her on to her servant's house in Chinatown to fetch the girl, then waits for Escobar. He tells the cop he will take them to Evelyn, but he takes them to Curly's house and uses the man to escape from the police.

Jake arranges for Curly to help get Evelyn and her sister/daughter out of the country, then sets up a meeting with Cross at the Mulwray house. There he confronts Cross and learns that the glasses in the pond were his. Without admitting to the murder, Cross explains his plans for the valley and the need for the water supply. With Mulvihill's gun to his head, Jake leads Cross to the house in Chinatown, where he also finds Escobar with his associates. While he futilely tries to explain to the police that Cross is behind it all and that he killed Mulwray, the rich and powerful man accosts his two daughters beside their car. Evelyn pulls a gun and shoots her father in the arm and drives off in the car. Though Jake tries to stop them, the police shoot after the car and it stops. There is Evelyn, shot through the eye, and the sister is screaming. Cross takes the girl away and Escobar sends Jake away with his associates, who tell him, "Forget it, Jake, it's Chinatown."

PROTAGONIST AND OBJECTIVE

This is clearly Jake's story. He is the man caught in the early deception, the one trying to clear himself of the embarrassment and the detective trying to solve the mystery. His objective is to solve the escalating mystery, which he was drawn into by the initial deception.

OBSTACLES

Obstructing Jake's path to solving the mystery are Evelyn, Yelburton, Ida Sessions, Cross, and others who are lying to him. In addition, he has

Mulvihill and the little man (played by the director) opposing him on the one side and Escobar and the police hemming him in on the other. And he has to solve the mystery of who the girl is and what she has to do with the rest of it. Behind all that, there is a full history between Cross and Mulwray to fathom, along with a burgeoning plan for the northwest valley that is actively being kept secret.

PREMISE AND OPENING

Again, much of the premise predates the opening of the story. In a time of drought in L.A., the head of the water utility is trying to track down water discharges, while his former partner is trying to enact a massive plan for a desert area adjacent to the city that has little water supply. And Jake is a successful private detective who seems to specialize in domestic work, but takes pride in his profession, his professionalism, and his honesty.

For his opening, Towne chose to show Jake at his regular work, displaying both his effectiveness and his version of sympathy for a distressed client. Immediately on the heels of this introduction to Jake's private detective world, the fake Mrs. Mulwray appears, water and power are brought up, and Jake is unknowingly swept into a web of intrigue much bigger than he had ever anticipated.

MAIN TENSION, CULMINATION, AND RESOLUTION

Because this is a mystery story, the main tension is created when the full situation of the mystery is established. When Jake declares that he intends to clear himself of the embarrassing debacle surrounding Mulwray and the girl—even after Mrs. Mulwray suddenly drops her lawsuit—his quest and the main tension are established when she hires him to find who hired the fake Mrs. Mulwray. It ties them together and creates the tension, "Will Jake be able to find out what is behind this embarassment to him and Mulwray?" As the story progresses, with Mulwray's murder and the various assaults on Jake, plus Ida Sessions's murder, the stakes are raised but the same basic dilemma continues; Jake still hasn't completely solved the mystery—what's it all about and who's behind it.

The culmination comes when the major part of the mystery is solved—that is, when Evelyn reveals that her father is also the father of her daughter, and that what it has all been about has been her attempt to keep the girl away from her father. Though not every loose end is yet tied, the major threads are clear: he knows more or less who killed Mulwray, why he was hired by the fake Mrs. Mulwray, and, especially, who is behind it all, Noah Cross.

This means that there is a particularly long second act, with a relatively brief third act. In a mystery story where we have an active detective delving into the past, it is not only easy but necessary to delay much of the exposition into the second act, where it takes on the form of clues and twists and turns. And because there is such a fully developed subplot, the love story with Evelyn, which cannot begin until her character is introduced. This also expands the second act. The very labyrinth that Jake seems to have fallen into, with its many corridors, locked doors, and dead ends, is so interesting that it never occurs to the audience that it is taking so long to get to the end of the mystery. This has partly to do with the theme of the story (see below) and with the fact that the audience is led into the same feeling the characters have—we think we finally know what's going on, but we really don't. Once this state of mind is established, it is deliciously elaborated on by Towne and Polanski.

The resolution is that Jake is unable to alter the course of events: Evelyn is killed; Cross gets the girl, gets away with the murder of Mulwray, and will ultimately get away with his plans to grab power and control in the valley.

THEME

Thematically, this story is very interesting because the story creates and defines its own theme rather than exploring a familiar part of human existence. Stated most simply, the theme of *Chinatown* is "Chinatown"—that is, the state of mind of thinking you know what's going on while you really don't. Though all of us may know that feeling from time to time, we have never put a word to it and probably have never been immersed in a world that will allow no other feeling. This is what *Chinatown* does to us. The deeper we dig to discover what's at the bottom of it all, the more we know and the more we don't know, and the more we must conclude we still don't know what's going on. It is a powerful and effective state of mind to put an audience in, as evidenced by the enduring popularity and widespread admiration of this film.

"Chinatown" is also a metaphor (see "Planting and Payoff"), one that has been specifically created to represent the theme of this story. Jake has known the feeling of "Chinatown" and is happy to have escaped it when the story begins. He is equally disappointed when it returns in full force. Evelyn is in a similar state. Though she often lies to Jake and exchanges old lies for new lies, she too doesn't know all that is going on—what her father is up to, and what her husband was doing that got him killed. To a lesser extent, even Noah Cross is put into this state of being. He knows full well what was behind the murder and the plan in the valley, but he doesn't know what Evelyn and Mulwray were up to with the girl, and he doesn't know where she is. And Escobar is hopelessly at sea on a feeling of "Chinatown." Most of the time he's entirely on the wrong track, and even when he's dead right about Jake, he's still wrong about what's behind it all; when he thinks he positively knows what's going on is exactly the time when he is most wrong.

UNITY

As with all stories that have a single strong central character, the unity here is one of action. Jake's pursuit of a solution to the mystery is the unifying element, and his varied approaches to gaining insights and the many obstacles to that information constitute the story.

EXPOSITION

We are lulled into much of the early exposition. We think we are merely watching the practice of the craft of detection while Jake tails Mulwray, slips watches under his tires, and has his associates take pictures of him with an as-yet-unidentified Noah Cross. But at the same time we are getting some of the context of the story—the drought, the plight of farmers, the politics and past of water management. We are also being introduced to locations such as the dry riverbed and the reservoir, which will play crucial roles later on. Towne wisely delivers just enough exposition to get us through the first act; then, once the mystery is fully set up, we get more snippets of exposition doled out as we need them, often using conflict or humor and often coming in the guise of clues and "breakthroughs" in the investigation.

A superb example of exposition, using both conflict and humor, is the scene in the hall of records which is discussed at length earlier in this book in the essay on exposition. Another example of the same technique is the scene in Yelburton's waiting room, when Jake irritates the secretary in order to get information out of her about Noah Cross, the history of the water department, and Cross's relationship with Mulwray.

CHARACTERIZATION

From the very opening scene, Jake is shown to be a man who is confident to the point of cockiness about his assessments of people. He reads Curly like a book, chooses an inexpensive liquor to ply him with, and delights in his own seemingly vast understanding of human nature. This is again evidenced as he waltzes the fake Mrs. Mulwray through her confessions about her husband's purported infidelity. Jake's ability to read other people is the stock in trade of a private detective, and is the very essence of what is first embarrassed and then challenged in him. Because he is a proud man, he rises to the challenge. It is the collision between Jake's self-image and the circumstances that attack it that creates this story.

Evelyn is characterized by a sometimes profound lack of confidence, a sharp contrast with Jake, though she does occasionally surprise him, herself, and us—as when she saves Jake at the rest home. But most of the time she is unsure of what she is saying, hesitant and equivocating, easily forced away from a simple declaration into a modified or alternate view. What we see at work here is her history, the living vestiges of her traumatic relationship with her father and her longtime dependence on her husband.

Noah Cross and Jake share a distinct resemblance and one major divergence. Like Jake, Cross is totally confident that he can read the character of all those around him, and is dogged in his pursuit of what he wants. But where Jake has a history of genuinely wanting to help clients or people in trouble, Cross has no interest in anyone other than himself. His whole motivation is to amass power, while Jake, on a rudimentary level, wants to be appreciated, wants to feel that he has a positive impact.

DEVELOPMENT OF THE STORY

This story develops precisely in such a way as to extend Jake's and the audience's feeling of being in "Chinatown." It alternately delivers us moments when we think we know what's going on and moments when we must admit that we don't. Like Russian nesting dolls, inside each mystery's solution is a new mystery. With amazing regularity, Jake thinks he's got it all figured out—Evelyn is holding the girl captive, or Evelyn got jealous and accidentally killed Mulwray—but each time he seems to get grounded in the story, the rug is pulled out from under him.

DRAMATIC IRONY

We are put directly into Jake's shoes in this story, through how it is told and how it is shot (see "Visuals"). Jake doesn't know anything that we don't know, and almost all the time we know only the same things he knows. This diminishes the use of dramatic irony, at least in terms of the central character. The one major exception comes in the scene when Jake is telling Duffy and Walsh a dirty joke and we see Evelyn well in advance of his realizing she is there. We don't know who she is or what it means, but we are aware of her presence and this existence of dramatic irony is what makes this scene effective and memorable.

And with other characters we do sometimes have the creation of irony, particularly with Escobar. Almost every scene with Jake and Escobar utilizes irony because we know how far off base the policeman really is. This use of irony not only strengthens our admiration for Jake, but our sympathy for him as well, since he is unjustly accused of extortion and other crimes. Scenes with Yelburton also use dramatic irony extensively.

PREPARATION AND AFTERMATH

Mood and atmosphere are very important to the experience of this film, and as a result, preparation and aftermath have been used very effectively. When Jake first visits the Mulwrays' house, there is a fairly long preparation with the drive up, the cryptic Chinese servant, the wait at the door, the driver polishing the car and making squeaking sounds. What follows is an introduction to a vastly different Evelyn, one more true to her real character. And this is also when the twisting and turning of the story begin in full force.

When Jake first goes out to the valley, there is preparation in setting the locale and showing the tranquil and nonthreatening orange groves. After his interlude with the farmers, there is a scene of aftermath when Jake wakes up and finds Evelyn bending over him. While he fully digests what has happened, we also are given a moment of aftermath.

When Jake and Evelyn go to the rest home, there is moody preparation of the location, the driveway and the building, there is preparation between the two of them for the lying they are about to do, and a setting of the atmosphere inside the home. Later, after the fight and their narrow escape, there is a silent moment of reflection in the car as they drive off.

PLANTING AND PAYOFF

The most important planting and payoff in this story is the creation of the metaphor of "Chinatown." The physical place of Chinatown comes up early and regularly, increasingly with the addition of a feeling of not knowing what is going on, "even if you think you do." Eventually we come to relate the place and the feeling to each other; "Everyone felt that way," Jake tells Evelyn about Chinatown. By the end, when we are finally able to escape that feeling, albeit at the expense of Evelyn's life and the girl's future, we are given the moment when it fully reaches metaphor status: "Forget it, Jake, it's Chinatown." Perhaps this is why the line is so memorable.

Another memorable and effective use of planting and payoff is the line "Bad for glass." Accentuated when first spoken by the Chinese gardener and when Jake gets his first glimpse at what will turn out to be a pivotal clue, this line has a marvelous payoff when Jake realizes it refers to the pond being saltwater. It is also tinged with irony, since the clue found in the pool is a pair of glasses.

Other, simpler, uses of planting and payoff include Yelburton's business cards, "apple core" overheard in the fight between Cross and Mulwray, and the photos Jake took of Mulwray and the girl, which are later found in Ida Sessions's house and seem to implicate Jake.

ELEMENTS OF THE FUTURE AND ADVERTISING

Examples of advertising in this film include an early one in which Evelyn tells Jake he can find Mulwray at the reservoir; a later one, when she says that she wants to take the girl away; and yet another, still later, after that plan has become specific, when she says she has a five-thirty train to catch. A very strong moment of advertising occurs early in the sister/daughter scene, when Jake calls Escobar and gives him the address of the house he's in with Evelyn. This promises the moment when Escobar will arrive.

An eerie moment of foreshadowing happens when Jake and Evelyn are in her car outside the house where the girl is being kept. She has just declared that she wants to take the girl away and keep her safe when her head drops on the wheel and honks the horn. Without our fully realizing it, this moment points toward the final moments of the story when Evelyn dies trying to take the girl away, and her head rests on the horn, sounding our alarm.

PLAUSIBILITY

Again we have a realistic, real-world story in which there is neither the supernatural nor the unbelievable to get past. We fully believe that these events could happen and might have happened in just the way they are depicted. In addition, as the story unfolds, with each new lie or revelation and its new mystery, we have the feeling that it couldn't have happened in any other way; we have the feeling of inevitability.

ACTION AND ACTIVITY

When Jake pours the cheaper liquor for Curly, it is an activity, and that is all there is to it. Moments later, when he feigns surprise at "Mrs. Mulwray's" revelations, it is an action; he is trying to get her as a customer and, more important, one who will pay very well. When he is alone with Yelburton's secretary and smokes, whistles, and strolls around the office, these are not the activities they seem to be, but actions—concerted efforts to get her to reveal information and to get him in to see Yelburton.

When Evelyn cleans Jake's nose wound, it is an activity, but when Jake takes some of Yelburton's business cards, it is clearly an action; he is arming himself for an as-yet-unidentified need that we quickly see arise. When Jake and Evelyn are walking up the steps to the rest home and he holds out his arm for her to take, it is an action; he is enlisting her on his team, getting her to join him in the lying he is about to undertake to get information.

DIALOGUE

Dialogue is used quite effectively as part of the characterizations. Jake always has a smart remark, Evelyn has something of a stammer and tremor when she speaks of her father, and Cross bulldozes through people and callously ignores even the pronunciation of their names.

This film ends with one of the most memorable lines in cinema, but there are also some other moments worth noting. After going to bed with Evelyn and then having his suspicions seriously aroused about her because the girl seems to be held captive, Jake calls her "Mrs. Mulwray," betraying his feeling of distance from her despite their intimacy. The scene where Jake and Evelyn are talking their way into the rest home has some effective use of dialogue that shows off Jake's vast superiority to the manager who is trying to keep him out.

VISUALS

The visual design of this film is especially worth discussing because it puts the audience into the same circumstance the protagonist is in, yet it does so without using point-of-view (POV) shots. We do not see literally what Jake sees; rather, we see him seeing things. He is a voyeur of a sort, and we are made to be voyeurs to his voyeurism. For instance, early on he is following Mulwray at the riverbed. We see a shot from the bridge that might be a POV shot, yet as we pan across the action and the vista, we find Jake at the end of the shot, spying on the same things we have been spying on. This builds a bond between us and Jake, puts us in similar shoes. In an interesting corollary, in these early scenes we have Mulwray trying to solve a mystery and catch sight of something, we have Jake watching him do it and trying to solve a mystery, and we are watching both of them.

This voyeuristic aspect of Jake's role and ours is given another fine moment when he is spying on Mulwray and the girl at the apartments. As he is taking the picture that will appear in the paper, we see the couple reflected in the lens, and we see Jake using the camera. This is a marvelous way of putting us inside Jake and even inside his camera without using the usual POV matrix—show someone looking, show what he or she is looking at, show the person's reaction.

DRAMATIC SCENES

It's hard to think of a more memorable or dynamic dramatic scene than the sister/daughter scene. It has preparation and aftermath; it has actions and activities; it has not one but two twists; it has passion, pathos, and major shifts in the characters. We have preparation as he races from Mulwray's house to the other place, as he angrily parks and strides up to the door, even fighting with the screen door. When Evelyn comes down, she is putting on pearls and offering lunch, but Jake gets right down to business. His actions include the call to Escobar, asking about attorneys and laying out the glasses. Then the conflict escalates as he spells out in detail his latest conviction about what has happened. He tries cajoling, persuading, even putting the words in her mouth, but finally resorts to slapping her. Here she delivers the first twist, that the girl is both her sister and her daughter, and this prompts an immediate change in Jake. Once again, what he thought was the answer wasn't it at all. Then comes the second twist, which is that the glasses weren't even Mulwray's. The scene is essentially over, but we have an elaborated aftermath in which the girl is introduced and Jake is told the address where they will be meeting. It obviously has an impact on him, and he watches out the window as Evelyn and the girl drive off. This aftermath immediately evolves into the preparation for the next scene, when Escobar arrives.

SPECIAL NOTES

The irony that emerges in an extensive analysis of *Chinatown* is that in reality the story is quite simple. Two powerful men who built the water supply for L.A. have a falling-out over water. When the one partner's daughter bears a child by her own father, the daughter marries her father's partner. Many years later the father/partner embarks on a scheme to amass vast power and wealth by bringing L.A.'s water to a large inexpensive area nearby. Into this mess a private investigator is brought through deception, and he sets out to discover who did what to whom, and why. When he finds it all out, the story is over.

It is the telling of the story that is both complex and intriguing. As has been discussed, this is the essence of what makes "a good story well told"; there are no new stories, but there are new characters and new ways to make the audience experience a story. All of the lies and deceptions told to, and eventually by, Jake are understandable, given the lives and motivations of the characters. And lies and mysteries are what this story explores, the feeling of being in "Chinatown." So, in this very long—yet never dull—second act, the mysteries within mysteries within mysteries are drawn out to tantalize and intrigue us, to confuse and then clarify only to confuse once again.

This is a perfect example of something that is often overlooked in storytelling—that it is, in a very real sense, a game played between storyteller and audience. Both sides agree to play the same game, the purpose being to enjoy the experience of the story, to feel moved, to exercise our emotions and intellects, to inhabit a world other than our own, to live with and care about characters we would never otherwise be able to know.

The Godfather

(1972)
Written by Francis Ford Coppola and Mario Puzo,
from a novel by Mario Puzo
Directed by Francis Ford Coppola

An epic family saga made from the unlikeliest material, the world of organized crime in America, *The Godfather* not only enjoyed enormous box-office and critical success around the world, but helped lead the way for a whole new era of crime-based films not unlike the seemingly endless string of gangster films of the thirties and forties. With the release of this film, and its 1974 sequel, Coppola put himself firmly and forever on the film-makers' map. This film won Academy Awards for Best Picture, Best Script, and Best Actor (for its star, Marlon Brando), along with nominations for Coppola, Al Pacino, Robert Duvall, and James Caan. In a never-duplicated tour de force, *The Godfather, Part Two* won Oscars for Best Picture and Best Script, along with two others, including Best Director, and five additional nominations.

SYNOPSIS

Just after World War II, in a lavish Long Island estate, Vito Corleone holds court, dispensing favors and making deals on his daughter's wedding day. His two closest advisers are his son Santino, called Sonny, and his adopted son and lawyer, Tom Hagen. His daughter, Connie, is marrying Carlo Rizzi amid a huge party that is being spied upon by FBI agents while gifts arrive from senators and judges. Vito's war-hero son, Michael, arrives with his girlfriend, Kay Adams, and is greeted warmly. His boozy brother, Fredo, is an embarrassment, but the Don, as Vito is called, agrees when a famous singer who owes the family his career asks a favor concerning a movie role. Vito dispatches Tom to take care of the matter.

In Hollywood, Tom visits a movie studio and asks the head of the studio to cast the singer, but gets himself thrown off the lot. Later, after having found out who was behind Tom, the studio boss is conciliatory and proudly shows Tom his pride and joy, a race horse. But he still resists efforts to cast the singer because he ran off with the studio boss's protégé and made him look foolish. That night the boss wakes up in a bed dripping with blood from the severed head of his prize horse—it is "an offer he can't refuse."

The Don receives a call from a gangster named Sollozzo, who wants to bring him into his burgeoning narcotics business, but Vito turns him down. Instead he tells one of his men, Luca Brasi, to pose as a defector from his family to find out what Sollozzo is up to. But when Brasi meets with the narcotics group, he is brutally killed. Tom is kidnapped by Sollozzo, and then the Don is gunned down in the street. Michael is shopping with Kay when he finds out about the shooting of his father and calls Sonny, but is told just to go home.

With Sonny the heir apparent, Sollozzo makes a proposal to him through Tom that they must do business together, but then it is learned that Vito is still alive. Michael joins Sonny as his brother takes over and plans revenge. His men prepare for a war, first by killing off an untrustworthy man. Michael goes to the city under guard and sends Kay out of town while he goes to the hospital to visit his father. There he finds no guards on duty and figures the absent police are part of a setup. He moves his father to a safer part of the hospital and stands guard outside. Michael has a run-in with McClusky, a corrupt police captain, but manages to forestall the presumed murder attempt.

The hotheaded Sonny still wants revenge, while a calmer Tom counsels that it must be business first; they can't afford to get revenge on Sollozzo or McClusky, his police accomplice. Michael confidently lays out a plan in which he will kill both Sollozzo and McClusky at a proposed meeting with the gangster and the cop. He shoots them both, and knows that he must hide out for at least a year. This leads to a war among the five mob families, but Vito heals during this time and is finally brought home.

An uneasy triumvirate now seems to control the family—Vito, Sonny, and Tom—while Michael hides out in Sicily, in the ancestral village of Corleone, where he falls in love with a lovely girl named Apollonia. He makes an offer to her father that he can't refuse, and courts the young woman. Back in New York, Sonny is furious when he discovers that Carlo has been beating his sister, Connie. Sonny beats Carlo up. Michael marries Apollonia while at the same time Kay makes inquiries about him and Tom refuses to tell her.

When Sonny finds out that Carlo has again beaten his sister, he storms out alone, against Tom's advice, and is executed by machine-gunners waiting in ambush. Vito learns of his son's death and says that this war must stop, while Michael makes plans to return after hearing the news. He prepares to send his new wife back to her father when she is blown up in his car. The Don makes a tenuous peace with the other family dons, but realizes that the family behind the drug pushing and Sonny's death is not the one he thought it was.

Michael returns and goes to work for his father, then proposes to Kay. She hesitates, but consents when he says that the family will be legitimate in five years. Michael is now the heir apparent, and he sends Carlo and Tom to Nevada to run their new operation there. Fredo, who has been in Las Vegas for some time, is nervous when Michael visits, and gets soundly rebuked by his brother. Michael is asked to be the godfather of Connie and Carlo's child, then meets with his now aged father, who warns him against a meeting in which his opponent will try to kill him. The Don dies and is mourned by the family and friends.

Michael identifies who will betray him in the meeting his father spoke of, and while he is in church, standing as godfather to Connie's child, his men execute all of his enemies. After the baptism, Michael gets Carlo to admit that it was he who set up Sonny to be killed. Michael's men kill Carlo for his betrayal. Connie hysterically calls her brother a killer and is carried out. Kay asks him insistently, and Michael assures her he did not have Carlo killed, and they embrace. But when she sees him now being addressed as "Don Corleone," she is hardened.

PROTAGONIST AND OBJECTIVE

Sometimes even the simple questions are not easily answered. The title of this film refers to Vito Corleone at the beginning and Michael Corleone at the end. And it is both of their stories. But it's not quite that simple, because they are not dual protagonists of the same story. Each is the protagonist of his own story; there are two complete, three-act stories told in this nearly three-hour epic. A similar story structure is evident in another epic, *The Bridge on the River Kwai,* where there are two intertwined stories, each with its own protagonist who is a significant character in the other person's parallel story.

This is the story of a transfer of power. We first learn through Vito's story what the power is, how it is handled, and how encompassing it is; then, through the course of the story, we slowly identify Michael as the one who will try to hold on to the power, after his own fashion, and we experience what he must go through to do that.

In the two stories, the protagonists have similar and related objectives, but they aren't quite identical. Vito wants to maintain his power and wield it according to the traditions and expectations of his highly ritualized organized-crime upbringing. Michael is faced not so much with an established and stagnant power base as with one that is eroding; his objective is to recapture and consolidate that power base.

OBSTACLES

For Vito the obstacles revolve mostly around the fact that the world is changing, even in organized crime, and that the direction of the future is one that he wants no part of. He refuses to get involved in narcotics dealing, and this leads to the remainder of his obstacles, which come in the form of rivals in the underworld and in other families, as well as defections and betrayals in his own family.

For Michael the obstacles are both internal and external. Because he is not established as a godfather, he must first come to terms with himself and his decision to take over the role, then he must win the support of the rest of the family, and then, on top of all that, he comes to power in the midst of an all-out underworld war filled with the same treachery that proved in part the undoing of his father.

PREMISE AND OPENING

The leader of a powerful American crime family, who wields incredible power according to an elaborate set of rules and etiquette, hands over the power of the family to the son he never expected to take his place.

For their opening, Puzo and Coppola chose to give a demonstration of just how a godfather operates, the arcane rules of behavior and the near ominipotence of his position. The undertaker who makes a request of the Don, without really understanding the ways of the family and the incredible importance placed on respect and attitude, helps to indoctrinate us into what is expected and how this world really works. By showing us the gala wedding party in parallel action to the Don doing business in his study, the filmmakers give us a fuller sense of the context in which this story is taking place. The wedding provides the opportunity for the filmmakers to flesh out the entire family—for *family,* in this film, means not only the particular organization of criminals, but also the actual relatives and extended family of the Corleones, including the new brother-in-law and Tom, the adopted brother.

MAIN TENSION, CULMINATION, AND RESOLUTION

The main tension of Vito's story has to do with maintenance of his already established power base. Though he seems to be able to do anything—and that is surely the impression given to those making requests of him—there are FBI agents nibbling around the edges of his empire, and all the politicians and judges he seems to own are afraid to come to his daughter's wedding. From a generalized feeling of the tenuousness of power, Vito's story gets very specific when he turns down the deal from Sollozzo and feels the need to send in Brasi to spy for him. So the main tension could be "Will Vito be able to retain this incredible power?"

The culmination of his story comes when Vito, recovered from the assassination attempt, calls the meeting of the heads of the five Mafia families. In an effort to save Michael from the fate that came to Sonny, he agrees to a truce that includes involvement in the drug trade in exchange for no harm coming to Michael. While he retains considerable power, it is no longer what it once was, and he has had to back down—a very humiliating experience with his elaborate set of rules.

And the resolution of Vito's story is that he hands over the reins to Michael and no longer wields the power. In fact, though he still sometimes analyzes all the treachery of the people in and around his world, he is losing the power of his own faculties before his eventual, peaceful death.

The main tension of Michael's story really has more to do with the degree of his involvement in the family business. When he first tells Kay about offers that can't be refused, he distances himself from the family and its ways. When he decides to kill McClusky and Sollozzo, he weds himself to his family's ways, yet there still seems to be some hope that he will not become what his father has been. He is more intent on love than on power when he is in Sicily, until Sonny's murder. So the main tension might be phrased, "Will Michael become inextricably mired in the family's criminal business?"

The culmination of his story comes when Michael meets privately with the aging Vito, who laments that he had wanted to spare Michael this life, that he had hoped Michael would be a senator or a governor. Michael has just been asked to be a godfather of Connie's child, and he is now tacitly accepted by his father as the head of the family. His life has become inextricably tied to that of the family and its criminal business.

The resolution of Michael's story occurs when he shows absolutely no mercy when it comes to "business." After having all his enemies gunned down and having stood as godfather to his sister's child, he has his own brother-in-law killed for having set up his brother's murder. He is the complete godfather, literally, figuratively, and in the minds of all the members of the family.

THEME

Though whose story this is might be a complicated question, what it is about is as simple as can be. This is a story about power—the exercise of it, the gaining of it, the desire for it, the abuse of it, the limits of it. At every turn, power is the ultimate question throughout this story. Vito wants to keep it; Michael doesn't think he wants it; Sonny can't control it; Tom teeters on the razor's edge of having it or not having it. The battles are over power, all the treachery is about power, all the excuses and rationalizations are about power—"It's only business, I always liked him."

UNITY

Because this is an epic story painted on a very broad canvas, and because there are two interwoven stories, the issue of what gives the whole a unity is compounded. There is, of course, unity of action in both Vito's and Michael's stories. Yet surrounding both of those is actually a larger unity, that of the family, both literally the Corleones and, figuratively, the crime organization they head. Because this is about the "godfather" of this family—the outgoing leader, the transitional team, and the incoming Don—it is the goals of the family that remain constant, that hold the whole of the story together.

The unity of Vito's action is always identical to the family's action, while Michael needs to be brought into the inner circle of the family's action. He is brought in with his decision to commit the double killing, but it is only on his return after Sonny's death that his action becomes one with the family's. It is especially evident in the transitional phase when Vito, Sonny, and Tom are grasping for a way to lead the family that the narrative thread is the unity of the family's power and its interests. At the beginning and the end, this power and action of the family is bonded with the old Don and the new Don, but it is the family that gives the story its cohesiveness from beginning to end.

EXPOSITION

The opening sequence, the parallel action between the power-brokering in the study and the wedding party, is a particularly effective exposition of the world this story will take place in. Much of the time there is a conflict within a scene that helps mask the expositional quality of the scenes—such as the opening scene involving the undertaker and his misunderstanding of the rules, formalities, and expectations of his relationship with the Don. Also, there is the conflict with the FBI in the parking lot, the turmoil of Luca Brasi and his rehearsed words, and Johnny Fontane's display of weakness. At other times we have Kay as the newcomer trying to grasp this huge family she is being introduced to. Much of the conflict comes from Michael—his defensiveness about his family and how they act, as well as his desire to make Kay feel like a member of the family.

CHARACTERIZATION

Vito is characterized most vividly by the elaborate and very strict code of behavior to which he adheres. He is always in control, but that is just another manifestation of the code. It is this almost maniacal fixation on doing everything properly, the antiquated and stylized formality of the rules he lives by, that gives consistency to his characterization. Sonny is an impetuous hothead. Whether he is having a frantic tryst during his sister's wedding, or running off to beat up her husband, Sonny is ruled by his emotions. That is why he has such heated run-ins with Tom. Tom is shown to have studied the controlled side of Vito. He has the same cool, rational side; everything is always "just business" to him. Yet what Tom lacks is Vito's code, which is the real source of his cool and rational behavior. Fredo is a weakling, from the time he is shown drunk at the wedding to his later attempt to serve two masters in Las Vegas, Moe Greene and Michael. And Michael is characterized most by his love, not by a code or business. He meets a woman and he wants to love her, and in fact he marries both women in whom he ever expresses any interest. Yet, more than any other, he is dominated by his love for his father. After Vito is shot, Sonny plots revenge while Michael goes to be with his father, to support him, to love him, and ultimately to save his life—a sharp contrast between the two brothers that goes to the core of who they are. The same event also shows the other brothers' personalities: Fredo breaks down and cries; Tom figures out the political ramifications within the crime families.

DEVELOPMENT OF THE STORY

The whole story grows logically and inexorably out of the collision of two strong forces: Vito's old-fashioned adherence to the rules of behavior for a crime family against the tide of postwar change as evidenced by the proposed move into narcotics. When Vito says no to this new direction because of his old ideas, it sets in motion the chain of events that grow logically one from another. Sollozzo makes a power move and shoots Vito; Michael is the only one who can take revenge and maintain the family's dominance, which leads to a long-standing feud that gets Sonny killed and brings Michael back in to take over the family from the ailing Vito.

DRAMATIC IRONY

A marvelous example of the use of dramatic irony for heightening the tension of a particular scene occurs when Michael is visiting Vito at the hospital and discovers the guards are all missing. He knows that moving Vito will only temporarily keep him safe, but when Enzo, the grateful baker whom the Don saved from deportation, shows up with flowers, Michael hatches a plan. We know these men are unarmed and are as unlikely a pair of bodyguards as could be found. Yet they stand on the front steps of the hospital and look just threatening enough to scare off an entire carload of presumably heavily armed assassins. If we had known only what the killers knew, there would be little tension to the scene. But by knowing what odds Michael is up against, and by knowing that Enzo only too late figures out what danger he's in, our interest and tension in the scene are greatly increased.

Another example of well-used irony comes with Michael's plan to kill the cop McClusky and Sollozzo. He is known in the underworld as a "civilian," a nonparticipant. And he has had his cheekbone broken by the cop. Yet we know he has courage—he was a war hero—and we know the full details of his plan to kill the two men. Once this dramatic irony is established, it is milked for a good deal of tension. McClusky is brusk, confident, even cocky with the younger Michael. We are made to dislike him completely, and we already know that Sollozzo is treacherous. The minutes drag on and we wonder whether the gun will be in place, whether Michael will be able to do it, and whether either the cop or the gangster will figure it out—and all the while we are really anticipating, we are experiencing a great deal of tension created primarily through the use of irony.

PREPARATION AND AFTERMATH

A film as textural and vivid as this uses preparation and aftermath extensively, sometimes for setting up a mood, sometimes for contrast, and often for establishing the context of a sequence. When Tom goes to Hollywood, there is a lyrical introduction to the studio that contrasts with his reception by the studio boss. Then there is a very long, slow buildup to the discovery by the boss of the horse's head under his bedcovers that is a preparation for the shocking revelation.

Michael and Kay going Christmas shopping and then the Christmas song playing while Luca Brasi prepares for his fateful meeting are preparation by contrast for what is the first really violent moment in the film and the beginning of the war that will drive the rest of the story. When the Don goes to buy fruit while Fredo waits in the car, this is also a preparation by contrast, but in this instance, coming as it does on the heels of Brasi's death and Tom's kidnapping, it is filled with foreboding as well.

PLANTING AND PAYOFF

Two people introduced in the very opening of the story come back much later and function as plants and payoffs. Enzo is saved by Vito from being repatriated to Italy after the war, and his little visit of gratitude to the hospital much later becomes instrumental in saving the Don's life. And the undertaker who begins the whole story and is told that he will be asked to return the favor sometime is brought back into the story and asked to try to cover up the marks of Sonny's violent death so his mother won't know.

Planting and payoff can come in the form of a line of dialogue that recurs and has new meaning. The often-repeated phrase "Make him an offer he can't refuse" is explained by Michael at the outset and demonstrated in action with the movie mogul and others in the course of the story. But for Michael, when he first explains it, the phrase is something he uses to distinguish himself from his family. He tells Kay that is the way of his family, but not his way. By the end of the story, they have become the words he lives by.

ELEMENTS OF THE FUTURE
AND ADVERTISING

Michael's plan to kill the cop and Sollozzo is a form of advertising. He tells us what he wants to do and plans for it, training with the gun and so on. The question of his being able to pull it off is brought up and heightened, but all the while we know that at least his attempt to enact the plan will be dealt with in the story. The same goes for his being told he will have to hide out for at least a year. We know that the action of the story will include his hiding.

When Vito tells Michael that there will be a traitor among the men he most trusts, it is a prediction and therefore an element of the future. When, after the Don is shot, Sonny orders Clemenza to get rid of Paulie, the Don's errant bodyguard, it is advertising, but when Sonny threatens to kill Carlo if he ever beats his sister again, it is a warning, an element of the future. One we know will be carried out within the context of this family, and the other is a kind of prediction.

PLAUSIBILITY

It is the subject matter and context that create the problems of plausibility that must be overcome in this film. Although we are all painfully aware of the existence of organized crime in America, and can believe that there are people who exercise brutal power with utter callousness, it is a different matter entirely to see that these things are done by people we "know" and come to care about as we do the members of this family. So the question is not so much that we are inclined to disbelieve that anyone would do these things, but that we tend not to believe they could be done by the kind of people we would want to identify with.

We are seduced into the possibility with our primary holdout against that kind of behavior, Michael. For his part, Vito is quite removed from the violence, and even declares that "we are not murderers," despite what the undertaker thinks. The first evidence of violence is the severed horse's head; though despicable, the killing of the horse is done off screen and is not quite on a plane with murder. Then the first acts of violence we witness have people we know as victims rather than as perpetrators. Luca Brasi is brutally killed and then Vito is shot. These incidents promote our sympathies, and Michael's pain at the near death of his father is very real and heartfelt, as is his desire to guard him.

When he decides to go on the offensive, then, we have seen that he is not naturally inclined to be a killer, that he has love and emotions, admiration for his father, and a protective family sense. He is not a monster from whom we instinctively distance ourselves. And the two men he kills we are encouraged to despise, though that doesn't really lessen the impact of the brutality of the double killing. But by now we have been seduced into believing that this holdout for decency—or some semblance of it— would believably become a part of this brutal life.

An interesting paradox lies beneath the surface of Michael's descent into the family business and its murderous ways—how did someone like the Michael we first meet grow up in this world and in this family? With his college education, his enlistment in the service, and his becoming a war hero, he seems like a very odd bird in the family. Though this is not a problem we necessarily wrestle with during the film, there does seem to be an answer that comes out in the final meeting of Vito and Michael, in which the old Don says that he had hoped to see Michael become a senator or a governor. Tellingly, these are both positions of extreme power, the only valued commodity in Vito's worldview. Perhaps this implies that Vito trained him for that kind of a life, that he took a hand in shaping him, at least early in his life, and kept him free of the taint of the family. Without its being dramatized on screen, we come to suspect that Michael's innocence at the outset might have been Vito's doing, and that it might be part of the love they share, which he doesn't seem to have with his other sons.

ACTION AND ACTIVITY

The ritual kissing of the Don's hand as a sign of respect is an activity most of the time. Yet for the poor frightened undertaker in the opening, who probably sees his life passing before his eyes, the moment when he kisses the Don's hand is very much an action. Behind it is his desperate attempt to get himself out of the hole he has dug himself into, and perhaps to salvage his request for justice.

When Fredo arranges a party and prostitutes for Michael's arrival in Las Vegas, it is very much an action. He is trying to please his brother and at the same time show that he is powerful in this world. The elaborate party for Connie's wedding is, for the most part, an activity. And when Apollonia's family has a party for the beginning of Michael's courtship of her, it is an activity for them. But Michael's formality and ritualized sociability with the family is an action; he is in pursuit of his goal of winning Apollonia's hand in the old Sicilian way.

The baptism of Connie's child, with Michael as godfather, is very much an action for him. Not only is he giving himself a perfect alibi for that time of multiple murders, but, more important to his way of thinking, he is becoming a true godfather and ascending to the full power of the position in everyone's eyes.

DIALOGUE

This film added a saying to the American lexicon that has lasted twenty years and quite probably will be permanent: "I made him an offer he couldn't refuse."

But well beyond memorable and quotable lines, the dialogue in this film is a very effective tool both for characterization and for showing power dynamics at work. Vito has his strict rules of propriety, which include language. Tom talks of everything as business, while Sonny is prone to fly off the handle with his volatile emotions. Michael's language tends toward control; even when he is disavowing his family, he does so with cold assurance. And the dynamics of who is powerful in a room color the language as well. Tom and Sonny can fight and make up like brothers with no sense of formality. But when Tom is acting as *consigliore* and talking to "outsiders," he does so with the utmost formality.

VISUALS

The brutality of Luca Brasi's murder is made all the more horrifying by the relentlessness of the camera, which will not cut away from his death throes.

The same kind of forthright and unblinking approach is also used in Sonny's death. Yet, ironically, an opposite technique is used to great effect in the fight between Connie and Carlo. She does most of the damage—to dishes and the dinner table—in the early part of their fight. Once Carlo takes a hand to her, the action goes into the bathroom and we are horrified to hear the beating he is giving his very pregnant wife. Not allowing us to see the gruesome details, but forcing us to imagine what he is doing to her, makes the violence of this nonlethal assault match the murders we see on screen for intensity and visceral reaction from the audience.

There are striking visual contrasts between the darkened backrooms of power-brokering and the scenic and open vistas of Sicily, where Michael meets and falls in love with Apollonia. The same darkness that characterized Vito as the Don in the opening scenes enshrouds Michael during the baptism and then when he takes over the den of the family house and for the first time is called "Don Corleone." He no longer is seen out under the sun; he has taken on the devil he renounced in the baptism, and lives in the same dark shadows of power his father did.

And there is a very effective use of visual grandeur to establish the kind of wealth the family has amassed. From the home furnishings to the wedding party to the house and estate, we are always being shown their power through their wealth.

DRAMATIC SCENES

A very effective dramatic scene with complete preparation and aftermath comes when Sollozzo proposes the narcotics deal. We are shown Sollozzo coming to the meeting and have a preparation showing Vito and his coterie of men—Tom, Sonny, and Clemenza. When Sollozzo meets the Don, he knows the routine and gives every deference to Vito's position and power. This is further demonstrated with Sonny's outburst, which Vito squashes and apologizes for in a formal way. And there is a scene of aftermath when Vito chastises Sonny for arguing with him in front of Sollozzo.

The scene at the restaurant, when Michael is about to kill McClusky and Sollozzo, is fraught with an undercurrent because of the irony of our knowing Michael's plan. Another dramatic scene tinged with irony that has full preparation and aftermath occurs when Vito comes home from the hospital. There is considerable elaboration of his return home, the visits from the grandchildren, and his welcome there. Then Tom and Sonny tell him that it was Michael who killed the two men and is now in hiding while the five families go to war, news that pains the Don. Then there is an aftermath between Sonny and Tom, where Sonny tells Tom he isn't a wartime *consigliore.*

A very moving dramatic scene comes when Tom must tell Vito that Sonny has been killed. There is irony because we know of the death, and there is a very palpable reluctance on Tom's part to deliver such bad news, but the Don is accustomed to having his way, and Tom is accustomed to letting him. In the end he accedes and tells the painful truth. This is the moment when Vito fully changes from the man in complete control to the one who is willing to give in to the other families to protect Michael.

SPECIAL NOTES

Perhaps of all the masterfully executed aspects of this film, the most purely cinematic and effective one is the utilization of parallel action for a variety of effects. Parallel action—the simultaneous development of two or more threads of action intercut to keep each in progress—is established, from the very opening sequence, as a part of how this story will be told. We cut from Vito's study to the wedding party in progress, and back again. Here the parallel action is used to help set the context of the story. The façade and the reality are contrasted, and the scale of the story is established.

Later, when Michael is in Sicily and the war is raging back home, the parallel action is used as a strong contrast between who Michael really is— a young man more interested in love than in power—and the results of what he has set in motion. He is not yet part of the very thing he helped to create, and only at the end of the parallel action, when his new wife is killed, does he become part of the fight back home.

And of course, with the famous and memorable baptism sequence, the payoff on the style of using parallel action is complete. Here again we have a contrast between the façade and the reality—renouncing Satan and or-dering murders. And this time the contrast is much starker than at the beginning of the story. By tying together these two sides of Michael's new life in simultaneous development, with music and words carrying over from one to the other, this sequence caps off the transformation of Michael into the full role of the Godfather.

One Flew Over the Cuckoo's Nest

(1975)
Written by Laurence Hauben and Bo Goldman,
from the novel by Ken Kesey
Directed by Milos Forman

Only the second film ever to win the top five Academy Awards for Best Picture, Best Screenplay, Best Director, Best Actor, and Best Actress (*It Happened One Night* was the first, and recently *The Silence of the Lambs* duplicated the feat), *One Flew Over the Cuckoo's Nest* is hardly a feel-good movie in terms of catering to an audience's desire for escape and fantasy. Yet, as adapted from Ken Kesey's extraordinary and blistering novel, it enjoyed enormous critical and box-office success. It managed this without any of the usual trappings of mainstream Hollywood fare; it did it with only one recognizable film star and a nearly unknown (at the time) foreign director, and despite a depressing setting and a decidedly downbeat ending. The key was a compelling story of a sympathetic character up against seemingly insurmountable odds and an execution of that story with superb performances by all of the principal creative people involved.

SYNOPSIS

R. P. McMurphy is brought to a mental hospital, and the moment he is released from his handcuffs, he leaps for joy. He is led into a mental ward, where the first internee he meets is Chief, a huge, mute Native American. The first to talk with him is the stuttering Billy Bibbit. McMurphy comes over and disrupts the card game being played by Harding, Cheswick, and Martini. When McMurphy interviews with Dr. Spivey, we learn he has been sent from the work farm where he was held on a statutory rape charge, and where he has been fighting. He will be in the hospital for a while to determine whether he is feigning mental illness. McMurphy is enthusiastic to cooperate in this observation.

During group therapy, Nurse Ratched encourages discussion of Harding's marital problems, and it turns into a shouting match with Taber, while Ratched remains unmoved by these men out of control. McMurphy checks out the security fences around the grounds, then tries to get Chief to throw a basketball into the hoop. During a poker game, McMurphy wants to hear a baseball game, but the "tranquil" music playing on the ward is too loud. He enters the nurse's station to turn it down and gets into a battle with Ratched over the music. When chided about his fight with her, McMurphy makes a bet that he'll wear down the nurse in a week.

With the sides drawn, McMurphy sets out to take on Ratched, starting with trying to get work assignments changed so the inmates can watch the World Series that is about to begin. But when it is put to a vote in group, he has only two backers. In the tub room, McMurphy bets the men he can pick up a sink base and throw it through the window to make an escape. When he can't budge the marble base, he says that at least he tried. And when he brings up the second Series game to get a vote, this time he has votes from all nine men in the group. But Ratched changes the rules and says the other men must be included. McMurphy tries everyone to get just one more vote, but she closes up the group meeting before he gets Chief to vote. He goes to the blank TV and starts calling out a play-by-play of a made-up game and gathers a cheering crowd of all the other men, getting them unusually excited.

McMurphy tells the doctor that Ratched isn't honest, that she likes a rigged game. Then later, with Chief's help, he gets over the fence, gets all of his buddies on board the hospital bus, and drives off without the driver. He picks up his girlfriend, Candy, and together they bluster their way onto a deep-sea fishing boat. He shows them how to bait hooks and go fishing while he retires to the cabin with Candy. But with everyone watching through the windows, the boat goes out of control and he must stop his tryst and get things in order. By the time they return to port, where police and onlookers await them, they have several trophy fish to show for their day.

McMurphy's psychiatrists agree that he isn't crazy, but that he is dangerous and should be sent back to the work farm. Ratched, however says she thinks they can help him, and persuades them to keep him in her ward. McMurphy finds out that the time he is spending in the hospital doesn't count toward his prison sentence, and brings it up at group. He is surprised to find that most of the other men are there voluntarily. He tries to convince them that they're no crazier than most people on the outside, and that they should just go. Cheswick gets belligerent about wanting his cigarettes, and Ratched eggs him on until finally McMurphy breaks into the nurse's station to get cigarettes for him to try to end the battle. When the orderlies come to subdue McMurphy, Chief joins in the fight, and suddenly all three men are led off in cuffs.

While Cheswick is dragged off for some kind of treatment, McMurphy finds out that Chief's deaf-mute routine is all a sham, that he can both hear and talk. Together they plan to escape and get to Canada. But when Mc-Murphy is led in for his therapy, it turns out that it is electroshock therapy (EST), horrifying and graphic. When he is led back to group some days later, he walks like a zombie, but suddenly lights up and is as lively as ever.

In fact, right away he arranges to have Candy drop by with some booze for a party—a going-away party, because he and Chief will be leaving. They bribe the night guard with cash, booze, and a woman, and the men of the ward have a riotous party of drinking and trashing the place. But Billy is growing very enamored of Candy, slow-dancing with her. He asks McMurphy if he's going to marry her. McMurphy gets the idea that Billy should have a "date" with Candy just once before they go. Billy is reluctant, but is led into a private room with her while the others resume their partying.

When the orderlies arrive in the morning, everyone is asleep, including McMurphy and Chief. With Ratched in charge, the men are rounded up and the open window is relocked, but Billy is missing. When he is discovered in bed with Candy, Ratched lays into him about telling his mother, brutally manipulating Billy into losing control. He is locked in the doctor's office with an orderly, but McMurphy still has the night guard's keys and tries to break out. The orderly runs to stop McMurphy, and there is a scream.

They discover that Billy has killed himself, and McMurphy blames Ratched. He very nearly strangles her to death before he is pulled off her. Life seems to have returned to normal around the ward, except that Ratched wears an orthopedic collar. The men spread rumors that McMurphy has finally escaped. But late at night he is brought back to his bed, and Chief finds out that he has been lobotomized. Distraught, Chief smothers him to death. Then he pulls the sink base from the floor in the tub room, throws it through the window, and makes good the escape he and McMurphy planned.

PROTAGONIST AND OBJECTIVE

This is McMurphy's story; he is the person whose powerful want and *joie de vivre* create this story. If he were even remotely like any of the other men on the ward, there would be no story here. His objective begins as a very simple one: to get out of the work farm, he pretends to be crazy. All he really wants to do is finish his time and get on with his life.

OBSTACLES

McMurphy's primary obstacle is clearly Nurse Ratched, but in a sense she is the embodiment of the larger institutions and the whole system of authority against which he rebels. She is supported by this system, and a significant aspect of her as an obstacle is that she likes to cheat—she likes a rigged game, as McMurphy tells the doctor. Ratched, the conditions of the hospital, and authority in general are McMurphy's external obstacles, but he also has his internal ones. His objective is to get through his time with ease in the psych ward; if he were capable of being meek and passive like Harding, it would be a cinch. So McMurphy's own liveliness, energy, and manic spirit are part of his own downfall, and become one of his worst obstacles.

PREMISE AND OPENING

The premise here predates the beginning and is only waiting for the collision of the two forces, McMurphy and Nurse Ratched. Ratched runs a mental-hospital ward of men whom she controls and dominates with a clever disguise of calm supportiveness. McMurphy is a free spirit, a man who loves a good time, who is full of life and energy and bonhomie, a man who is a natural leader and booster. He is also a convict who is serving time for statutory rape.

For their opening, Hauben and Goldman chose to give a very brief introduction to the general landscape, then get right inside with the daily routine of the passive, obedient patients. McMurphy is immediately brought into this world, and the second he is freed from his handcuffs, we see the first glimmer of his manic spirit and energy.

MAIN TENSION, CULMINATION, AND RESOLUTION

The main tension of this story begins when the battle lines have been clearly drawn between the two adversaries. After the fight over the music, when McMurphy makes the bet that he can rattle Ratched's cage within a week, we have the two principals poised and ready for battle. Clearly the story evolves far beyond his attempts to shake her control, but the main tension has been established at this point: Will McMurphy be able to win in this battle with Ratched?

The culmination comes when McMurphy and Chief have everything set for their escape. It is the completion of the main tension, because Mc-Murphy has changed his want from bucking the system (and Nurse Ratched) to escaping it. Early in the party he has the wherewithal to make good on his new want: he has the keys and the ability to escape. But McMurphy stays to give a going-away party for his friends and then to give a "present" to Billy that just might solve his problem. The window is open,

206 ■ The Tools of Screenwriting

the escape is possible, and his escape would constitute a defeat of Ratched. Yet the humanitarian side of McMurphy, which we have seen throughout, needs to do something for his friends. This is his downfall.

The resolution comes when Chief smothers McMurphy and makes the escape alone that they planned to do together. At least one caged soul has been liberated by McMurphy's actions. He lost in the flesh, but won in the spirit.

THEME

This story is about freedom; Nurse Ratched is a jailer of the human spirit who pretends to be helping when she is subjugating with her every move. The battle fought between the two principals is over freedom, literal and figurative. And two sharply drawn subplots, involving Harding and Billy, also deal with it. Both are voluntarily committed. Harding chooses to stay, for he is afraid of freedom and prefers the safety of captivity. Billy would really rather leave, but doesn't feel he's ready. In fact, his problem is that he is a prisoner of his mother—and her surrogate, Ratched. Even if he were to leave physically, he would still be a prisoner of his dominating mother. The third subplot, that of Chief, also deals with imprisonment. At first, Chief's prison seems to be that he is deaf and speechless. But in fact he is a prisoner of his own self-doubt, his own lack of faith in himself. And he is the one who is set free by McMurphy, who is given the confidence to escape his private prison, making his subplot the one with the greatest thematic resonance.

UNITY

The unity here is one of action, because we have a strong central character. But in this case, action includes reaction. About half the time McMurphy is actively trying to pursue his own aims, which include making his stay easier, guaranteeing that he will be able to stay, winning the leadership of the group, and eventually trying to escape. And half the time he is reacting to the workings of Ratched, often in defense of his cohorts, whom she is torturing.

EXPOSITION

The early exposition on McMurphy is dealt with in the first interview with the doctor, where there is a conflict in the subtext. Though their exchange is treated playfully, the doctor has quite rightly guessed what McMurphy is up to, feigning mental disturbance to get out of work and the work farm. McMurphy wants to be able to stay in the hospital, and thus there is a test between the men concerning whether he will get away with his plan at all.

The exposition about the rest of the men is largely delivered through the group-therapy sessions. In each of these, there is some major conflict, and our discovery of the expositional material seems incidental. The exposition about Ratched, in terms of how she deals with the men, is brought out in the same way. There is no exposition dealing with her personal life or accounting for why she is the way she is. This absence of any background information on her helps to make Ratched a more evil character, for we are given no mollifying details from her own life and experience to explain her behavior.

CHARACTERIZATION

The characterization of McMurphy starts from his very first scene, when he is unshackled, leaps at the guard, and kisses his forehead. He is almost larger than life, a very demonstrative and energetic man. But he is also a man of determination, as his attempt to move the marble sink base shows. This is a telling moment for McMurphy and for the story, as he attempts the impossible with all his heart.

Nurse Ratched is shown to be cold and indifferent to the sufferings of all her charges, while wearing a mask of concern. In fact, early on we see how she revels in her power to divide and conquer all these men. It is their disunity that gives her her power—which is why McMurphy's leadership is such a threat to her.

Chief is shown to be stolid and unaffected at first, but in the basketball game he comes into his own, and this shows the growth in the man that the ending will finalize. Billy is a timid stutterer with a history of suicide attempts and a problem with his mother, something Ratched uses to keep him in his place. Harding also has a problem with women, especially his wife, again giving Ratched the lever she needs for control.

DEVELOPMENT OF THE STORY

This story can be seen as a battle for control of the psych ward, between the nurse who has controlled it and the natural leader who comes in and threatens her position. With that in mind, we can see that the story is really a series of battles—skirmishes at first, then openly declared warfare later on, the push and pull between two warriors, with the various other men shifting from one side to the other and back again. In this context, the battle over the World Series is won by McMurphy, as is the grand escape to go fishing. But Ratched wins with the electroshock therapy and of course, ultimately with the lobotomy. She wins control of the ward in the end, but one spirit escapes: Chief. He is the "One" of the title.

DRAMATIC IRONY

There is relatively little use of dramatic irony in the telling of this story, and what there is of it is generally quite short-term. This is perhaps because the storytellers preferred to withhold irony until the series of major and horrifying ironies dawn on us as we leave the theater: If he had only stayed at the work farm, McMurphy would have been free; if he had only cared for himself, he could have escaped in the bus or at the party; the true humanitarian is called a criminal, and the sadist is called a humanitarian. These powerful feelings, which can haunt us long after the film is over, are not delivered as dramatic ironies while the story is in progress. Rather, we discover them more or less with McMurphy. The big difference is that we have been filled with a far greater foreboding than he has most of the time. (See "Elements of the Future and Advertising," below.)

There are little uses of irony, however. When Harding slips a lit cigarette into Taber's cuff, we have the revelation and await Taber's recognition. When McMurphy comes stumbling back from EST looking like a zombie, there is a momentary irony when he reveals the truth to Chief before he does to the others. After the big party, when Billy is missing, we know, along with all the men, exactly where he is, but Ratched and the orderlies do not. This is the most protracted use of irony in the film.

PREPARATION AND AFTERMATH

There is a marvelous example of preparation by contrast in the scene before the EST. McMurphy and Chief are alone and he finds out the deaf-mute business is a sham. He gets excited and plans the escape to Canada, and everything seems to be set as far as McMurphy is concerned. He leaves giving the thumbs-up to Chief. The horrifying scene of electroshock therapy comes right on the heels of this high moment.

And there is a marvelous scene of aftermath at the very end of the story. After Chief has escaped and is loping across the field toward the mountains, Taber wakes up and begins to howl in delight, waking the whole ward with his excitement and causing a slight upturn in our own emotions, despite the disappointment of McMurphy's defeat.

PLANTING AND PAYOFF

There are numerous effective plantings and payoffs. When McMurphy first meets the doctor, they talk about deep-sea fishing, and that is where McMurphy takes his buddies when they escape. McMurphy's awareness of the bus leaving the hospital from outside the fence is planted and paid off with the great escape sequence. Chief's deafness and silence are a plant, and there is a marvelous payoff outside the electroshock therapy room. Billy's attempted suicides are planted and have a horrifying payoff.

One plant takes on a metaphorical level by the end. It is McMurphy's attempt to pull the sink base from the floor of the tub room. It seems to be an impossible task, and it subliminally gives us the idea of McMurphy as Sisyphus. After McMurphy's death in the end, when Chief yanks the sink base up and carries it to the other room, the impossible is being done; someone else is carrying McMurphy's torch, and the sink base has become a metaphor.

ELEMENTS OF THE FUTURE AND ADVERTISING

The first advertising comes in the scene with the doctor who tells McMurphy he will stay awhile, and the staff will evaluate him and make their determination. This not only gives us our first time frame, but it also leads us to anticipate their evaluation and determination—both of which we see. Another advertisement comes when McMurphy calls Candy and says the party's on for tonight, thus promising us those scenes.

Elements of the future are also used. Perhaps the most effective is the sense of foreboding that comes over us all too often. When McMurphy and Chief wait outside the EST room, we suspect something terrible is coming, yet he does not. When they escape and go fishing, we suspect there could be terrible consequences, but McMurphy says they'll just be treated like they are crazy and nothing will happen. The irony is that this is true of everyone but him.

Other elements of the future occur when McMurphy makes the plan with Chief to escape to Canada, when he tells the doctor to "get to the bottom of R. P. McMurphy," and when he lays out the whole plan for escaping by throwing the sink base through a window, which is eventually used at the end.

PLAUSIBILITY

This story is distressingly plausible. The conditions depicted aren't even the worst that mental patients suffer through, and the actions of the staff, hated as they are in the course of this story, pale by comparison to real-life horror stories in the daily paper. The actions of the principal characters are thoroughly motivated and logical, while their dialogue, their problems, and their strengths are all firmly within the realm of believability.

ACTION AND ACTIVITY

The first time McMurphy asks the group session to vote on changing the schedule, he has dim hope of getting to watch the World Series. His primary interest, his action, is in getting to Ratched, since this comes right on the heels of his bet about riling her. The second time, the voting is still part of his plan to get to her, but he genuinely believes he will get to see the second game. When he goes to call out the play-by-play in front of the empty TV screen, it is a strong action to defeat Ratched on this same issue.

When McMurphy tries to teach Chief to play basketball, it is only an activity; there is no other meaning behind it. But when he enlists Chief's help in getting over the fence, it is clearly an action. And the escape to go fishing itself is an action as a whole. He is threatened with being found to be "not crazy," and he sets out to show them that he is. And when he is setting the men all up with bait and rods and getting Cheswick to steer, it is action. He is trying to get them all busy so he can go belowdecks with Candy.

DIALOGUE

The dialogue is realistic—gritty and rough, believable within the setting and the context. Though it doesn't seem poetic in the usual sense, the raucous barroom rhythms and terminology of McMurphy's language are filled with specific and evocative imagery. Ratched's language is all control-oriented, manipulative, and insidious. Harding is shown to be the kind of man who hides from himself behind his intellect and uses words to muddy the waters. Billy's stuttering is more important than his words, and Chief's muteness, once we know the truth, is eloquent indeed.

VISUALS

The visual style of this film could perhaps be characterized as hyper-real. The camera does not shy away from difficult and painful images. We see fishhooks go through fish eyes, we linger and close in on the horror of electroshock therapy, and we see clearly just how Billy kills himself. This is all used effectively in service of the story, a gritty and horrifying look at a reality that we would largely prefer to overlook. But here we cannot.

There are also lyrical moments and images. When McMurphy calls out the baseball play-by-play and the men all gather around, we see their reflections in the dead TV screen. When Chief learns how to play basketball, we see him stride up and down the court with growing pride and finally run with a new-found self-confidence. When the partying inmates awaken in the morning and the orderlies lock the window, the lock is right over the heads of the two men who had meant to escape. The image adds another note of irony to the moment.

DRAMATIC SCENES

A marvelous dramatic scene is the first group-therapy session. It is Ratched's scene, and she is ostensibly trying to get the group to talk about Harding's marital problems, but in reality what she is doing is exercising her power over the group through distancing them from each other. There is a brief preparation as they all do stretching exercises and McMurphy shows himself to be lazy indeed. She needles the men until they are ready to throw their discord at each other, and then she does nothing to stop the ensuing shouting match. Although she is obsessed with control, this ability to make the men go out of control at her whim is her greatest tool. A marvelous aftermath follows, in which she and McMurphy stare each other down, each aware that the other knows exactly what has just happened.

Another effective dramatic scene is the second vote on the baseball game. McMurphy thinks he has a trick up his sleeve and seems to deliver when he gets a unanimous vote from the session, only to have Ratched change the rules. Even when he accepts the new rules and goes out in search of another vote, wheedling and cajoling the more "out of it" patients to vote for the game, she just changes the rules again and ends the session. In fact, the whole scene where McMurphy calls the plays of a fictitious baseball game is a protracted scene of aftermath to the fight with Ratched.

SPECIAL NOTES

One of the most important things to note about this film has already been alluded to in the "Dramatic Irony" section above—the fact that we are left to discover the many ironies and tragedies of the situation and the story for ourselves after it is over, rather than experiencing them as ironies during the course of the story. When each of us comes to realize that the "criminal" is the humanitarian and the "humanitarian" is the criminal, the discovery is greater for our having had to work for it, rather than having it revealed during the story.

Another aspect of this story well worth discussing is the fact that it was very successful, yet it has a central character who is not especially admirable and it has an ending that is bittersweet at best. McMurphy is lovable and sympathetic, even though we don't especially admire who he has been prior to the story or even in the early scenes. The sympathy comes from his *joie de vivre* and his good heart, which is evidenced early on. Still, he is hardly someone most in the audience would choose to emulate. That does not in the least stop him from being a powerful protagonist, one capable of eliciting major emotional responses from the audience.

And in a time when it seems that almost all films have to have a happy ending in order to sell tickets, it is well worth noting that a satisfactory resolution and a happy ending are not necessarily the same thing. Some satisfactory resolutions are happy endings, but by no means all. The audience needs to feel a sense of completion, a sense that the story won't simply go on without us. At the same time, people fail, people are not up to the tasks they set for themselves, people deliver too little too late, or they realize their error only when it is too late. These people can still be the stuff of first-rate drama.

A relentlessly downbeat ending would perhaps be too much for the audience. If Chief smothered McMurphy and then got caught trying to escape, was tried for murder and executed, it would be difficult to feel any sense of satisfaction and completion when leaving the theater. But with just a hint of an upturn at the end, even the death and defeat of our protagonist can be a satisfactory resolution.

Thelma and Louise

(1991)
Written by Callie Khouri
Directed by Ridley Scott

There's an old saying that controversy is good news at the box office. There are film producers who go out of their way to create controversy, there are films that by their very nature must become controversial, and there are others, such as this one, which find unexpected controversy. The irony in the case of *Thelma and Louise* is that the controversy surrounding its release is the result of the very same sexist thinking that the film decries. If it had been Butch and Sundance, there wouldn't have been a single editorial, but because in this film two women take to the road and defy the law, there was a great deal of furor surrounding its exhibition. And yes, it was good for the box office.

But well beyond the fact that it prompted arguments, letters to the editor, and ticket sales, this is a well-crafted and unusual film. In an era dominated by macho leading men, it gives us two female leads who are assertive without being macho, who march to their own drummer without being crazy, and it offers a resolution that is just as defiant of the recent laws of the box-office-pleasing happy ending as its heroines are of the laws of several Southern states. *Thelma and Louise* received six Academy Award nominations, including two for Best Actress as well as Best Directing, Best Editing, and Best Cinematography, while the script won the Academy Award for Best Screenplay. This film poses considerable dramaturgical problems as well. It could prove to be an example of what the 1990s might bring to film storytelling.

SYNOPSIS

In Arkansas, Louise is a waitress in a busy diner. She calls her friend Thelma to check on their plans for a weekend at a borrowed cabin in the mountains. Thelma is a bit harried in her own kitchen, and it is the obnoxious and oppressive behavior of her husband that seems to make her that way. She is supposed to ask his permission to go on the little trip, something she has put off already. And when it comes down to it, she can't ask. But Louise goes home from work and packs while Thelma does the same—taking nearly everything in her house. She packs her gun, which she can barely stand to touch, and tells Louise it's to protect them from crazed killers and bears. Thelma puts it in Louise's purse.

They leave town and head to the mountains, but Thelma wants to stop for some fun on the way, saying that she's never been out of town without Darryl, her husband, and she's intent on having some fun. They stop at a western bar in trucker's territory and start drinking heavily. Thelma seems to encourage the attention of a good old boy, Harlan, and they accept drinks he sends to the table. Thelma dances with him while Louise worries about the time. While Louise goes to the bathroom, Harlan ushers Thelma outside for some fresh air because of her drunken dizziness.

But in the parking lot he starts making insistent advances on her. When she fights him off, he hits her hard and then starts to rape her. Louise shows up and, holding the gun to Harlan's ear, makes him stop. But his verbal abuse continues, and something snaps in Louise. She fires the gun, hitting Harlan in the heart. She sends Thelma off to get the car, then gives a final reprimand to the corpse before she hops in the car and they speed away. Thelma thinks they should go to the police, but Louise says they won't believe he tried to rape her, she was dancing close with him all night. Instead, Louise tells Thelma she has to think about what they will do.

They stop for coffee, and Louise concludes the cops won't know it was them. At the bar, Hal Slocum of the state police views the body and interrogates their waitress, who says it wasn't Thelma and Louise who shot him, but probably Harlan's wife or the husband of one of the women he's been with. On the road, Louise figures that they need more money. They decide to check into a hotel and think. There Louise calls her boyfriend, Jimmy, and asks him to loan her a large sum of money against her savings, and he says he'll wire it. She tells him to send it to Oklahoma City. She gathers up Thelma and they race off toward Oklahoma, while Louise concludes that she will go to Mexico. It is uncertain whether Thelma will go.

Thelma meets J. D., a cute young cowboy, who asks for a ride, but Louise nixes the idea and they drive off. Hal finds Louise in the police computer. Meanwhile the women decide to take secondary roads to Mexico, figuring it will decrease their chances of being caught. Hal goes to Louise's house and then her work, asking questions. When they spot J. D. hitchhiking again, Thelma moans like a puppy until Louise agrees to pick him up. When Hal tries to explain to Darryl what his wife is mixed up with, he is disbelieved. J. D. charms Thelma and discovers that the women have a serious aversion to the police. Meanwhile, Hal learns that Louise did bring her gun from home; it's the right caliber.

When Louise goes to pick up the money in Oklahoma City, she finds that Jimmy has brought it in person. They send J. D. away while Jimmy rents them two motel rooms. Louise gives Thelma the money from Jimmy for safekeeping, and then goes to Jimmy's room. J. D. shows up at Thelma's door and she invites him in out of the rain. As they get to know each other, he tells her he's on parole and then explains in detail how he commits his armed robberies. Jimmy wants to know if Louise is in love with another man and gets angry when she refuses to tell him about her real troubles. After fighting, he offers her the engagement ring he had brought and asks her to marry him. Thelma and J. D. make passionate love while Louise and Jimmy come to an understanding and go to bed.

In the morning Louise worries about the future, then goes to breakfast with Jimmy. She agrees to keep the ring and says good-bye to Jimmy. Thelma floats in, ecstatic after her night with J. D., but when Louise finds out she left him in the room with the cash, they run out. They discover that J. D. has stolen their money, and Louise simply loses control and the will to go on. It is Thelma who has to motivate them.

Hal and the FBI go to Darryl's house and tap the phone. They tell him that when Thelma calls, he should be nice on the phone so she won't suspect anything. Thelma stops the car and goes into a market, then comes running out with a bag of money and booze. The police, the FBI, and Darryl watch on the store's videotape as Thelma robs the market just the way J. D. told her he did it. As they drive on, the women have a run-in with a particularly lewd truckdriver.

Jimmy gets picked up by the cops on his return home, and Louise figures that Thelma's home phone will probably be tapped, now that the charges are first-degree murder and armed robbery. J. D. is picked up by the police, and when questioned by Hal, he finds out that they already know about the cash from Jimmy. It is also clear that Hal really wants to help the women, not just catch them. When he is led away, J. D. taunts Darryl about his wife.

Thelma calls Darryl and knows immediately from his niceness that he knows. She hangs up. Louise calls back and asks to talk to the police. She talks with Hal and learns that he knows they plan to go to Mexico. It's clear that J. D. has been picked up, and Louise is angry with Thelma. As they drive into the night, Thelma figures out Louise's past problem in Texas— she was raped there—but Louise won't confirm it. They get pulled over by a trooper for speeding and Thelma pulls a gun on him, disarms him, and locks him in his own trunk.

Louise calls Hal, wanting to convince him it was an accident, which he says he believes. But when he asks her if she wants to come out of this alive, she says they will have to think about it. This time the police phone trace works, and Hal asks to be there for the arrest with the FBI so that he can protect the women—they've been hurt enough.

After their third run-in with the lewd trucker, Louise pulls off the road to meet him. She demands at gunpoint that he apologize for his behavior, but he won't and she shoots out his tires. When he gets even more abusive, both women shoot at his gasoline truck and it explodes. They drive off, leaving billowing smoke. But the FBI and Hal land at a nearby airport, and soon a platoon of police cars spots the women and chases them overland at high speeds. Through some pretty fancy driving, Louise manages to lose them. But now they are being pursued by helicopter.

Racing away, they barely manage to stop the car at the edge of a huge cliff. When they back off the cliff, they find that dozens of police cars have caught up with them, along with the helicopter carrying Hal and the FBI. They are told to give up, and they are surrounded by high-powered weapons with scope sights aimed right at them. Hal wants to keep them from being killed. Thelma doesn't want to be caught, and she convinces Louise that they have to go on with the journey. Louise floors the accelerator and the car sails over the cliff.

PROTAGONIST AND OBJECTIVE

There seem to be three possibilities for how this story is structured: it has dual protagonists; it begins with Louise as the protagonist, but somewhere in the middle it shifts to Thelma; or perhaps it is Thelma's story all along, and she is simply dominated by Louise (as she has been for a long time by her husband) for a portion of the story. Cogent arguments can be mounted for any of these three story structures.

The usual test to determine the protagonist is which character makes the decisions that propel the story, but even here there is a little difficulty. The pivotal incident in this film occurs when Louise shoots Harlan after his attempted rape of Thelma. Here we have both women's complicity in creating the circumstance that makes the story happen. Thelma's innocence helps get her into the predicament, which brings out something in Louise that she had pretty thoroughly sublimated. Louise wouldn't have killed Harlan if it hadn't been for Thelma, and yet Thelma's story would have been radically different if Louise hadn't been there. So the question at this pivotal moment in the story is which decision is the fateful one—Thelma's decision to get involved with Harlan and place herself in a vulnerable position with him, or Louise's decision in the heat of the moment to shoot him.

So perhaps the digging has to go deeper. What about other pivotal decisions? Stopping at the bar instead of going straight up to the mountains is Thelma's decision. Not going directly to the police is Louise's decision. Picking up the hitchhiker J. D. is Thelma's decision. Robbing the market is Thelma's decision. Avoiding Texas on the way to Mexico is Louise's decision. Driving the car off the cliff rather than giving up in the end is Thelma's decision. The balance seems to go toward Thelma, but it isn't an overwhelming dominance. So the next thing to look at is which character undergoes the greater change.

The character arc seems to make clear which character really dominates. While Louise changes during the course of the story, her character arc pales by comparison to Thelma's. The latter goes from a submissive and utterly dominated—if deceptive—housewife to her own self-defined person. Here it becomes clear that the character with more at stake, the one with the greater change and the greater link to the theme of liberation or self-definition, is Thelma. A look at the title might be a shorter route to the same conclusion—that this is Thelma's story.

If we accept that proposition, it becomes clear that the fateful decision, the moment that creates the rest of the story, is not Louise's decision to kill Harlan, but Thelma's decision to let Louise do her thinking for her, as she has done with Darryl for a long time. In the aftermath of the murder, while Louise is trying to decide what they will do, Thelma is horrified to be thought of as the cause of the predicament and immediately calls Darryl to do her thinking for her. When he isn't at home, she decides to give that duty to Louise and thus signs on for the ride. This demonstrates her complete passivity, her way of dealing with the world. To its core, this film is an exploration of the role of the subjugated and the dominated; its plot is the eruption of rebellion against domination.

The key to understanding Thelma's objective comes when she reveals to Louise that she didn't ask Darryl's permission to go. She says he wouldn't have let her go, and yet she wanted to go. In her view of herself at this time, she was supposed to ask and yet she wants to have a good time, something he would surely have denied her if she'd asked. So she didn't ask. Her objective is to have a good time, to get out of town without Darryl for the first time in her life, and, in a way, to try on a new persona. She plays at smoking, looking at herself in the mirror. Her reaction to the murder is that it's not the fun she expected. Yet later she keeps coming back to the same theme—that she's enjoying this, that she has a knack for it, that J. D. and sex are fun, robbing a store is fun, blowing up a gasoline truck is fun.

OBSTACLES

If Thelma's objective is as simple as just having fun, then the obstacles in her way must be the real source of conflict. Her first obstacle is Louise's desire just to get on with the trip to the mountains. Harlan becomes at first a source of fun, but he wants his idea of fun, not hers, and he becomes a major obstacle. When Louise kills him, that deed becomes the central driving obstacle to Thelma's objective. Yet, surprisingly, she doesn't abandon the objective. All the remaining obstacles stem from the fact that they have left a dead man in their wake and have police searching for them. While sporadically Thelma achieves her objective, it is not a permanent condition, and new obstacles arise along the way.

In an interesting addendum, Louise also has her own objective that surfaces in the aftermath of the murder—to get to Mexico. While Thelma is more or less in accord with that objective, she is really more along for the ride, as she says at the end. She has always been less intent on making the destination than Louise; it is getting there, the moments along the way, that Thelma is after.

PREMISE AND OPENING

A woman and her best friend go on vacation, but when she is nearly raped and the man is killed, they hit the road, hoping to escape responsibility, only to become the objects of a massive manhunt. The collision of three critical elements in the parking lot outside the western bar is what creates this story: Thelma's innocence and passivity; Harlan's relationship to women and force; and Louise's suppressed past, apparently having to do with similar circumstances. Each of these elements predates the start of the story, but it is the intersection of them that forces the story to happen.

For her opening, Callie Khouri chose to introduce both of the women in their daily environments. We see Louise waiting tables in a diner and displaying a certain equanimity in the distracting place. By contrast, Thelma is frazzled while alone in her kitchen, frantically moving around, preparing breakfast for her husband. In their interaction we see just how dominated Thelma is by Darryl, and how willing she is to accept his abuse. We also see that she doesn't have the fortitude to ask his permission to go on the weekend trip to the mountains she plans with her friend Louise.

MAIN TENSION, CULMINATION, AND RESOLUTION

The main tension here isn't so much whether they will get away with the murder, but what will happen as a result of their decision not to go to the police after the shooting. Thelma, as a passive central character, leaves this decision in Louise's hands in the immediate aftermath of the murder. By doing so, she signs herself on for a journey and a whole slew of troubles that would not be hers if she had had the strength and sense of self to make her own decision.

The culmination comes when Louise has been talking with Slocum and is contemplating giving up, but Thelma hangs up the phone on her and then makes her friend promise that she isn't going to stop now. Thelma's character arc is complete; she has become an active central character, and a true test of this new state of being is that her friend's conviction is wavering. Thelma has seemed to be an active character since the time of the market robbery, yet the real issue in this story is between the two women, not between them and the law. Thelma allowed herself to be dragged into troubles that weren't her own by her passivity, by allowing Louise to decide for her. Now she has taken those troubles on herself; she has become the decision-maker and she is the one who is dragging her friend into completing what they have begun.

The resolution comes when Thelma suggests that they not allow themselves to be captured despite the absolutely insurmountable array of police power that surrounds them. Once freed of her shackles, Thelma is not about to return to some other form of subjugation, and proves herself willing to take the action that is the only logical solution to her dilemma. She is the one who prompts Louise to drive the car off the cliff; she has the courage to act on her hard-won sense of self, her independence, liberation, or freedom.

THEME

Thelma and Louise are in analagous positions rather than identical ones. Thelma is obviously and overtly oppressed by her husband, and she has accepted this position. She is not openly rebellious against it, nor does she feel that she is getting less than her due—at least at the outset. Louise's subjugation is subtler and takes much longer to surface. It is not the nature of her job or her relationship with her boyfriend. It is her past—the thing that happened to her in Texas—that presses in on her and finally explodes when Harlan is trying to rape Thelma.

Thematically, then, the two women are closely linked. This is a story about liberation, not in a political or physical sense, but rather it is about liberation from one's view of one's self. Louise's line, "You get what you settle for," quite clearly states what both women are coming to terms with in the story. Thelma has settled for too little for too long, and now she wants more. By the third act she actively wants to grab a whole lot more for herself. She comes to feel "more awake" than she has ever felt in her life. Louise has also settled for something—running from her past in Texas. But the nightmare has followed her, and when it resurfaces with Harlan, she runs again. When she finally has the obnoxious trucker pull over and demands an apology, she has turned around and faced her demon. When the apology doesn't come, she coolly shoots at his truck and blows it up. Though she hasn't gotten what she was after, within herself she has stood up to it rather than running away. She has made life take her on her own terms.

And this gets us to the theme, self-definition. Thelma escapes from being the wife that Darryl forcefully demands she be, and becomes who she needs to be. Louise quits running from the demon in her past and sets her own course. The fact that self-definition comes at such a high price to both women, and only after so much destructive and illegal activity, serves to underscore just how intractable is male dominance of women.

And this is probably the root of the controversy surrounding this film. Reviewers and editorialists ask if it is necessary to turn women into criminals in order to free them of domination, in order for them to define their own lives. This is the very question this film was meant to make audiences think about. We were meant to feel the injustice that Hal talks about in the last scene. The fact that the reaction to the film was so strong is a testament to the power of the story to provoke emotions and to challenge the prevailing assumptions of much of the viewing audience.

UNITY

Here we have the unity of action, though, in a way, it could be called the unity of *re*action. Through much of the story, Thelma isn't so much actively chasing down her objective as reacting to all the changing events that clearly interfere with her objective and usually place her in danger. But there are plenty of times—J. D. is a fine example—when she is back to pursuing her objective regardless of what else is going on around her. Still, it is the consistency of her character that gives this story unity.

EXPOSITION

The early exposition, especially about Thelma, is delivered through conflict: Thelma argues with Louise over when she will ask Darryl, and submits to Darryl's abusiveness when she can't bring herself to ask. Thelma's obliviousness of life's realities comes through in the contrast between her reaction and Louise's to Harlan's first approach.

A particularly effective scene in which exposition of a complicated backstory is given without seeming like exposition comes in the scene with Jimmy and Louise after he has delivered the cash to her in Oklahoma City. He thinks her secrecy is because of another man, and he has come to ask her to marry him. We learn a great deal about their relationship through the conflict in the scene.

Another interesting back-story development has to do with Louise's mysterious past in Texas. First it is simply alluded to when she says she shot a gun before in Texas, then it is brought up when she doesn't want to go through Texas to get to Mexico. Finally Thelma figures it out and says that Louise must have been raped in Texas. Louise never admits it, but it seems clear from the vehemence of her denial that Thelma has hit the nail on the head. This is an interesting variation on exposition through conflict. Without the person who knows the background ever revealing it directly, we have learned as much as we need to about that part of her past.

CHARACTERIZATION

Louise is characterized as world-wise and a bit world-weary. This comes out clearly in the first meeting with Harlan and her impatience with him and her disbelief at Thelma's openness. Thelma is characterized as innocent, believing, and trusting, and all of that emerges in that same scene with Harlan. Later, in the parking lot, her eyes are really opened, but she still displays many of the same qualities when she meets J. D.

Hal is sympathetic and understanding, which comes as a surprise, and he is more on their side than he is given credit for. Darryl is insufferably selfish, abusive, and demanding, as is made clear in his opening scene with Thelma. Jimmy is another sympathetic male, sensitive and, despite his one outburst, rather gentle, giving, and understanding. J. D. appears to be gentle and gentlemanly with all his politeness, yet on closer inspection he resembles Darryl more than Jimmy. Each of the men is characterized most by what he wants: Hal wants to help the women by stopping their flight; Darryl wants Thelma's obedience; Jimmy wants Louise's love; J. D. wants anything and everything Thelma will let him have.

DEVELOPMENT OF THE STORY

Most of the story stems from the collision of Thelma's character and her objective with the realities of the world. The rest is due to Louise and her baggage. Thelma is a bit naive and she wants to have fun. But she picks the wrong man to be that way with, and it nearly gets her raped. Louise, baggage and all, steps in to save her friend, but the moment goes wrong and triggers something from Louise's past that turns a bad thing into a tragedy. And here the two characters' natures conspire to create the rest of the story. Louise is accustomed to running away from bad things, and Thelma is accustomed to having other, more dominant people around her do her thinking for her. Thelma gives that power to Louise, who is inclined to run, and we are on the road for the rest of the story. While Louise remains more or less true to her past self, Thelma grows out of her past and becomes her own person, taking the initiative and actually becoming the dominant member of the partnership.

DRAMATIC IRONY

Sometimes dramatic irony can be used for the creation of a single moment rather than a protracted dramatic scene. A fine example of this occurs when Thelma calls Darryl and he is nice on the phone. She immediately knows that he's on to everything and hangs up. The irony is that the police didn't know about Thelma and Darryl's relationship and counseled him to be nice to her. This is so out of keeping with her experience of her husband that it becomes a dead giveaway.

Another effective use of dramatic irony comes in the scene when the state trooper pulls them over for speeding. He has no idea that he has a tiger by the tail. He just clocked them at 110 miles per hour and is doing what he would normally do. The trooper's transformation from strutting, controlling confidence to whimpering and begging comes from the unexpectedness of their reaction—which is perfectly expected and logical to us who know about them.

And another use of irony comes in the scenes with Jimmy, when he wants to know what's going on and Louise refuses to tell him. Because he doesn't know, he jumps to the conclusion that it is another man, and has come prepared with a whole plan for what he wrongly assumes is going on. He has the ring and asks her to marry him. It is such a non sequitur to what is really happening to the women in this story, and yet it is so true to his character and his relationship with Louise, that in a way, this irony helps point up the wrong turn that these women have taken.

PREPARATION AND AFTERMATH

The scenes at the bar where the two women meet Harlan have effective preparation and aftermath. After they decide to stop before going up to the mountains, they drive through trucker country and then enter the western bar's parking lot, helping to set up something of the masculine-dominated environment they are entering. When they speed away after the murder, there seem to be trucks everywhere with angry, aggressive horns blasting at them, helping to drive the unsettling events deeper into our psyches.

Two nicely contrasted aftermaths come in Oklahoma City. After her night with Jimmy, Louise is up early and looking back out to the road, worried. Later, after Louise and Jimmy have said good-bye, Thelma arrives with a radically different aftermath to her night of oblivion. She is rapturous and wears it on her sleeve—or, in this case, on her collar. These demonstrable results of their nights in bed with men tell more than whole volumes of words could say.

PLANTING AND PAYOFF

The clearest plant and payoff has to be the gun Thelma daintily takes from the drawer when packing. Its payoff is obvious, if disastrous, when Louise uses the gun on Harlan. A more complicated, if just as effective, plant occurs when J. D. tells Thelma in considerable detail about how he would conduct his armed robberies. The two payoffs come in rapid succession. The first payoff is when she commits the armed robbery and races off in giddy delight with Louise at the wheel. Then the full disclosure of the event on the video screen is another payoff, for she performed the robbery precisely the way J. D. had inadvertently taught her.

ELEMENTS OF THE FUTURE
AND ADVERTISING

There are almost innumerable instances of the use of elements of the future. Thelma and Louise are always talking about what they are planning to do, about getting to Mexico, about not going through Texas, about what might happen, what they fear or hope might happen. When Louise says, "Why go to the police? Give them enough time and they'll come to us," it is an element of the future. Louise worries out loud that this could get them killed, and then later Hal asks her if she wants to come out of this alive. She says that they will have to think about it. When Thelma asks if Louise has something to look forward to, the retort is "We'll be drinking margaritas by the sea, Mamacita." All of these have the force of driving our thoughts forward in the story without guaranteeing us that any of them will really happen.

A very effective instance of advertising comes when Jimmy agrees to wire money to Louise and gives her the specific place in Oklahoma City. We feel certain that the story will take us to that place for the pickup of the money. We have no way of knowing how that event will transpire, and are surprised by Jimmy's arrival, but we feel that the story will at least take us to that point.

PLAUSIBILITY

In the beginning there is no problem of believability about the characters. Louise is quite familiar; Thelma and her passive acceptance of Darryl's abuse is distressingly common, as is his unacceptable behavior. And we see Harlan coming from the first minute we lay eyes on him, just as Louise does. So not only is he believable, but we are filled with a certain dread about the intersection of his believably macho worldview and Thelma's innocent and accepting attitude. It is when we get to the murder that the willing suspension of disbelief must be worked through actively.

Louise's action comes at a time in the incident when the danger is over. If it didn't, they would be utterly wrong to run and stupid to think they wouldn't be believed. Khouri and Scott chose to play the moment for shock value, for its element of surprise—placing us in Thelma's shoes. The price they had to pay for the surprise was that they couldn't prepare us for this thing in Louise that snaps at that moment. They are locked into explaining it after the fact. We have been prepared for her personality, her forthright way of shutting a man down and her distrust of men, but nothing that would say she might kill a man.

This is where the mystery from Louise's Texas past comes in. It is there to give credence to her having taken such a drastic action. Khouri and Scott are aided in this strategy of suspending our disbelief by Thelma, our central character, whose shoes we have just been in. She can't quite believe it either. But as she comes to her own conclusion to let Louise do her thinking for her, she accepts the fact that Louise had to shoot the gun. She continues to ponder the dilemma and comes back to the incident in Texas several times as she wrestles with it. Though we might not ever get a full delineation of the facts, we choose to go along with Thelma's acceptance of Louise's action. Explaining a major motivation only after a pivotal moment is a very tricky solution to the problem of suspending disbelief and one that is doomed to failure more often than success, but it works well in this instance.

ACTION AND ACTIVITY

A fine example of actions that are disguised to appear as mere activities comes with J. D.'s politeness and his apparent willingness to walk away with "Have a nice day." He is always in pursuit of a goal—a ride, getting into Thelma's bed, putting down the cops—but he is masking it as gentlemanly politeness, as innocence. Louise sees through it immediately, as she did with Harlan, but Thelma buys it.

A nice contrast of the same action being activity and action in different circumstances comes in two parallel scenes. Jimmy shoves bottles on the floor and overturns a table in his fight with Louise about what he thinks is another man. This is an action, for he is trying to show just how deeply he is hurt, how angry he is. Next door, on another table covered with bottles, J. D. sweeps them to the floor in an activity, simply to clear a place to make love.

DIALOGUE

There are numerous effective uses of dialogue for goals well beyond just advancing the plot and conveying short-term information. Louise's line, "You get what you settle for," becomes more than just a line of dialogue. It becomes something of a statement of their lives, almost their mantra. When Hal says, "Brains will get you only so far and luck always runs out," it is a prediction, an element of the future, and it is also a statement of what we already see happening with the women. When Louise says to Thelma, "You've always been crazy . . . this is just your first chance to express yourself," it is a reflection of the change that has taken place in Thelma, a summation of the story that comes very near the end.

VISUALS

Of course, the final image of this film is one that few people forget after seeing it. It so aptly sums up what has really been taking place ever since the shooting—a great ride that will have a horrible end. Other visuals are used in the same vein, as summations or shorthand for various elements. The view from high above of the women's car racing across a field with a dozen police cars in pursuit says in one image what might have taken many cuts and lots of dialogue to get across otherwise. The view of the front wheel going over the cliff near the end is a summation of their situation—they have come face to face with their own personal abyss. The image of the defiant truckdriver standing in front of his gasoline truck as it explodes seems to have two functions. First it tells how far Louise is willing to go to get "justice" in the guise of his apology. It also foretells the price of defiance—what Thelma and Louise face for their defiance of the law and what is expected of them.

DRAMATIC SCENES

Two similar scenes, both with good dramatic emphasis, also point up the differences between two similar characters. When Harlan first approaches the women in the bar, Thelma welcomes him and opens up to him. Louise squelches it and sends him away. Harlan recedes, but, like a shark, is only looking for another approach to his attack. When J. D. asks for a ride, Thelma welcomes him in a similar way. Again Louise nixes the idea, but J. D. really is willing to take no for an answer and does not circle to attack another way. They are men with similar intentions, but they are different, as shown by these two scenes. Later, when he is given another chance, J. D. is immediately back into the same mode, but one feels that he is not the sort who, like Harlan, would resort to physical and verbal abuse, because he has proven that he can take no for an answer.

A first-rate dramatic scene occurs when Jimmy asks Louise to marry him. And its power is sharpened by the contrast to the scenes of J. D. and Thelma getting friendly and then making love. Jimmy is living under a mistaken notion that Louise can't seem to set right, given her desire to keep what is really going on secret. When he presents the ring, under circumstances that fight his intention all the way, the mood shifts and they start to talk of how they met. When he really does know the color of her eyes, her final defense falls and they make love. The ups and downs, the misunderstandings, distrusts, gained trusts, and shifting power between them as the scenes unfold all make this a powerful and poignant moment in the story.

SPECIAL NOTES

This film is a fine recent example of how a film can make a strong and controversial social statement without being either boring or preachy. Injustice in men's perception and treatment of women is at the core of this story, and we can't help but feel it and come away from the film thinking about it. Yet, as the story is unfolding, we are only aware that a good story is being told; we want to know what will happen and we can't predict it.

Too often, particularly in the last decade or so, there has been a separation of films that entertain from films that make us think, as if thinking were something that we must stop doing in order to be entertained. Yet the whole history of storytelling and theater and cinema say the opposite. The films analyzed in this book urge us to keep our minds awake while the show is going on, but many of them are also rather old by today's standards. Yet here is a recent film that did very well at the box office, won critical acclaim and several Academy Award nominations, and also requires that we think and feel while we take the roller-coaster ride.

Diner

(1982)
Written and directed by Barry Levinson

So-called "ensemble" films are made rather frequently, and a few, such as *Diner, American Graffiti, The Big Chill,* and *Nashville,* gain a level of considerable distinction, while many more sink into oblivion. This sort of film fails more easily than a traditional story with an easily identifiable protagonist, because it is very difficult to get an audience to identify with a number of characters more or less equally and still care about what will happen. Levinson managed quite well in this clearly autobiographical and immensely well-observed film that was his debut as a director.

SYNOPSIS

On Christmas night, 1959, in Baltimore we follow a young man, Modell, into a dance in an upstairs gymnasium, where he finds his friend Boogie. Boogie in turn discovers his friend Fenwick in the basement, drunkenly breaking windows. He learns that Fenwick "sold" his date for five dollars, but Boogie sweet-talks her into going home with Fenwick anyway. But on the drive from the dance, Fenwick pulls a stunt in which he fakes an accident. Shrevie and his wife, Beth, are also driving home at the same time, but by the time Boogie, Fenwick, Shrevie, and Modell gather in the diner, where they meet up with Eddie, the women have been left at home.

Boogie owes money to the diner owner, but has nothing to pay it back with, while at the same time an older diner habitué, Bagel, reveals that Boogie has a two-thousand-dollar bet on a basketball game. Boogie claims it's a rigged game and the bet is a sure thing. But when he tries to enlist his buddies in the bet, he can't cover much of his action. Instead he brags about his upcoming date with Carol and makes bets about how far he will get her to go on a first date.

In the dead of night, the guys break up, but several go to the train station to meet Billy, who is coming in as a surprise to his best friend, Eddie, several days in advance of his wedding. They tell Billy of the football test that Eddie is giving his fiancée; if she fails, the wedding is off. Billy goes to wake up Eddie and agrees to be best man. Eddie torments his mother, who loves Billy, but in the end gets his way. Shrevie sells electrical appliances and has a visit from Fenwick, who is already drunk, saying that the "verification" of Boogie's bet about Carol will be at the movies tonight. While playing pool, Eddie reveals to Billy his insecurity about getting married, his uncertainty that it is the right thing to do.

That night everyone gathers at the theater to see if Boogie will get Carol to touch him, while Beth is kept in the dark about the whole situation. Boogie succeeds, after a fashion, in getting Carol to do what he wagered she would, by slipping his penis into a box of popcorn. She is justifiably offended, but he runs after her and in a twisted but smooth effort at logic and explanation, he gets her to believe it was an accident and was due to his attraction to her. She comes back to the theater with him for the end of the film.

Outside the theater, Billy decks a guy in settlement of a many-year-old grudge. The next day he looks up Barbara at her job at the local television station and establishes their long-existing friendship. The next night, Fenwick drinks and stares at the town creche while Eddie asks Shrevie about marriage. At first saying it's great, Shrevie eventually admits that he and Beth can't talk about anything, then ends up by saying it's great. At the diner, Boogie finds out that he lost his two-thousand-dollar bet, and then his buddies grouse that he cheated in the bet about Carol. Finally he ups the ante by betting them all that he will make love with her on the very next date. They all take bets against Boogie.

As the sun rises, the guys all leave the diner. Boogie and Fenwick drive into the country, where Boogie sees the real girl of his dreams on horseback on a huge estate; she is clearly a rich girl who seems to have little interest in him. Billy finds out that Barbara might be pregnant from their one encounter several weeks ago. She laments six years of a platonic relationship, one night and disaster. Billy wants to marry her, but she says their night in bed was a mistake.

Watching TV at home, Fenwick outsmarts both teams on the television show "College Bowl," while Boogie tells his mother of his debt and tries to raise some cash. Fenwick says he will talk to his brother, a truly horrific prospect, about borrowing some money. Shrevie picks a fight with Beth about his compulsive organization of record albums, and storms out of the house just before Boogie arrives to see him. Boogie comforts her, while Shrevie looks quite disturbed as he drives about trying to pretend that he is having a good time. Fenwick tries to beg money from his older brother and gets severely rebuked.

Billy takes Eddie to a Bergman film, which puts him to sleep until they are fetched by Shrevie. They find Fenwick nearly naked, lying in the manger of the creche. He drunkenly fights them off and destroys the manger setting, which gets them all arrested. The other three fathers come to bail out their sons, but Fenwick's father leaves him in jail overnight to "teach him a lesson."

Eddie admits to Boogie that he's "technically" still a virgin, while Billy tries to get Barbara to agree to marry him, but he gets a flat no. Boogie gets beaten up by the man to whom he owes the two thousand dollars, and then finds out that Carol has the flu. In desperation to win his bet about Carol, he sweet-talks Beth, who was once his girlfriend and who is unhappy with Shrevie, into going out with him tonight while everyone else is at Eddie's football test. Friends and relatives gather to listen in as an unseen Elyse answers incredibly difficult football questions, but still fails by just two points, at least one of which is in contention.

Beth goes out with Boogie, who brings a wig for her to wear, saying it is so no one will recognize her, but it is meant to make her look like Carol. Fenwick is to verify the event to settle the bet, but Shrevie tags along. While those two hide in the closet, Boogie takes Beth nearly to the door before he calls it off. He admits to her what was happening and tells her that she will always rate right up there, but that she and Shrevie should work things out between them.

In a strip bar, Eddie and Billy commiserate that neither of them has an impending marriage. Eddie admits to his sexual ineptitude as a kid, while Billy becomes increasingly agitated. Finally he joins the band on stage and livens up the music so much that Eddie dances with the stripper, who eventually gets into it. Boogie arrives at the diner to face the music, but finds out that Bagel paid his debt off—out of respect for his father. Boogie punches out the man who beat him up, then makes a deal with Bagel to work as a salesman for him in the home-improvement field to pay off the debt. Eddie, Billy, and the stripper go out for coffee, and Eddie says that he's giving Elyse the benefit of the doubt and that his wedding is on. Billy is asked if he ever really showed Barbara that he loved her.

Boogie rides in the country on horseback until he meets the girl of his dreams and manages to sweet-talk her. Eddie gets married with a football team song in lieu of the wedding march, and all his friends are there with him. At the reception, Beth and Shrevie start to work things out, Boogie brings his new girlfriend along to the party, and Fenwick talks about going to Europe. Billy and Barbara dance without talking, and it seems they won't marry. When Elyse tosses her bridal bouquet, it lands on the table before all of the guys assembled together.

PROTAGONIST AND OBJECTIVE

In this film there isn't a single central character; rather, there are five stories interwoven, and each story has its own protagonist. It's interesting that there are six buddies and proportionally they don't all have equal screen time, but the differences are not really pronounced. Yet one of the friends, Modell, does not have his own story. He is there and he participates throughout, yet we are not made curious about his life, nor are we made to participate in his troubles. The five protagonists are Boogie, Eddie, Shrevie, Fenwick, and Billy. Even among the ones who have complete stories, there isn't absolute equality. Boogie's and Eddie's stories are more fleshed out and demand more of our attention than do the other three.

Their situations are similar, their settings are pretty much the same, their problems are related, yet their objectives are all different. Boogie wants to keep ahead of his gambling debts. Eddie wants to figure out whether he's doing the right thing by getting married. Billy wants to work something out with Barbara. Fenwick wants attention, and Shrevie wants to be appreciated.

OBSTACLES

The obstacles, like the objectives, are different for each of the guys. Boogie likes a stacked deck, yet his every effort to rig a bet seems to run into failure. Eddie's primary obstacle stems from his ignorance; he is a virgin and he hasn't dated very much, so he has no idea whether what he is doing is right for him at this time. Billy's obstacle is that he is in love with a self-possessed and strong woman. Unlike Beth and the unseen Elyse, Barbara thinks for herself, and though she has a long-standing friendship with Billy, she knows enough to know that it won't work between them. Fenwick's obstacles come down to the fact that he can't figure out how to get any attention other than a negative kind. Shrevie's obstacle, again, is the woman he loves. He wants to be appreciated for what he can do and what he knows, but she places no importance on those things.

PREMISE AND OPENING

Five guys who are just past college age in Baltimore, in 1959, languish in their lives, both fearing and hoping for change, while they hang out together in a diner rather than really communicating with the women in their lives. The pivotal issue in each of their lives predates the start of this story.

For his opening, Levinson chose to introduce us to the time and context of the story rather than the diner setting itself. The music, the dress, the setting of this little Christmas-night dance, all help to place us in the time period. We first see the one friend without his own story—he is more of a commentator on all the stories—who leads us to Boogie, who in turn leads us to Fenwick, already out of control. We quickly learn that Boogie is a smooth talker, that Fenwick will do anything for attention, and that Shrevie can't open up about anything to his wife. Only after the context and several of the characters are introduced do we then adjourn to the diner to find out the place it holds in their world.

MAIN TENSION, CULMINATION, AND RESOLUTION

Each of the five stories has its own three act division, yet the two more important stories are much more fleshed out than the other three, and those two characters also go through the greatest changes.

The main tension of Boogie's story has to do with his gambling debts. The culmination comes when he can't go through with the date with Beth, even though it would mean he would have the money to pay off enough of the debt to buy more time. And the resolution comes when he makes a deal with Bagel to utilize his demonstrable talent—his smooth talk—to pay off the debt that Bagel has assumed.

The main tension of Eddie's story is his decision about getting married. He tries to make himself believe that the decision is out of his hands, yet he is obsessed with finding out from each of his friends whether this is the right thing for him to do. The culmination comes when Elyse fails the test and he calls off the wedding. The resolution comes when he concludes that he will give her the benefit of the doubt and then goes ahead and marries her.

The main tension of Billy's story arises from his relationship with Barbara. Even before he knows of the possible pregnancy, he wants more from her, and the news just gives him a good reason to push for more. The culmination comes when she gives him a flat refusal, and the resolution comes at the wedding reception, when he seems to accept the fact that she is right and they won't marry.

The main tension of Fenwick's story is his poorly articulated need for attention. From breaking windows he goes right into his fake car accident, which he seems to hope will elicit the sympathy and caring that lie behind the attention he seeks. The culmination of his story comes when he gets himself and his friends arrested for destroying the manger scene. Rather than receiving attention from the person he wants it from—his father—he is left to rot in jail.

The main tension of Shrevie's story has to do with his feeling unappreciated and misunderstood by his wife, Beth. The culmination comes, without his knowledge but with his almost being a witness, when Beth goes out with Boogie and almost makes love to him in front of her husband. And the resolution, equally outside of Shrevie's control, comes after Boogie persuades Beth to try harder with Shrevie, and the two start to communicate at the wedding reception.

THEME

The five stories are variations on the same theme of growing up. Each in his own way, these young men are coming to grips with the reality that they must start to become adults. The diner has in part enabled their protracted adolescence—their inability to communicate with women, to see women as people, to grasp life's responsibilities, to take control of their own lives. At the diner they have a safe haven from women and adult responsibilities. There they find the understanding and appreciation they must sometime learn to gain elsewhere. They have camaraderie and a sympathetic ear when they stay up all night at the diner. So, in a sense, the theme of their growing up as individuals is directly linked to their weaning themselves from the diner or remaining tied to it and thus not fully growing up.

UNITY

Unity in this kind of story is particularly crucial since, like *Rashomon*, it does not have a single central character. But unlike the Kurosawa film, here the unity stems not so much from time as from place. The diner of the title is the main unifying element, but it is supported by the whole era, the syndrome of protracted adolescence that all the young men share, the entire context in which the story takes place. In other words, the place in time, exemplified by the diner, is what holds these stories together—along with a strong thematic link.

It is interesting to note how many of the films that are built on interwoven stories share nostalgia as an inherent part of their makeup. This seems to be because the re-creation of an era—the music, the clothes, the dialect, the social rules, rituals, and context—leads in the best films to an especially vivid portrait of a place in time, and this in turn helps the various stories to coexist and coalesce.

EXPOSITION

Much of the exposition of the place, setting, and context comes "on the fly" while the stories are building in and around the diner. For instance, Boogie owing money to the diner owner shows his financial straits just before his two-thousand-dollar bet is revealed. And a great deal of the exposition is delivered through using Billy, who has been out of town. He must be brought up to date on Eddie's football test, and his disbelief helps us to grasp the situation. Beth is married into the core group, but is systematically kept out of it. Nonetheless, she is close enough to ask what is going on, and her persistence in trying to understand—and Shrevie's defense of his buddies—also helps expose what we need to know about the lives of these characters.

There are some marvelous scenes of bickering, particularly between Eddie and Modell, which don't so much flesh out back-stories on the individuals as they help to show the depth and length of the friendships and broaden our experience of the world we are being delivered into.

CHARACTERIZATION

Boogie is characterized by his ability to talk nearly anyone into nearly anything, and by his preference for a rigged game. From his initial big bet, which is supposed to be on a game where the teams are shaving points, to his trick on Carol in the movie theater, to his scam with Beth playing Carol without knowing it, Boogie is always trying to take the risk out of his bets, to stack the deck in his favor—after his silver tongue has gotten him into the bets and into trouble.

Billy is presented as a strong contrast in character to Boogie, who lies, exaggerates, and manipulates, especially with women, and enjoys a great deal of success with these tactics. Billy, on the other hand, has a long-standing platonic friendship with a woman and is able to communicate with her openly and honestly, yet can't get her to do what he wants, no matter what he tries.

Shrevie, too, is characterized by his inability to connect with a woman, his wife. He bemoans the days before they were married, when all their talk centered around finding a time and place to "do it." Now he feels there is nothing left for them to talk about, though with his friends in the diner he can stay up all night jabbering.

Eddie's inability to communicate with Elyse doesn't take the form of talking, but is characterized by his absolute demand that she pass an absurd test about football. This demand, coupled with his guarded, but regularly revealed, uncertainty about the step he is about to take, show what really makes him tick through most of the story: he wants someone else to make this crucial decision for him.

Fenwick doesn't distinguish between men and women in his inability to communicate. Though he is a welcome member of the boys' club, even his buddies think he's crazy, and none of them ever gets into any depth with him. His most profound miscommunication is with his brother, who accuses him of not being bright and not reading books, when we know Fenwick can beat the scholars on "College Bowl." When it comes to getting what he wants from life, Fenwick is characterized as being utterly inarticulate.

DEVELOPMENT OF THE STORY

Each of the five stories stems from something that happened (or evolved) before the film starts. The time frame of the film covers the week from Christmas Day, 1959, to New Years Day, 1960, and each story comes to a head during this time. Boogie's troubles all stem from the bet he placed before this story starts. Eddie has demanded the football test for Elyse months before this Christmas week, but now it has to happen. Shrevie has long since lost his ability to talk with Beth. Billy's desire to have something more with Barbara is a feeling that he has harbored for a long time. While he considers their night in New York the start of something more, she thinks it was a mistake. And Fenwick has become increasingly estranged from his family and alienated from his world, to the point where we first see him breaking windows just for the hell of it, and we only know him as an alcoholic.

DRAMATIC IRONY

A marvelous example of the use of dramatic irony occurs in the movie-theater scene where Boogie is trying to win his bet about Carol. We are let in on his secret trick—and have all manner of commentary and anticipation from his buddies in the theater. And all the while, Carol blithely nibbles on popcorn while we wait for the inevitable moment of discovery. This scene shows how effective irony can be, and how long our anticipation can be prolonged by it. We seem to spend forever waiting for her to dig deep enough into the popcorn box, yet no one is bored. From the moment of revelation to the audience, we are waiting with bated breath for the inevitable moment of recognition by the one character who does not know the secret.

Another superb use of dramatic irony comes when Boogie is trying to pass Beth off as Carol. He tells one story to Beth, while the other guys only know the original plan. Only Boogie and the audience know the whole truth. From the revelation of the irony we begin to anticipate recognition from both sides, and that anticipation is increased when Shrevie, the one who stands to lose the most, invites himself along, not knowing what he might be about to see. This compounds the irony, because Boogie has no idea that Beth's husband is hiding there, ready to watch his show. Even after Boogie thinks better of his plan and reveals what he knows to Beth, a new irony continues: he never finds out that Shrevie was hiding in the closet with Fenwick and that those two think Boogie has failed, an ironic knowledge we share with Boogie.

PREPARATION AND AFTERMATH

The same scene in which Boogie is about to show up at Fenwick's apartment with "Carol" has marvelous preparation. From the moment Shrevie invites himself along, the two friends treat this as a caper, some clandestine thing that seems like great fun. They scamper into the building and set up a perfect hiding place for themselves. They help set up the whole plan, and it is their larkish quality that makes this a preparation by contrast. The contrast is between what we know to be true and our foreboding at Boogie's actually going through with it. Not only would he be abusing Beth horribly, but he would inadvertently be compounding it with her husband watching—two events we strongly hope will not happen.

The entire scene in the strip joint between Eddie and Billy is, in a way, an aftermath of both of their marriage decisions—decisions that were "out of their hands" because Elyse failed the test and Barbara adamantly said no. They commiserate, they drink, and they have a great deal of energy that they have to let off—all of which are kinds of aftermaths to the trials they have been through. In a nice scene that recaps their circumstances and advances the story, they go out with the stripper, and Eddie decides he will get married while Billy acknowledges that he won't.

PLANTING AND PAYOFF

Fenwick's consistent fascination with the community creche is a kind of planting that is paid off when he strips off his clothes and lays himself down in the manger. And the utterly senseless, irrational side of his attention-getting is also planted with his first introduction, where he is breaking windows. This gets its final payoff also at the manger.

The woman on horseback and how she seems to embody Boogie's big dreams is a plant for his continuing to chase his dreams at the end—by going after her and perhaps not going after any more stacked decks. And Bagel's admiration for Boogie's father is planted early in the story and paid off when he pays Boogie's gambling debt.

ELEMENTS OF THE FUTURE
AND ADVERTISING

Eddie's big football test for Elyse is, of course, advertising that is brought up regularly, and is something that we fully expect to see within the film. The final outcome of Boogie's two-thousand-dollar bet is another advertisement, since we expect to know how it goes. When he loses the bet, it is another advertisement, because we expect to find out how he will pay off such a huge debt. The same goes for all of Boogie's bets. When he bets about his first date with Carol, we fully expect to find out what happens, just as we expect to find out about his second date with her.

Eddie's mother's strong desire to see him leave the house at long last is an element of the future. She is predicting that she will be ecstatic when he leaves. And of course in the end she is already inviting him back at his wedding reception. When Fenwick's brother says that their dad ought to change Fenwick's trust fund, it is a prediction, not an advertisement. In a way it comes about when the father leaves Fenwick in jail overnight, but it isn't a literal event so much as an emotional equivalent.

PLAUSIBILITY

Films in which interwoven stories of several characters are used to make one larger story usually take place in a relatively short span of time. *American Graffiti* was one night, *The Big Chill* a weekend, *Nashville* a week, and *Diner* also a week. In these films we have no real trouble believing in the events of the interwoven stories. What usually needs to be done is to convince the audience that it is believable that all of these different stories would come to a head in such a short period of time.

In *American Graffiti,* that one night was the last night two principal characters were going to be in town; the action had to take place then or it would have to wait. In *The Big Chill* the characters haven't seen each other in a long time and there is a sizable backlog of old business that naturally comes out at once. In *Nashville* there is a political rally and the preparation for it, which provide a time frame to intensify the actions.

Here the same method of time compression is used. The story takes place during a holiday week, and at the end of it a wedding is planned. Billy hasn't seen most of the people for a while, and the big test has been put off until this week; both help to intensify the events. Shrevie's crisis is a result of Boogie's crisis, and in fact the last straw for Fenwick is the fight with his brother, which is also the result of Boogie's dilemma. And Boogie strikes us as someone who has always been just one step and two smooth lines ahead of serious trouble, so it doesn't seem unbelievable when his lying and cheating ways start to backfire on him.

ACTION AND ACTIVITY

When Modell and Eddie bicker over food and rides at the diner and in the parking lot, it is activity. This is how these guys relate to each other, and there is no hidden agenda—although Modell's mode of asking for a ride or a part of a sandwich are ways of masking his action of asking for what he wants. But when Boogie is cajoling his friends into betting about his romantic prowess with Carol, it is most definitely an action. He wants to get them to bet big money so that he can pay off part of the large bet he lost.

When Eddie's mother pulls a knife on him in the kitchen, it is an interesting interplay between activity and action. We come to see this scene as a normal part of their daily interaction, yet it isn't really just activity. The mother pulls the knife not because she wants to stab Eddie, but because she wants to communicate her displeasure at the way he lives and how he treats her. Eddie goads her and leads the frantic chase around the table not because he doesn't understand, but because he wants to show off for Billy.

DIALOGUE

Quite often in this story, the characters express the essence of their dilemma or a central aspect of their characterization in dialogue. When Boogie tells Bagel that without "good dreams, you got nightmares" he is expressing what keeps him running just a step ahead of his deceptions. When Shrevie tells Eddie about how he and Beth used to talk about places to "do it" and now they have nothing left to talk about, he is spelling out his dilemma while at the same time denying its existence.

Two scenes with Fenwick reveal his internal inconsistency. We see him top the students on "College Bowl" in one scene, then tell his brother he never reads and doesn't know anything. From what he says and what we know to be a lie, we come to understand why he is misunderstood and how he revels in it.

VISUALS

Part of the richness of this film is the accumulation of well-observed material. It is a telling detail that these guys all wear jackets and ties throughout, except for Billy, who is the one who seems to be moving away. Watching Eddie dress in dirty clothes, partially buttoned shirt, and pre-tied necktie tells us more than endless dialogue about how he lives. Shrevie's album collection and his care of it show us his nature. The guys leaving the diner at dawn becomes a recurring image, one that underlines just how much time they waste there.

The visuals can be used to convey a joke as well. After the big fat man has eaten one of every item on the diner's menu, he drives off in the smallest car available in America in 1959 and it becomes a joke.

Another use of the visuals is to make contrasts and parallels between film and television clips we see on screen and the lives of the characters in the story. In the movie theater, in the appliance store, and in the television station, there are visual images and bits of dialogue from the fictions on screen that are used in counterpoint to, or to underline, the situations of the characters in the story.

DRAMATIC SCENES

An effective and uncomfortably amusing dramatic scene occurs after Carol has stormed out of the movie. Boogie tries to do the impossible and succeeds. What is particularly noteworthy about the scene is how effectively it shows this smooth talker taking what is an obvious disadvantage and twisting it to his own ends. Clearly there can be no excuse, yet he turns that into a compliment to her. He takes what should be his profound embarrassment and turns it into a tool to manipulate her. This scene reveals a great deal about his character as well as his persuasive abilities.

A similar but considerably more sinister example of the same thing comes in the scene when Boogie talks Beth into meeting him on the sly. We know her and have sympathy for her circumstances. And we know just what he is up to as he tells her about how good the old days were, how she ranks right up there, and he gets her to suggest that they meet tonight. While this is an exercise of the same talents, this scene has another element that the first didn't. With Carol, part of us wanted him to get away with it. No harm done. With Beth we fear that he will get away with it, and perhaps even worse, we are terribly afraid that he will go through with it. So, even though the scene with Beth is Boogie's scene—he is in pursuit of her as a solution to his problem—our allegiance shifts over to her entirely, whereas with Carol our allegiance remains with Boogie.

Another effective dramatic scene for showing how a simple and seemingly small conflict can escalate occurs when Shrevie finds that Beth has put away some of his albums in the wrong places. Not only do we learn what is important to him by hearing about his elaborate system and the passion with which he pleads his case, but we find out about Beth as well, in her responses to the barrage and her assertions of how meaningless it all is. This scene has a preparation when Shrevie is organizing the albums, and it has a particularly moving aftermath when Boogie shows up and quite sympathetically consoles Beth.

SPECIAL NOTES

Nostalgia was discussed as an aspect of what helps to unify this kind of a story—not in all cases, certainly, but in a great many of them. But nostalgia is often abused and sometimes misunderstood. Nostalgia doesn't necessarily mean falsely remembered, seen through rose-colored glasses, or cloyingly sweet. Here we have a fine example of nostalgia at its best. There is a quality of fond remembrance about this story, but the memories are clear and sharp and not sugar-coated. There isn't any of the aspect of wish-fulfillment that is so often associated with nostalgia—making believe life was perfect at another time and place. Here, life in 1959 is recaptured with complexity, base emotions along with the better moments, the bitter with the sweet.

False nostalgia, which implies that a particular place and time were somehow perfect, utterly destroys drama. Drama depends on good and evil, internal conflicts, desires that must be resisted, and resistances that we hope will be lifted. It depends on rounded characters who stand in the mud and look to the sky, on whom rain falls, and whose hopes and wishes are capable of not coming true. Without these things, there can't be conflict and there can't be drama. False nostalgia is a kind of self-deception that forbids the onlooker to admit to the reality of life and conflict. Without conflict, there is no drama. Without reality—in some guise or another—we don't really care enough to invest our emotions.

Rashomon

(1951)
Screenplay by Akira Kurosawa and Shinobu Hashimoto,
from a story by Ryonosuke Akutagawa
Directed by Akira Kurosawa

When *Rashomon* won the top prize at the Venice Film Festival and then
the Academy Award for Best Foreign Film in 1951, it opened the world's
eyes to filmmaking in Japan, and it made its co-writer and director, Akira
Kurosawa, a major force in world cinema. This film is notable for its psychological realism, its masterful use of the camera, and its visual style, as
well as its superb use of music to heighten the different versions of the
same events. But above all, it is known for its approach to the telling of
what would at first seem to be a simple tale of lust, betrayal, and murder.
It is the way in which this story is told and the juxtapositions of the various
accounts of the "truth" presented in the film that account for its enduring
importance and popularity.

SYNOPSIS

A priest, a woodcutter, and a tramp gather under the decrepit Rashomon
Gate to get out of a thunderstorm. The priest and the woodcutter are be-
moaning the terrible events of the day, and the tramp, wishing only to pass
the time of the storm, urges them to tell him the story that has them upset.
The woodcutter describes how he was walking through the woods when he
found first a woman's hat, then a man's hat, then a piece of rope and an
amulet. At the end of this trail of discoveries, he found a corpse and raced
through the woods to report it to the police.

In a flashback, the priest tells the police how he saw the murdered man
and his wife, astride a horse and wearing a veiled hat, on the road shortly
before the death.

The notorious bandit Tajomaru is brought before the same police inquest
and testifies that he killed the man, and that if it hadn't been for a cool
breeze, he might not have killed. He tells of first seeing the man and his
wife, Takehiro and Masago, on the road, and of the breeze blowing aside
her veil. He thinks he has seen an angel and vows to himself that he will
have her. He cuts them off on the road, then shows his Korean sword to
the gentleman, saying that he has found a hoard of such items and will sell

them cheap. He lures the man into the woods, jumps him, and ties him up. Then he goes back for the wife and gets the notion that he would like her to see that her husband has been humiliated this way. He lures her into the woods, and when she sees her husband, she attacks the bandit with her dagger. He disarms her and kisses her, and she succumbs to his kisses. When he is about to leave, the wife pleads with the bandit that she cannot stand the double humiliation, saying that either he or her husband must die. The bandit frees the man, they fight valiantly with swords, and Tajomaru is the victor, stabbing the man with his sword. But when it is over, the woman has fled.

Back at the Rashomon Gate, the tramp suggests the bandit probably killed the woman too, but the priest says she also testified at the inquest, and recounts her tale. In the subsequent flashback, which tells the woman's version, the bandit attacks her and then afterward sneers at her husband before running off into the woods. She goes to her husband and finds only cold hatred in his eyes, no understanding or compassion. She cuts his ropes and begs him to kill her, but not to stare at her anymore with such hatred. She approaches him with the dagger, but then faints, and when she wakes up, her husband is dead. She finds herself by a stream and throws herself into it in a failed suicide attempt.

The tramp complains that the more he hears, the more confused he becomes. The priest goes on to recount the murdered man's version, as told through a medium at the inquest. After the bandit attacks the wife, he consoles her while the man thinks his wife never looked lovelier than at that moment. But then she begs the bandit to kill her husband and to take her away with him. Even the bandit is taken aback by this demand, and shoves her to the ground. While the two men wonder what to do with such a woman, she flees. Tajomaru frees the man before running off himself. Left alone, Takehiro finds his wife's dagger and, consumed with remorse and humiliation, plunges it into his own heart.

The woodcutter says that both the dead man and the medium must have lied, because the man was killed with a sword, not a dagger. The tramp uses this assertion to elicit from the woodcutter that he knows a lot more than he told the police. The woodcutter says that after finding the woman's hat, he saw the bandit consoling the woman and vowing his love for her, his desire to marry her. In the woodcutter's version, she grabs the dagger and cuts her husband's ropes, only to hear him say that he wouldn't fight over such a woman, that she should kill herself. She taunts both of the men, assaulting their masculinity and provoking them into a fight over her. Both are timid and rather pitiful in their protracted fight, but in the end the bandit gets the upper hand and plunges his sword into the husband. The woman runs off and the bandit limps off alone with his own and the husband's swords.

The tramp accuses the woodcutter of lying about everything, but as they argue, they hear a baby crying. They discover an abandoned infant, and the tramp steals half its clothes. The woodcutter attacks him as being despicable, but is accused in turn of having stolen the dagger and probably having lied about much of his story. After the tramp runs off with the child's clothes, the priest is disconsolate about the nature of mankind. When the woodcutter goes to take the baby, the priest accuses him of wanting to steal what little the child has left. But the woodcutter simply wants to add the child to his own large family. The priest gives up the child and feels reaffirmed in his faith in mankind by this simple act of kindness and selflessness.

PROTAGONIST AND OBJECTIVE

Because this story comprises four interwoven versions of more or less the same events, there is no central character to the overall story. See the "Unity" section below for a discussion of what holds this story together without a protagonist.

However, when this story is broken down into the four versions, three of them have their own protagonists, in each case the person recounting his or her version of the events. Tajomaru is the central character of his version, and his objective is to get the woman—with or without having to kill the husband. Masago is the protagonist of her version, and her objective is to get back what was lost—her husband's respect and admiration. As with the others, Takehiro is his own central character, and his objective is to make up for his disgrace and humiliation—which he does by killing himself.

Only the woodcutter's version is without a protagonist, which is why, at first glance, it seems to be the truest and most forthright. While the woodcutter recounts the events, he is in no way a participant in them. This gives his account a kind of anonymous quality; there is no point of view, so we are not made to identify with one character more than the others. This sort of story would fail miserably if it were the whole film or even if it were the first version presented. But because it is the last, and we have been made to identify in turn with the bandit, the wife, and the husband, we are already invested in their lives and the course of events that is given its last twist in the woodcutter's version. Because this identification and empathy have already been created, this last version can stand alone without a protagonist.

OBSTACLES

In the three versions that have protagonists, there are clearly defined obstacles. Tajomaru's obstacles are, first, the husband's distrust of him, then the wife's assault on him, and finally the wife's plea that one or the other of them must die because of what has happened. This leads to his last and biggest obstacle, that the husband is a samurai and a good swordsman. Masago's principal obstacle is the fact that rather than the sympathy and understanding she seeks from her husband after the assault, she is met with cold hatred. She tries to break through her husband's shell, but fails. And Takehiro's primary obstacle is not the bandit but his own wife. When she demands that the bandit kill him, his humiliation is redoubled, his tragedy compounded by her betrayal.

PREMISE AND OPENING

A man, his wife, and a bandit are involved in an incident in the woods in which the wife is raped or seduced by the bandit and the husband is stabbed to death. His horse and sword are stolen and found on the bandit, while the wife is found elsewhere.

For their opening, Kurosawa and Hashimoto chose the meeting of three characters who are, at best, peripheral to the main events of the story. Because this is a story about the recounting of events and the unreliable nature of memory or a person's "honest" version of past events, they chose to put all of the events in the past and to have them recounted one step further removed from the major participants. In their own way, these three men under the Rashomon Gate are the audience: our moral stance is embodied in the priest, our selfish side in the tramp, and our mixed-up, troubled, and cowardly aspects in the woodcutter. They help to guide our responses on the journey through the murky moral waters this film explores.

MAIN TENSION, CULMINATION, AND RESOLUTION

Again, because of the nature of this story and its lack of a protagonist, the overall story is told without these three tools. But the individual stories have their own points, however briefly they may be told. The most fully developed version of the events, Tajomaru's, is the clearest. The main tension of his story might be "Will he get the woman, and at what price?" The culmination would occur after he has had her and is about to leave, at the moment when she says that one or the other of them must die. And the resolution is that he prevails in their swordfight and kills the man in a fair and honorable way.

THEME

In each of the stories told about that day's events, the teller proclaims the "truth." And in his questioning of what he hears from the priest and the woodcutter, the tramp is constantly questioning what is the truth, what is a lie. Together the three men under the gate philosophize on truth and lies and why men tell lies. To its core, this film is an exploration of perspectives on truth, on how an individual misperceives or knowingly distorts reality because of his or her own inner needs.

UNITY

Because there is no single protagonist, this film does not get its unity from action, from the pursuit of an objective by a central character. Here the unity is one of time. Specifically, the tie that binds this into a cohesive story is the afternoon of the fateful events. Everything keeps coming back to these few hours in which all of these lives changed forever. As we go from the bandit's version of the events to the wife's to the husband's, what makes this a single story rather than four unrelated stories is that they all focus on the same specific time and place. As the versions of the events in that time and place sometimes support and sometimes contradict parts of the other versions and the layers of our understanding and questioning of those events build up, we unconsciously come to accept these widely varying accounts as parts of the same whole.

Clearly a more difficult form than the unity of action, and for that reason less frequently attempted, the unity of time (or, if you prefer in this case, time and place) can create a cohesive, compelling, and effective drama. Although it is perhaps more difficult to generate as intense an emotional response in the audience without a main character to identify with, the ability of this kind of story to generate a thoughtful and lingering response is quite clear.

EXPOSITION

The basic exposition is delivered first by the woodcutter and then by the priest. The woodcutter sets the locale and finds the hats and rope and then the corpse in his first flashback. The priest introduces us to the man and his wife and gives us another crucial bit of information, that it was the husband who died. The remaining exposition is delivered in Tajomaru's version of the events.

An interesting variation on delivering exposition through conflict comes with the woodcutter's walk in the woods. There is no conflict inherent in the scene, but we have seen both him and the priest commiserating over how horrible it was, how nothing was ever worse, and so on. With this preparation, a simple walk in the woods can be filled with foreboding and the audience will feel a sense of conflict, though the actual events on screen don't have any.

CHARACTERIZATION

There are four accounts of the three principal players' actions at the same place and time. The characterizations of these three people vary from one account to the next. The cumulative effect of these layers of sometimes conflicting and sometimes supporting versions is that each of the characters takes on a complex and in some ways inconsistent characterization. Yet within the individual accounts, there is a simple consistency.

For instance, in his own account, Tajomaru is troubled by itches, bugs, and other things that pester his person from the beginning of his tale to the end. In the others' accounts of his actions, those other people telling about him are not inside his skin, and thus there is no focus on his personal hygiene or these petty annoyances.

What is perhaps more interesting than the deviations in the characterizations from one version to the next is the way in which the three principals characterize themselves in their own versions. It is quite telling that in each of the three accounts the protagonist of that version does what is the most honorable thing given the circumstances. In his version, Tajomaru seduces the wife—neither having to kill the man nor rape the woman. When he is cajoled into fighting for her honor, it is a valiant battle and he wins, fair and square. In Masago's version, she is assaulted and then she is wronged a second time by her cold-hearted husband. She prefers to die than to withstand his hatred, and asks him to kill her—the honorable thing to do, from her point of view. And in Takehiro's version, his humiliation is doubled by the bandit and the betrayal of his faithless wife. He does the only honorable thing, which is to kill himself.

DEVELOPMENT OF THE STORY

All of the versions of the events of that afternoon are developed from the same two desires coming into conflict. Tajomaru wants to have Masago, by whatever means are necessary. Masago and Takehiro both want honor and propriety. In each of the versions of the story, everything grows out of the collision of these two wants. The differences from one version to another depend mostly on the perceiver: The person who is telling the story, the character whose point of view is being represented, even in the woodcutter's version, where he isn't a principal player in the drama, his perception seriously colors how we are given the events. He sees none of them as honorable, and he portrays the bandit as lacking the courage to follow through (until the very end of the fight) with his avowed desire to use any means necessary.

DRAMATIC IRONY

The telling of this story does not depend heavily on the use of dramatic irony. This is mostly because of the territory being explored in the film— what is true, what do the characters really want, and what do they do to get it. This exploration presupposes that there isn't an absolute truth that can be known and then balanced against what a character knows or doesn't know.

At the same time, within the individual accounts, there is some effective use of dramatic irony, particularly in Tajomaru's version. When he first approaches the couple on the road, we know that he is after the wife. Yet he does not reveal this want. Rather, he finds a way to win a little bit of the husband's trust by offering his sword and presenting a plausible, and believably dishonest, little scheme—the sale of goods he stole from a grave. With this ruse he lures the man away from his wife so that he may attack him unawares. Then, when he gets back to the wife, he uses the same trick once more, again creating a dramatic irony. This time he tells her the man was bitten by a snake and he lures her back to the same spot, so that she may see her husband's humiliation. In both cases, the use of irony greatly increases the dramatic impact and also gives us insight into the wiles of this bandit.

PREPARATION AND AFTERMATH

Most of the aftermath moments in this film belong either to the three men under the Rashomon Gate or to the individual giving testimony to the inquest (including the medium in the place of the slain husband). These moments help us to digest the new twists the story has taken and the implications of those twists, and to prepare us for the next variation. So some of the preparation also takes place with these three men.

But much of the preparation occurs within the characters' stories. Again, because Tajomaru's tale is the most elaborate, richly developed, and complete, it uses the tools of screenwriting more than the others. When the bandit is sleeping under the tree with no greater want than to keep up with his scratching, it is an introduction to his indolent life, but it is also preparation by contrast for the scenes to come. When the veil blows aside and he sees Masago, he leaps into action, races down the hill, and becomes a manic and persistent interloper in the travels of this couple. Later, when he has lured the woman into the woods on the pretext that her husband was bitten by a snake, they rush through the woods, directly preparing us for the energy of their fight, when she tries to stab him.

PLANTING AND PAYOFF

The woman's hat, the man's hat, the rope, and the dagger are all planted very early in the film—in the woodcutter's account of finding the body. These items, in particular the dagger, all have later payoffs in the various versions of events. The dagger is the most critical item, because it plays a role in every single version of the events and even comes into play in the framing story of the three men at the gate, since the woodcutter is accused in the end of stealing it.

ELEMENTS OF THE FUTURE
AND ADVERTISING

Within the early part of the recounting of the stories, we come to learn the style of the storytelling—that we will get various versions of the same events. When the priest and the woodcutter commiserate over these horrible events and speak of all three people, it is a form of advertising that lets us know to expect at least those versions, though it still comes as a surprise that one version is told by a ghost. The woodcutter's story is not advertised.

And the testimonies of the three principals before the inquest all have elements of the future in them. At the very least, we already know there was a murder, but at first we don't know who died, and all along we're not quite sure how the death occurred, and by whose hand. When Tajomaru testifies that he killed the man, it pushes us into the future of his story by making us curious about how and why and under what circumstances. When Masago testifies, she says that the bandit sneered at her husband and she ran after him. This too gives us an impetus into the story, something to anticipate and wonder about. And when Takehiro testifies through the medium that the bandit consoled his wife, we wonder what direction this version will take.

PLAUSIBILITY

The vast majority of events in this story are fully within the realm of believability; even among the conflicting statements, each version of events seems at least plausible. The only area where suspension of disbelief is required is in the testimony of the slain husband through the medium. The three men under Rashomon Gate take this testimony as a matter of course, implying that this is a completely acceptable thing in their world, in the twelfth century. But this alone is not enough for a modern film audience.

Instead, the entire matrix of the film helps to persuade us to accept this as readily as the three men do. This is a story about perception and reality, about what is true versus what is believed to be true, what one person accepts that contradicts what another person accepts. Because these questions and issues are already in the audience's mind and are being actively wrestled with through two already disparate versions of the events, it is a relatively easy leap for us to go one step further and accept the medium/husband as a witness. We do so not because we believe it is true, but because we believe that *they* believe it is true. We are given three other conflicting stories, each told with heartfelt earnestness; why should this one be singled out for a special degree of disbelief?

ACTION AND ACTIVITY

This is a film in which the action is much more important to the storytelling than is the dialogue. A marvelous example of an action with a purpose behind it comes when Tajomaru offers his sword to Takehiro shortly after they first meet. He doesn't really want to sell him contraband, but he does want to inspire a measure of trust in a man who clearly does not trust him. There is no better way than by apparently disarming himself. Another example of an action comes in the woodcutter's account, when Masago taunts both men about their masculinity, about what real men would do in these circumstances. She is willfully inciting them to fight over her and her honor.

Examples of mere activity come when the tramp tears wood off the building to make a fire, when he wrings his clothes and dries them over the fire. These are actions he takes for no purpose other than what is on the surface of the act.

DIALOGUE

For the most part, the telling of the various tales does not depend too heavily on dialogue. Yet under the Rashomon Gate, where the three members of the "audience" react to and try to make sense of these conflicting stories, dialogue takes on a more important function. It is here that they explore the deeper implications of these events and what they mean to their own versions of the world. They are exploring the theme, but the tramp continually stops the priest from turning it into a sermon. Several lines of dialogue reflect back on the theme: "Men are only men. That's why they lie. They can't tell the truth, even to themselves"; "Men lie to deceive themselves"; and "We all want to forget something, so we create stories." These come dangerously close to stating the theme in forthright and thesis-like form, yet because the three characters are in conflict themselves, and because none of them dominates the other two, the writers manage to avoid the pitfall of preaching directly to the audience.

VISUALS

The visual design of this film is stunning. Every shot and every movement of the camera seem to support the actions of the characters or the reactions of the audience—us or the on-screen audience under the gate. This is true from the stasis of the testimony shots to the camera racing with the action running through the woods. Different visual compositions are used for the various versions. In the bandit's version, two-shots of him and the woman or of him and the man dominate. (A two-shot is a shot in which only two people are in the frame, most often tightly together.) These two-shots support his contention that he takes them both on separately. In the man's version, two-shots of the bandit with his wife are contrasted with singles (one person in the frame) on him. This helps to demonstrate visually that he feels his wife and the bandit are against him. In the wife's version, the bandit barely exists, leaving a few two-shots with her and her husband, but a predominance of singles depicts the wife-versus-husband conflict. And in the woodcutter's version, the three-shot (all three characters in the frame at once) dominates, almost always with the woman between the two men, visually depicting the conflict dynamics, showing the triangle this story is about.

But, well beyond these patterns, the camera, the staging, and the choices Kurosawa makes help to point up the dynamics between people. When the tramp is trying to weasel the story out of the woodcutter, he is seen practically perched on his shoulder like his conscience. When the woman succumbs to the bandit's kisses in his version, the "ceiling" of the forest and the flickering light through it help to give a little lyricism or romance to what is inherently an ugly reality. When, in the woodcutter's version, the woman provokes the men to fight, there is a marvelous shot of her between the two swords poised for battle, which separates the men behind them and puts her at the core with the weapons; it is her battle they are fighting. And another time in the same version, she is between the men, prostrate between the bandit's legs, with her husband in the background, again visually clarifying the very nature of the conflict.

DRAMATIC SCENES

A particularly marvelous example of a well-made dramatic scene occurs when the bandit first confronts the man and woman in the woods. We know that he is after the woman, and we watch with fascination as he does not betray his want even while in pursuit of his opportunity. It is fascinating to see how this seemingly shiftless man sets the samurai ever more at ease. He is obviously a bandit and would not be believed by the man if he didn't act like one. So he acts like a bandit, but one who is none too clever and then one who willingly disarms himself. Once the samurai has accepted the sword to look at, the bandit has won; he has gained the man's confidence by admitting to a level of dishonesty, but one that has nothing to do with his real intent. The fact that this is done with only modest use of dialogue makes it a scene well worth studying.

SPECIAL NOTES

This film is an exploration of the relative nature of truth and a search for an absolute truth. It graphically depicts how reality is filtered through the point of view of the perceiver. In other words, more than just beauty is in the eye of the beholder. What is real and what is believed actually to have happened seem to depend on who saw it and how that person filtered it through his or her own perspective. These are the questions the viewer is left to wrestle with upon seeing this film, and it is a testament to the effectiveness of the filmmaking that we aren't so much given "answers"—the filmmaker's philosophy—as that we are given intriguing questions and a perfect context in which to grapple with them.

Here each of the stories told about the same events is distorted by the point of view of the different tellers: the bandit sees it as a valiant fight, and that he has won the woman's love; the woman feels that she has been wronged by the bandit and then wronged again by the cold, hateful husband; the husband also feels that he was wronged by the bandit, but instead of deserting his wife, he feels betrayed by her; and the woodcutter sees the fight as cowardly on both sides and perceives all three of them as weak and treacherous. Each of them is "right" about the truth of his or her tale from his or her own point of view. And each of them does the honorable thing in his or her own version. This goes back to what the tramp says: "We all want to forget something, so we create stories."

Another interesting offshoot of the dramaturgy of this film is the fact that there is only resolution in the framing story. What we are left with from the main story—the four interwoven stories about the same events—is a host of questions and some opinions, which we will discover are different from the opinions of others in the same audience. This story sparks intellectual and philosophical curiosity and rumination, but it is not fully resolved. In the framing story, however, the three men discover the abandoned child and each of them acts in a different way toward it. Here we are given something that is not a "solution" to the dilemma of belief and conscience that the main story has provoked. Rather, we are given an opportunity to feel that there is at least some hope for mankind: however difficult the problems of communication and perception, however impossible the quest for an absolute truth, there is at least a sense of humanity still alive in the human spirit—in the twelfth century and in the twentieth. That is quite a feeling in the 1990s; imagine the impact it had just six years after the end of World War II, coming from filmmakers in a devastated and defeated land.

sex, lies, and videotape

(1989)
Written and directed by Steven Soderbergh

A very low-budget, independently produced film, and a first effort for its writer/director, this film took the world by storm when it was first seen at the Sundance Film Festival and then won top honors at the Cannes Film Festival. A talky and low-key film that is decidedly far afield from mainstream Hollywood fare, it won all this attention, and put Soderbergh on the map as a filmmaker, through the quality of the writing and the thoughtful story, as well as the performances he elicited from its small cast.

SYNOPSIS

While Ann Melaney discusses with her psychiatrist her obsession about all the garbage in the world and her sexual problems—both with her husband and by herself—her husband, John, is having a passionate tryst with her sister, Cynthia. At the same time, an unwanted house guest, Graham, a college buddy of her husband's, is heading toward their house and her life. After an awkward meeting of Graham and Ann, John comes home to find his former friend totally different from himself, not materialistic or ambitious, readily admitting all manner of faults, but protesting strongly that he is not a liar, he does not lie.

Ann helps Graham find an apartment in town; it seems he is moving back, perhaps to be near an old girlfriend who dumped him years ago. John picks this time, with Ann safely out of the way, to make love with Cynthia in his own bed. In a moment of surprising candor, Ann admits to Graham that she doesn't care much for sex, and Graham tells her that he is impotent, that he can't become aroused in the presence of anyone—though he wasn't always this way. The two of them strike up a friendship, while Cynthia asks both John and Ann about Graham, betraying intense interest in him, which both of them interpret as meaning that she wants to sleep with him.

When Ann visits Graham unexpectedly, she discovers a large collection of videotapes, which he reluctantly admits are interviews with women who tell him intimate details of their sex lives and sometimes do things for the camera, although he never touches the women. Ann runs off in horror. Cynthia's curiosity about Graham reaches critical mass when Ann won't tell her what Graham did that was so offensive, so she visits him. Once she finds out about Graham, his videotaping and his hang-ups, Cynthia can't resist making a tape herself, which turns out to be a particularly revealing exercise. When she admits it to Ann and John (separately), they are both aghast, but she is rather excited about it.

Ann's growing suspicions about John finally erupt, and she accuses him of having an affair and she even suspects it might be Cynthia. John looks her straight in the eye and lies, eventually convincing her it's all in her mind. When he meets with Cynthia, he lies to her as well. But Ann can't shake her feelings, and in a cleaning frenzy she finds one of Cynthia's earrings in her bedroom and knows she was right.

In a blind flight, Ann is surprised to find herself at Graham's house, and he confirms what she has just discovered; he knows from his interview with Cynthia that she is sleeping with John. Now changed—assertive and swearing—Ann tells Graham that she wants to make one of these videotapes and he reluctantly agrees. At home she drops a bomb on John, demanding a divorce. She tells him she made a tape with Graham and implies she made love with him, too. In a fury, John goes over to Graham's, throws him out, and views the tape of Ann. In it, Ann and Graham break down each other's defenses and come to grips with their own sexual problems. When they begin to make love, they shut off the video camera.

John leaves, devastated but no wiser as he tries to get a vengeful dig at Graham, who then tears up his collection of videotapes and destroys his camera. John loses a major client because he has been neglecting his work, and he lies to himself that he's better off without his marriage to Ann. And Ann goes back to work, feeling independent and strong, and as the story ends, she gets together with Graham for the beginning of a relationship.

PROTAGONIST AND OBJECTIVE

The protagonist of this story is less obvious than it is in a good many films, in large part because Ann is a passive central character, one who is not actually pursuing something different from what she has, but rather wishes only to maintain what she thinks she has. Ann is the central character, and the other three principal characters all gain their importance more through their relationships with her than with each other—her sister, her husband, and the guest in her house who will be the catalyst for her change. What she wants, what she actively tries to do, is to stick her head in the sand and avoid the spiralling realities of her life.

OBSTACLES

The obstacles to Ann maintaining what she thinks is her status quo are many, both interior and exterior. On the outside is the fact that her husband is unfaithful to her with her sexpot sister. On the inside are her obsessions, which she uses to hide from herself and from her growing suspicions, not just about her husband, but about herself as well. Add to this volatile circumstance a character from the outside who is capable of insinuating himself inside her world—and, more important, into her psyche—and he becomes an obstacle to her status quo as well.

The obstacles in this story have a particular importance because they come to Ann more than they stand in her way. She is the passive character who is put upon by circumstances and events that eventually force her into an active role in her own life and story. Just like Rick in *Casablanca*, Ann doesn't want to act and works very hard to avoid it, but circumstances— external and internal—will not allow her to remain uninvolved.

PREMISE AND OPENING

Ann, a lovely but neurotic woman, is married to a very successful and incredibly selfish man who is having an affair with her sister. At the same time, Ann and her husband are no longer making love, since, in part, she no longer wants him to touch her. She tells herself that she really doesn't care much for sex and even that happiness is overrated. Into this world comes an equally neurotic young man, one who is impotent and who videotapes women's private confessions.

Soderbergh chose to open with three parallel lines of action, held together by the dialogue from Ann's session with her psychiatrist carrying over the other lines. We are shown Ann's obsessions with the outside world, how she diminishes her lack of interest in sex and her inability to come to grips with her sexuality, even while alone. At the same time, we see her husband's command position in his law firm and his torrid lovemaking with Ann's sister. Also, we have Graham's arrival in town and preparation for meeting Ann and John. We learn of his quirks, his relative poverty, and his transient solitude.

MAIN TENSION, CULMINATION, AND RESOLUTION

The main tension asks whether Ann will be able to keep reality at bay once she has had an intimate discussion with Graham—more intimate, in fact, than she has ever had with John. We have seen her huge defenses at work, armor that neither John nor her psychiatrist seems to be able to penetrate. But in a simple, disarming moment of mutual revelation, Graham opens a chink in her armor that threatens to change her approach to life.

The culmination comes when Ann, after finding her sister's earring and putting two and two together, finally and definitively goes into action, shedding her passivity.

The resolution of this story comes chronologically a little sooner than it does in the telling of the story. In strict sequence of time, Ann and Graham shut off the videotape and make love before she confronts John, demanding a divorce, and before he knows how she came to this position. But because the telling of a story does not have to follow chronology, and events can be shifted around for maximum dramatic impact, Soderbergh wisely chose to delay the resolution until the other factors—John most particularly—were in place. When he views the tape of Ann and Graham, and then we go into the reality of their making the tape, we arrive at the resolution, which occurs when they make love.

THEME

Thematically, this story revolves around lying. Ann is a world-class champion at lying to herself, making herself believe that her foremost concerns are the world's garbage and babies dying in Africa, when those are but a smoke screen to mask her real concerns and terrors. John knowingly lies to everyone—his clients, his wife, his mistress, his old friend, his secretary. Cynthia also lies, but in a vastly different way. She is utterly honest with herself and her feelings—she is emotionally honest with John, she is forthright with Graham, and she is generally honest with Ann about everything from having made the videotape with Graham to her feelings about the present for their mother. And Graham calls himself a recovering pathological liar, someone who has now sworn himself to complete, if brutal, honesty.

UNITY

Action gives unity to this story, but because the central character is passive, there is a slight variation on the unity of action. It could be said to be a unity of *re*action; all the pressures that come to bear in the story revolve around Ann and her inability to face up to the realities of her life. She has a strong defensive shell; she comes out briefly when she and Graham talk about themselves, then scurries back in to safety, comes back out, only to be burned by the revelation of Graham's videotaping, then goes back in to safety, and so on. The unity then stems from the continuously evolving challenges to her armor and her reactions to these challenges. These reactions constitute a pattern of action—tentative forays outside of the shell, frantic dives back into it—which helps to give the story focus and clarity.

EXPOSITION

Even though a good deal of the early exposition is delivered primarily in dialogue, much of it effectively uses conflict to mask the expositional quality. In Ann's opening session with her psychiatrist, we learn a great deal about her life, circumstances, and problems. Yet the psychiatrist continually puts her on the spot and at times embarrasses her with his straightforward questions, creating within her palpable conflicts that make her revelations both difficult and reluctant. Because of this visible inner conflict, we don't see the exposition as too easy or convenient.

The exposition on John and Cynthia is shown much more with action, and is given irony by being played out in contrast to Ann's discussion with her psychiatrist. And the early exposition on Graham is delivered virtually without dialogue—shaving and changing clothes in a gas-station men's room, the stuff in his trunk, some of his quirkiness.

A deceptively simple example of exposition being delivered directly to the audience in dialogue occurs in the scene with Graham and Ann after they have found him an apartment. On the surface we have two people who willingly tell each other, and thus the audience, about themselves, revealing information that we couldn't have known otherwise. This is seemingly a weak circumstance. But because of the startling nature of the revelations, particularly Graham's, and the disarming candor of the delivery, there is again a very strong subtext of conflict, largely created within Ann. Her grappling with this unexpected turn of events is another effective use of an inner conflict that masks the expositional elements within the scene.

CHARACTERIZATION

Ann is clearly characterized from the opening scene through the use of her obsessions and with her self-consciousness even in front of her psychiatrist. These cut right to the core of her objective, which is to hide from herself, to throw up smoke screens. Later, Graham directly points out to her her self-consciousness, underlining its importance. Graham's solitude and rootlessness are also established very quickly and then given strength by his desire to "have only one key," not to burden himself with two, three, or four keys.

John is characterized in part by what he has—a "power" office with a commanding view, the trappings of success—and in part by what he does. Nearly his first act on screen is coming up with a lie to reschedule a client, then he smugly goes after what he wants—Cynthia. And Cynthia is characterized by what she wants—which, surprisingly, is not John. Rather, what she wants is to be desired, to be as prized by men as her sister is, and to have as good a time as self-indulgence can give her.

DEVELOPMENT OF THE STORY

Again, owing to the passivity of the central character, the development of this story is a slight variation from the norm. Ann is in active pursuit of escape from the realities of her life, so the development of this story deals in large part with escalations of the assault of reality upon her.

At first Graham seems like a perfect friend, sensitive and easy to talk to, and his impotence means he is not a threat to Ann's avoidance of sexuality. When she discovers that he makes these videotapes, he becomes a threat, which scares her off. Yet her reaction to that threat is what intrigues her sister, who has the opposite attitude toward all things sexual. When Cynthia acts out of her own character, not only making a videotape but openly admitting to Ann that she has done so, this increases the pressure on Ann.

When Ann finds Cynthia's earring in her bedroom, it prompts her into action, which to her at this moment translates into making her own videotape with Graham. But that act itself prompts the next development in the story. In the past, Graham's tapes have been made with women with whom he had no more relationship than he had with Cynthia, but now he and Ann have a friendship. As they attempt to make the tape, this connection and the changes going on inside Ann force the session to be radically different from past ones. They both come to grips with their sexual and relationship problems and see the solution partly in each other. And even the making of the tape, with its personal repercussions for Ann, is also the instigator of a further development, when John views it and it helps bring the marriage to an end.

DRAMATIC IRONY

From the very beginning, this film utilizes dramatic irony for a central element. We know from the opening parallel scenes that Ann's husband and sister are having an affair. This critical bit of information is dealt with and escalated throughout much of the story while we wait for Ann to figure out the truth, which she does upon finding the earring.

At the same time, there is another aspect of this story that we fully expect will be an irony, only to be surprised that it is not. When Cynthia makes the videotape with Graham and he has promised secrecy, we expect this tape and its existence to be an ironic underpinning of the rest of the story. But because of her nature, it is Cynthia who reveals to both Ann and John that she made it and everything that she did.

Because this is a story about lying, playing with the use of irony is an effective tool—both what we expect will be told and what we expect will remain a secret can have a significant impact on the audience. For instance, when Ann unexpectedly visits Graham and he is watching what we learn is a rather racy little homemade tape, we fully expect him to keep this knowledge from Ann. Yet his revelation to her is in keeping with his character, and it thematically ties with the story for him to be forthright.

PREPARATION AND AFTERMATH

A fine little scene of preparation comes the last night that Graham is staying at Ann's house. She gets up and goes to the side of the couch where he is sleeping and just looks at him, while music plays and moody, intimate lighting makes her and the whole setting seem romantic and peaceful and calm. The next scene is one with her psychiatrist, who asks about the unwanted visitor and Ann has to admit it wasn't bad at all—a statement that is vastly strengthened not only by the action of her staring at him, but by the setting and mood of the circumstances.

A good example of an aftermath of one scene being the preparation for the next comes when Ann accuses John of having an affair with her sister. He successfully lies his way through it, but still finds himself upset and he sits on the edge of the bed. With a nice transition, we see him sitting in a similar way on the edge of a bed, only this time with Cynthia, and the subject is very different, for she is revealing that she made a videotape with Graham. His aftermath of being upset from one scene carries over into another kind of upset in the next, as the transition turns the tables and transforms John from betrayer to betrayed.

PLANTING AND PAYOFF

The most crucial planting and payoff in the story is Cynthia's earring, which ultimately reveals to Ann that her suspicions are well founded. When Cynthia comes to John's house for the fantasy tryst of making love in her sister's bed, she takes her earrings off and the moment is emphasized. Later, when Ann finds one, we know exactly when it was lost.

A planting and payoff that eventually achieves the metaphorical level is Graham's videotape collection. Once the tapes are introduced, they become an element in the telling of the story, discussed, created, and found to be titillating or horrifying. But by the very end of the story, when Graham is tearing them apart frantically, they have come to represent his isolation, his distance from the world and women and relationships, the very things he has finally conquered with Ann. At this point a cinematic metaphor has been created.

ELEMENTS OF THE FUTURE AND ADVERTISING

There are numerous instances of advertising. There is talk of Graham finding an apartment and Ann helping him with the search. Cynthia says that she would like to make love at John's house in her sister's bed. And Ann suggests to Cynthia that they get a present for their mother together. Each of these points toward a future event.

An effective element of the future occurs when Graham tells John and Ann over dinner his first night there that he doesn't lie, that he never lies. This prediction of future behavior is put to the test later in the story.

PLAUSIBILITY

There is nothing in this story that couldn't quite believably happen. There is no story element that requires the audience to suspend its disbelief, and the whole sense of plausibility about the film is substantially aided by the naturalistic performances of the actors.

ACTION AND ACTIVITY

There are two interesting scenes in which the same moment is an action for one character and an activity for another. When John and Cynthia make love in Ann's bed, it is merely an activity for John; it has no deeper purpose than what is obvious on the surface. But for Cynthia, who is competing with the sister she has always envied, this is an action, a moment of triumph. A similar thing happens when she goes to make a videotape with Graham. He does it for the same reasons he has done it with other women; there is no other intention there. But Cynthia is again acting out that same competition with Ann, convincing herself of her superiority over her sister. This compulsion of hers to outdo her sister is why she finds it necessary to reveal the videotaping to her two intimates, Ann and John.

DIALOGUE

This is undeniably a talky picture, which makes it feel more like a European film than one made in Hollywood. Yet, surprisingly, even for American audiences, it doesn't seem slow and it doesn't seem as if there is too much talk. This comes from the fact that when a film has something in abundance that the audience wants or appreciates, the audience will overlook all manner of things that would otherwise bother them. In this case, the film delivers so much wit, humor, and, in particular, pathos, that we barely notice how often the scenes are just two people sitting and talking.

This sense of good, effective dialogue is greatly aided by the use of dramatic irony (see above), which helps tinge nearly every scene with double or even triple meanings, depending on which characters know what, and on what we know that they don't. This establishment of irony that continually changes can help dialogue immeasurably.

An example of a straightforward use of dialogue to help reveal character is Ann's aversion to four-letter words and any discussion that deals directly with sexuality. By the end, when she goes to Graham and insists on making a videotape to attack head-on this fear of discussing sex, she is using all the words she earlier abhorred. Thus the mere choice of words helps demonstrate her character change.

VISUALS

While this film doesn't have striking vistas or painterly compositions, there is a sophisticated visual style at work here, evidenced by the effective use of transitions that have a graphic and visual component. We are pulled into flashbacks through the video screen or through the camera itself, using the act of filmmaking to become a transition into the scene that was recorded.

Another effective use of a visual transition comes when Ann finds the earring and runs out to her car and holds her head. Suddenly she looks up and finds herself outside Graham's house without seeming to have driven. This visual transition emphasizes what is going on inside Ann—she hadn't consciously been aware of going to Graham's or even intending to go there, but rather seemed to wake up there. This makes the visual transition a subjective element that helps to put us inside the shoes of a character.

DRAMATIC SCENES

Sometimes the measure of the effectiveness of a scene is how much it can make the audience uncomfortable, squeamish, exhilarated, or excited—in other words, how aware we are of how viscerally we are reacting to the scene at hand. One scene that works very well by this measure is the first meeting of Ann and Graham, before John comes home. We already know that Ann dreads his arrival, and then, when he comes, the awkwardness between them becomes palpable. We desperately want them to find something chatty to fill the awkwardness and mask their discomfort, but the effectiveness of the scene comes from the fact that Soderbergh resists that want; he consciously and deliberately puts them through this awkward wringer, which has a lasting impact on us.

Another effective dramatic scene occurs when Ann comes to the bar to show Cynthia the dress that she bought for their mother. Two elements are added to this scene of conflict between the sisters. The first element is the drunk who insinuates himself into their interaction, heightening the stand-off between the sisters. The other is the phone call from John, which underlines the irony of the sisters' bickering over something rather inconsequential when there is a huge area that isn't being dealt with. It also lends a greater degree of subtext to Cynthia's remarks to Ann after the call.

SPECIAL NOTES

One of the more intriguing aspects of this film is not just that it got made at all, but that it enjoyed both critical and box-office success, in the United States and overseas. It has very little action, no special effects, no major stars, none of the elements traditionally thought to bring in an audience. What this film does have, however, is a story the audience can identify with; it has situations we have all felt—and suffered through; it has characters we recognize from our own lives; and, most important of all, the story is effectively told. Irony, revelation, and recognition, strong subtext, awkward and humiliating and difficult moments, surprises and startling revelations and marvelous naturalistic performances are all elements in making this story well told.

Annie Hall

(1977)
Written by Woody Allen and Marshall Brickman
Directed by Woody Allen

One of the most highly honored comedies of recent memory, *Annie Hall* is
perhaps the best achievement to date of one of the few true *auteurs* of
American cinema. As writer, director, and actor, Woody Allen has established himself as a complete filmmaker with an incredibly varied body of
work that ranges from manic silliness to somber, thoughtful introspection.
Perhaps because it is a delightful and delicate synthesis of the two extremes
of Allen's work, this film is considered by many of his fans around the
world to be his best. It won Academy Awards for Best Picture, Best Actress,
Best Screenplay, and Best Director, and Allen was also nominated as Best
Actor.

SYNOPSIS

Stand-up comedian Alvy Singer directly addresses the camera and tells
about his life, starting with an incident in his childhood that shows his
existential angst. We see his family in Coney Island, his childhood libido
in the classroom, and we see him on a television talk show as an adult.
While he waits outside a New York theater for Annie, he is accosted by
working-class fans and "rescued" when her cab arrives. But she is irritable,
which is only made worse when he refuses to see the movie they were going
to, because they missed the first two minutes. He cajoles her into going to
see *The Sorrow and the Pity* one more time, but while they wait in line, an
obnoxious patron behind them pontificates until Alvy brings Marshall Mc-
Luhan out of the wings to put him down.

Later, in bed, Alvy wants to make love with Annie, but she doesn't want
to, and brings up his first wife, Alison. A flashback takes us backstage at
an Adlai Stevenson rally, where Alvy meets Alison just as he is about to
go on as a comic. Later, in bed with Alison, who is now his wife, Alvy is
obsessed with the Kennedy assassination to the point where she accuses
him of using it as an excuse for not making love with her.

In a beach house, Alvy and Annie are enjoying their best times, having
fun trying to cook lobsters. Then, walking on the beach, Annie tells Alvy

about her old boyfriends and together they "visit" her past and look in on her with these other men.

With his second wife, the ambitious and "proper" Robin, Alvy is being conducted around a literary party while all he wants to do is watch a basketball game on TV or make love, despite the party guests. Later, while they are making love, Robin is distracted by a siren and cannot climax. She takes a Valium and he takes a cold shower. Alvy talks on about his Jewish paranoia while his buddy Rob talks on about going to California, the new mecca. They meet two women for tennis, and this is the first meeting of Alvy and Annie. They have an awkward meeting after the game and finally end up with her giving him a ride uptown. They keep starting to say good-bye and not leaving until Alvy winds up at her apartment. Over wine and an increasingly difficult exchange—counterpointed by subtitles of their thoughts contrasted with their words—Alvy finally asks her out.

Annie sings before an inattentive audience, then afterwards Alvy kisses her on the way to getting something to eat. Over a sandwich, Alvy discusses his ex-wives. In bed together, Alvy and Annie can't get over how good they were. As they get to know each other, Alvy recommends books for Annie with "death" in the title and they comment on all the "types" they see in Central Park before he declares that he loves her. But when she starts moving into his apartment, he seems to panic at the thought that she's giving up her own apartment, their safety valve. Back at the beach house, Annie pores over adult-education course offerings that Alvy has suggested, but he wants to make love—insisting she not smoke marijuana this time. While he starts to make love with her, her "spirit" gets out of bed and wants to know where her drawing pads are.

Alvy suffers through an interview with a horrible comic who is looking for a writer, then performs for a college audience in Wisconsin. Then he and Annie go to visit her family for a big Sunday dinner. He thinks Grammy Hall sees him as Hassidic, then contrasts his family with hers, showing both simultaneously through a split-screen. Annie's brother reveals a death-wish fantasy about driving, then terrifies Alvy by driving them to the airport in the rain.

Back in New York, Alvy is now jealous of Annie's apparent involvement with her adult-education instructor and she counters that he never considers her smart enough or intellectual enough. Annie returns from her first session with her psychiatrist, which Alvy is paying for. She seems to have made more progress in one session than he has in fifteen years with his psychiatrist. But Annie dreams that Alvy is suffocating her, so he interviews people on the street about the durability of love. In an animated parody of

Snow White, Rob suggests just the girl for Alvy to date. He and the woman, a gangly *Rolling Stone* reporter, go to see the Maharishi, then end up in bed. But Alvy gets an emergency call from Annie and rushes to her apartment only to discover the emergency is a spider in her bathroom. After he tangles with the spider, he and Annie wind up in bed and vow never to break up again.

Rob, Annie, and Alvy drive back to the old Brooklyn neighborhood to "visit" with Alvy's past. For her birthday, Alvy gives Annie lingerie and a watch. She gives a good performance of "Seems Like Old Times" at a nightclub, which attracts the attention of Tony Lacey, a record producer from Los Angeles. Alvy turns down Tony's invitation to a party. Then, in split-screen with their respective psychiatrists, Annie and Alvy complain about the "constant" and "hardly ever" lovemaking of their relationship.

Alvy is introduced to cocaine by friends, but ends up destroying a lot of it by sneezing into it. Then, in Los Angeles, he and Annie are shown the Christmastime sights by Rob. Alvy is in town to deliver an award, but feels deathly ill. When he is replaced on the awards show, he feels just fine. Rob takes them to a Hollywood party, only to discover that it is at Tony Lacey's house. Tony wants to cut an album with Annie and have her stay at his house for six weeks to do it. Alvy tries to put the kibosh on the deal, but when they are flying home to New York, he and Annie conclude that they can't stay together. They divide up their books, and Alvy is advised to see other women.

He tries to find the same old magic with another woman by cooking lobsters at the beach house, but she is no fun. He calls Annie in Los Angeles and asks her to come back, but when she refuses, he flies there. He drives to meet her for lunch and proposes marriage. She turns him down, and he smashes up his car in the restaurant parking lot right afterwards. Rob bails him out of jail. Back in New York, Alvy watches a rehearsal of his first play, which is nearly an exact replication of the last scene with Annie—except that the guy leaves her only to have her run after him and agree to marry him. Alvy tells us he saw her again and they reminisced about old times, and parted amicably. In the end, he concludes that relationships are irrational and absurd, but we need them.

PROTAGONIST AND OBJECTIVE

In most films where the title is the name of a character, that character is the protagonist. However, in this case the central character is Alvy, not Annie. This is the story of his life, and his objective is his quest for some kind of happiness, some means of finding or experiencing pleasure, love, and acceptance of life's limitations.

OBSTACLES

Alvy's most formidable obstacles to experiencing pleasure, love, and acceptance are his own neuroses. These are delineated from the very outset, from childhood and even from the jokes he tells. But Alvy's multiple neuroses are compounded by the women he falls in love with. We see how both Alison's and Robin's own problems conflict with Alvy's, convincing him all the more of the impossibility of his finding love and acceptance and the pleasure that should result from them. When he falls in love with Annie, he thinks that at last he has the key, only to discover that she has her own insecurities and hang-ups, which become obstacles to his quest, along with her growing sense of self and her ambitions.

PREMISE AND OPENING

A neurotic, Jewish New York comedian falls in love with a gentile midwestern singer in New York City and tries to find through this relationship the answer to his inability to accept and love life. Alvy's quest for love and understanding predate the start of the story.

For their opening, Allen and Brickman chose to have the central character speak directly to the camera, telling jokes that reflect on his life and philosophy. He alludes to a breakup with Annie, then turns to describing his childhood, complete with his budding neuroses and angst. These early, subjectively told scenes show not so much the reality of how he grew up, but rather the inner emotional state he brought from his childhood into his adulthood. This is evidenced by the end of this first childhood sequence, when he is on a TV talk show making jokes of his neurotic existence.

MAIN TENSION, CULMINATION, AND RESOLUTION

The main tension asks whether Alvy can find the key to his future happiness in this relationship with Annie. It begins when they meet and get together after tennis, even though we have known from the first scene that they would get together. The question is not whether they will have a relationship, but rather whether it will work for Alvy; therefore we must see the context before the main tension becomes clear—who he is, what his hang-ups are, what his past relationships have been like, and how he and Annie manage to get together at all.

The culmination occurs when they are flying back from Los Angeles and decide that they must break up. Our protagonist has gone as far as he can with trying to get what he needs from this relationship to fix his problem, and the attempt has failed.

The resolution comes after he rehearses his "improved" version of his affair with Annie in the play and he relives the best times they had while reminiscing with her. It is here that he concludes that there isn't a perfect key for him, there isn't a relationship that will solve his trouble with the acceptance of love and the experience of pleasure, but that love relationships are nonetheless worthwhile because "we need the eggs."

THEME

When this story was being written and shot, its working title was *Anhedonia*, which means the inability to experience pleasure. While it was quite rightly concluded that this was not a title that would attract a wide audience, anhedonia has remained as the theme of the story. Right from the opening direct-to-the-camera scene, Alvy talks about how miserable life is, and how it's over way too soon. At various other times he speaks of how we should be thankful when we are miserable because it could be worse, we could be horrible. And in the end he concludes that misery is worthwhile.

Annie has a different variation on the same theme. She too starts out with numerous hang-ups and difficulty with pleasure, not so much in accepting it as in allowing it. But as she grows and becomes more self-confident, she is able to enjoy the pleasure of her success and her new life. And Rob is the perfect contrast to Alvy. He is the hedonist, the exact opposite of the anhedonist that Alvy is. Rob lives only for pleasure, from fake laugh tracks to twins in bed to the feel-good life he always promotes to Alvy.

UNITY

Unity is critical to a story that is told in this manner, for it never follows chronology, and at first glance there doesn't seem to be a clear-cut pursuit of a goal. Yet with the illusion of the film screen broken, with the protagonist speaking directly to the audience, bringing alive his fantasies and his fears, standing aside and watching his own childhood or Annie with a past lover, we are constantly put into Alvy's shoes, inside his skin. So even though he might not always know what he is pursuing, we identify with him and see that his whole relationship with Annie has come to be what he thinks is his last-ditch effort to find pleasure, love, and happiness in this miserable thing we call existence. This pursuit, which he doesn't always understand himself, is the unifying element of the story, and thus it is the unity of action that holds the film together.

EXPOSITION

The exposition is always handled with humor and, more often than not, is dramatized rather than alluded to. We find out about his childhood by going there to his home, to his family, and to his classroom. We find out about Annie's old boyfriends by seeing them, standing aside and watching them. In all of these expositional scenes there is at least humor and most of the time conflict as well—sometimes between the "modern" Annie and Alvy and the "remembered" version, as in the scene where Annie and her actor boyfriend talk at a party. At other times the conflict is within the remembered moment, as when young Alvy asserts that the universe is expanding and the obnoxious doctor tries to chide him out of it.

CHARACTERIZATION

Alvy is characterized by his neuroses, his obsessions with death and guilt and *The Sorrow and the Pity.* He is a man who believes that all people are either miserable or horrible, who sees anti-semitism wherever he turns, who doesn't even allow his success as a comedian to cheer him up or make him feel good. By the end, when he is reminiscing about all the old times with Annie, he has come to realize that what may have seemed like misery to him at the time was really pleasure and that he can experience it, even if it is sometimes delayed.

Annie is characterized by her constant worry that she doesn't come off as intellectual enough. Like Alvy, she fails to see her strengths as strengths, she thinks that her utter charm is flakiness. She is vulnerable to his suggestions about adult-education classes because of this fear about her intellectual capacity, and she is touchy about his comments. Yet she is a much more open person; she is unfazed by referring to her "sexual problem" in public and is able to get more done in one session with her psychiatrist than Alvy has in years of therapy.

DEVELOPMENT OF THE STORY

This story develops completely outside the realm of the chronology of the events. By breaking the illusion of the film as "reality," by speaking directly to the audience and freeing up the storytellers to go wherever they want— past, present, fantasy, animation—they have made it possible for the development of the story to flow with the emotional side of the protagonist rather than the sequence of events. We begin with Alvy, his life and his obsessions and neuroses. When we first see Annie, we see no potential for her to help deflect his course from these problems. We learn of his past failures with former wives, and only later do we get the first meeting of Alvy and Annie, which promotes our hope that this will be the relationship that will help him overcome his anhedonia.

Once they are together and Alvy's problems are clear, we follow a somewhat more straightforward chronology, but still have detours into the past, and fantasy and animation come into play. But still the thread of the development is Alvy's emotional progress, not the sequence of events of his life with Annie. And the large leaps of time in the third act are made possible by telling the story with this freedom, this connection to the emotional rather than the temporal.

DRAMATIC IRONY

Dramatic irony is utilized in a number of ways. When Annie and Alvy are trying to impress each other shortly after they meet by talking about aesthetics, we see the subtitles of what they are really thinking as an ironic contrast to their mumbo-jumbo. Straightforward dramatic irony is used when Alvy gets out of bed with the *Rolling Stone* reporter to go kill spiders at Annie's house. Annie asks if he was with someone, and he lies, though we know the truth.

But there is also a kind of reflective use of irony employed in the telling of this story. Alvy asks people on the street to comment on the events of the story or aspects of their lives that reflect on the story. Also, through the use of split-screen contrasts—the two psychiatric sessions and the two families, even commenting on each other—Allen has employed an irony that involves the audience in the story and forces us to reflect on what is happening. Then there are the visits to his past, the adult Alvy in his school chair, Alvy and Annie watching a younger Annie and her actor boyfriend. In all these instances we are made privy to something that someone on screen doesn't know, we hear both the past and the present, we are made to reflect on both sides at once. In a sense we become part of the irony, we participate, which is one of the major goals of using irony, to involve the audience more deeply in the story.

PREPARATION AND AFTERMATH

The scenes of preparation used here are often quite traditional uses of the dramatic form, while the aftermath scenes are often very different. For instance, right before Annie is first introduced, Alvy is accosted by "the cast of *The Godfather*" outside the movie theater. He is put upon in a way that distresses him, and her arrival is seen as his rescue. But she is in a really bad mood and they are in instant conflict. The scene was one of direct preparation.

When Alvy and Annie walk on a pier and he declares that he loves her and "lurvs" her, it is a preparation by contrast for the scene to come when she is moving into his apartment and he goes into a panic about it. Late in the film, when he goes to California to ask her to marry him, there is a scene of preparation with the waitress before the scene. And here there is an effective and traditional scene of aftermath when he smashes his rental car into three cars in the parking lot.

But many other scenes of aftermath occur when he speaks directly to the camera or interviews people on the street. When he and Annie fight and she takes off in a cab, Alvy questions people on the street, who tell him that love fades and that shallowness works to keep a relationship together. After Annie has moved out of his apartment, a man on the street tells him she moved to California and a woman tells him to date other women. These aftermath scenes are another way in which the audience is enlisted to participate in the story.

PLANTING AND PAYOFF

A marvelous example of planting and payoff is young Alvy driving a bumper car at Coney Island. Throughout the story, Alvy's relationship with cars is emphasized—his terror at Annie's driving, his unwillingness to drive in California, and then his erratic attempt to drive when he comes to see her at the end. The payoff after she turns down his marriage proposal goes right back to his bumper-car days.

Another good example of contrasts making a plant and a payoff work effectively are the two lobster-cooking scenes. One of the best times we see Annie and Alvy have is their battle with the lobsters at the beach house. When he tries to re-create that same sense of fun with another woman it is a disaster. Another example of the same contrast between plant and payoff comes with her marijuana smoking when they make love. When they first make love, he finds it acceptable, but later it bothers him and it becomes a conflict, a distinct contrast is drawn. Books with "Death" in their titles form another plant, which we see in action early in their relationship; later it is paid off when they split up, when she turns down his proposal and he reuses it in his play that reconstructs that scene.

ELEMENTS OF THE FUTURE
AND ADVERTISING

From the very first time Alvy mentions Annie, it is in the context of breaking up, though for the most part the story is about their being together. So this early statement is a form of advertising. Rob constantly talks about going to California and urges Alvy to go with him. This is more of an element of the future, not a guarantee that the action will go to California but something of a prediction. And then, when they first meet Tony Lacey, he suggests they come to see him if they ever get out to California—another element of the future.

PLAUSIBILITY

We are never expected to believe that everything happens exactly as depicted. From the very first frame, this film breaks the illusion of reality that most films attempt to create for the audience. Rather we are encouraged to believe in the emotional reality of the experiences, while taking the actual depiction of events as exaggeration, hyperbole, and sometimes outright fantasy.

The method employed for getting us to suspend our disbelief is an interesting one. Here it is simply presented from the outset that this is the way this story will be told. If the protagonist talking directly to us isn't enough and if we believe that the young Alvy really did worry about the expanding universe just as shown, within a few minutes we have the adult Alvy sitting in his childhood school seat debating his interest in girls with his grade-school teacher. We have been led into a style of storytelling that does not ask us to believe anything happens exactly as presented, but rather that this is how the central character feels about what is depicted. His feelings thus become the governing factor in what we believe to be true or not.

ACTION AND ACTIVITY

A fine example of the difference between activity and action happens in the two lobster scenes. In the scene with Annie, for all the fun and happiness this scene represents, what happens in the scene is only activity. Beyond the surface level of just having fun together, neither of them has a hidden agenda, neither is pursuing a goal by trying to cook the lobsters. In the second scene, Alvy is trying to re-create a pleasant moment, to recapture something that the woman he is with knows nothing about. He has a goal, a hidden agenda, and therefore the scene shows him in an action.

When Annie calls Alvy in the middle of the night to come kill spiders, it is an action on her part. She wants them to get back together. The actual killing of the spiders is an activity, but the invitation and then her keeping him in her apartment are actions.

When Annie and Alvy offer each other rides after first meeting, it is action on both sides. Each of them wants to get a chance to get to know the other, and both are awkward about coming right out and saying it. So they banter about who will give whom a ride and who owns a car to prolong their interaction long enough to find a way to spend some more time together.

DIALOGUE

Witty and pithy dialogue occur throughout the story. From Alvy's speech about the miserable and the horrible to the *Rolling Stone* reporter's statement, "Sex with you is a real Kafkaesque experience," we see a sardonic wit at work. One of his best bits of dialogue is reserved for their decision to break up: "A relationship is like a shark, it has to keep moving or it dies. I think what we got on our hands is a dead shark."

But beyond the wit, dialogue is used effectively for contrasts and growth as well. When Alvy first suggests Annie take adult-education classes, he says that she "could meet lots of interesting professors." When she meets an interesting professor, Alvy lambasts adult education as being "such junk, the professors are so phony." Near the end, when Annie turns down Alvy's marriage proposal, she likens him to New York, a dying city. When he "fixes up reality" by redoing it in his play, he uses the same words, showing how much she has affected him.

VISUALS

The visuals of this film are constantly being used to break the illusion of reality. Just like the direct addresses to the camera and the "interviews" of people on the street, the visuals—and some of the paradoxes created by them—are in the service of maintaining this style of the story. When Alvy appears in his school seat and debates with the teacher, there isn't anything terribly stunning in the look of the moment, but it is the beginning of the freedom the camera has to show us things that are not really possible: Annie and Alvy watching her with another man in the past; "visiting" Alvy's old neighborhood by actually standing there in scenes from the past. It is also this same freedom that enables the split-screen contrasts of the psychiatric sessions and the two family dinners. And it also makes possible the fantasy side of what we can see—Alvy as a Hassidic Jew at the Halls' dinner table, the animated sequence, Annie's spirit getting out of bed while her body remains there.

DRAMATIC SCENES

The scene of Annie and Alvy after the tennis match is an incredibly memorable and vivid dramatic scene. Awkwardness is a very effective tool for revealing character because not only does it show us what makes someone awkward, but their attempts to overcome it can compound the discomfort and at the same time shed light on the nature of their character. This seemingly simple scene of offering a ride is both beautifully performed and marvelously conceived. She seems interested in him and he catches her in apparent inconsistencies or contradictions. For her part, she is nonplussed and resorts to affectations that are both endearing and charming—"la-de-da." We find ourselves hoping they will muddle through their impasse long before they finally conclude that she will give him a ride uptown. In a funny bit of staging that ends the scene, Alvy accidentally "pokes" her with the handle of his tennis racket on their way out the door. Alvy would surely admit to the Freudian implications, but it also hearkens back to his joke about the woman he dated briefly during the Eisenhower administration.

Another marvelous dramatic scene is the one at the beach house when Alvy doesn't want Annie to smoke marijuana before they make love. His want and hers are in direct conflict, and his attempts to distract them both from the fact that they are fighting, not making love, demonstrably fail when her spirit gets out of bed and wants her drawing pad. His desire to re-create their lovemaking to fit his fantasy—complete with red light and no marijuana—is at the heart of their conflict and is the very thing that is soundly defeated.

SPECIAL NOTES

There are many memorable moments in this film: Marshall McLuhan coming out from behind a sign to put down a pedantic nuisance; the subtitles contrasting real thoughts with the words the lovers say to each other shortly after meeting; Annie's spirit getting out of bed and debating with Alvy while her body is still there; Alvy enlisting people on the street into his problems and into the story. But perhaps the most important aspect of this film that makes it memorable is the way it literally externalizes the internal.

Externalizing the internal is a perennial problem for the screen story-teller—how do we know what someone really feels or thinks? Usually this is solved through putting characters into action so that what they do tells us what they feel and think, regardless of what they might say. This method is used at times in this story, but often we have the internal literally performed. Asking people on the street or bringing in Marshall McLuhan are fantasies literally acted out in the story. Going back to debate the school-teacher, criticizing Annie's old boyfriends as they pontificate, and talking directly to the audience are all extensions of the protagonist's fantasy life as well. We are made privy to his inner thoughts and feelings by being there, seeing them acted out and dramatized.

This would not work in every film, and it takes a confident filmmaker to attempt to lead the audience into accepting it as the way in which a story will be told. When it works, as it does here, it is absolutely marvelous. When it fails, as it often does in lesser hands, it can be dreadful and can send the audience literally or figuratively running for the exits.

Hamlet

(1948)
From the play by William Shakespeare
Directed by Laurence Olivier

Hamlet is, of course, at once a theatrical masterpiece, great literature, and one of the most popular and frequently performed plays ever written. It has also been successfully adapted to the screen on more than one occasion, and thus provides us with an opportunity to explore which of the ideas in this book are universal to drama and which are particular to cinema alone. The play was written to be performed before an Elizabethan audience, one accustomed to suspense melodramas and the lurid trappings of regicide, vengeance, madness, and assorted acts of violence. In short, it is perfectly tailored to the audience of today, if only we can get beyond the language in the dialogue and the moviegoing public's fear of literature. The play has a great many scenes, which in the theater have come to be grouped into five acts, though in the film versions these act breaks are blended into the continuum of the action, which covers a wide range of time and locations.

The film version we are working from won the Academy Award for Best Picture, as well as Best Actor for Olivier and Best Art Direction. It also garnered nominations for the costumes, for Olivier as director, for William Walton for the music, and for Jean Simmons as Ophelia.

SYNOPSIS

(Note: When the full text is performed, *Hamlet* is a very long play. Many of the more recent stage versions and most of the film adaptations of the play have abridged the text, often in differing ways. The following synopsis is for the entirety of the play and thus may include scenes or moments not evident in the film version you might watch. In the Olivier version of Hamlet, the Fortinbras and the Rosencrantz and Guildenstern story lines are excised completely, while other areas have been truncated in more subtle ways.)

A ghost resembling the late king has been seen walking the battlements of Elsinore. Horatio, a trusted friend of Prince Hamlet's, has been summoned to confront the ghost. While waiting, he speaks of the recent conflict between Denmark and Norway and worries that Fortinbras, whose father Hamlet killed in battle, might be preparing to retake the Norwegian lands lost to Denmark. When the ghost appears on schedule, it will not speak, and Horatio decides that Hamlet must be summoned.

The newly crowned king, Claudius, sends ambassadors to the king of Norway to persuade him to restrain Fortinbras, then grants permission to Laertes, son of his counselor Polonius, to return to his studies in France. With the support of Gertrude, his new queen and the mother of Hamlet, Claudius urges Hamlet to end his prolonged and excessive mourning for his father. But alone in his thoughts, Hamlet is repulsed by his mother's quick remarriage to his uncle Claudius, a man far inferior to his father. His rage over this marriage has left Hamlet bitter and disgusted with life itself. Later, Horatio tells Hamlet of the ghost of his father, and he agrees to join him in the watch to meet the ghost.

Laertes says good-bye to his sister Ophelia and warns her that Hamlet's attentions to her should not be taken seriously. Polonius gives Laertes advice on his journey, then insists that Ophelia not see Hamlet anymore. When Hamlet joins Horatio on the watch, the ghost appears and beckons him. Hamlet cannot be restrained from following the ghost. Once alone with it, Hamlet discovers the ghost is indeed that of his dead father, and the old king commands his son to avenge his murder. The ghost says that Claudius seduced his wife, Gertrude, then poured poison into his ear, killing him. The father-ghost urges leniency for Hamlet's mother, and Hamlet swears vengeance on Claudius for the murder. The ghost disappears and Horatio finds Hamlet, who refuses to tell him what happened. But he does demand a vow of secrecy, no matter how strange his actions might become.

Polonius worries about Laertes's life in France and sends a servant to spy on him. Then Ophelia reveals to her father that she encountered Hamlet acting irrationally. Polonius sees this supposed madness as the result of his unrequited love for Ophelia, and decides to tell Claudius. Meanwhile, Rosencrantz and Guildenstern, two old friends of Hamlet's, are brought to Claudius and instructed to find out what they can about Hamlet's strange behavior.

The ambassadors sent to Norway report that Fortinbras has been persuaded to make war on "the Polack" instead, but to do so he must cross Denmark. Claudius is delighted by the success of his mission. When Polonius tells Claudius that Hamlet has been driven mad by his unrequited love for Ophelia, Claudius is doubtful, but agrees to spy on an arranged meeting between Hamlet and Ophelia. When Polonius encounters Hamlet, his behavior confirms Polonius's idea that the prince has lost his reason.

Rosencrantz and Guildenstern find Hamlet, who guesses at the true reason for their visit and they cannot deny it. Polonius arrives with a troupe of traveling actors, and Hamlet welcomes them warmly. A speech from one of the players prompts Hamlet to think of a way to prove Claudius's guilt. He asks the players to perform a specific play and insert some lines he will write for them. Alone again, Hamlet worries about the actors playing a fiction with no meaning to themselves while he must bottle up his own true emotions. Hamlet believes that if Claudius's response to the play betrays his guilt, this will give him the courage and the will to act in his promised revenge for the murder.

All that Rosencrantz and Guildenstern can tell Claudius is that Hamlet has become interested in a play to be performed that evening, and the king is pleased that Hamlet is getting beyond his own melancholia. Ophelia is sent to meet with Hamlet where Claudius and Polonius can spy on them. Claudius admits to his own feelings of guilt before hiding. Hamlet enters alone and ponders suicide, but he is stopped from it by the fact that he has not fulfilled his promise to his father and the thought that even death might not end his misery. Ophelia finds him and returns the gifts he has given her. Sensing her betrayal and that his promised revenge dooms their relationship, he tells her in a venomous and insulting way that he doesn't love her. He rails on against Polonius as well, and hints at a threat to the king, leading Ophelia to conclude that he has lost all reason. Claudius and Polonius discuss all that they have overheard, and the king decides that in his present state of mind, Hamlet is too dangerous to have at court, so he decides to send the prince to England. Polonius holds to his unrequited-love theory and suggests that after the play tonight, Gertrude might speak to her son.

Hamlet prepares the players by speaking on acting, then tells Horatio that he must observe the king's reactions to the play. The court assembles for the play, whose story closely parallels Claudius's murder of his brother. The king is disturbed and runs out of the hall, confirming for Hamlet and Horatio that the ghost was telling the truth. Rosencrantz and Guildenstern report to Hamlet the king's anger and the queen's desire to see Hamlet in her chamber. Hamlet is contemptuous of his former friends, then Polonius comes to bring Hamlet to his mother. In his thoughts, Hamlet vows not to allow himself to be so overcome with emotions that he kills her.

The king orders Rosencrantz and Guildenstern to take Hamlet to England, while Polonius comes to say that the prince is on his way to visit the queen, an encounter that Polonius intends to eavesdrop upon. The king is trying to ease his conscience by prayer when Hamlet comes upon him. It is an opportunity to exact his revenge, but Hamlet cannot kill Claudius during a moment of repentence, because it would send the king to heaven instead of hell. But in the end we learn that the king has been unable to pray.

Hamlet confronts his mother in such a way that it alarms her and she calls for help, which is echoed by Polonius, who is hiding behind a tapestry. Believing the intruder is Claudius, Hamlet stabs him through the tapestry and discovers he has killed the counselor, the father of Ophelia and Laertes. He turns his venom on his mother, who is consumed with shame and terror until the ghost reappears, distracting him from his fury at his mother and reminding him that his vengeance is not yet done. Because Gertrude cannot see the ghost, she interprets Hamlet's actions as proof of his lunacy. Hamlet urges his mother to repent from her degrading marriage, then tells her he has been ordered to England, where he expects Rosencrantz and Guild-erstern to try to kill him. He resolves to turn the tables on his friends.

Claudius is told of the death of Polonius and sends Rosencrantz and Guildenstern after the prince, who taunts them and leads them on a chase. Finally Hamlet is brought before the king and ordered to England with his two escorts. Claudius says that with the death of Polonius, this is for Hamlet's own safety, and the prince has no choice but to go. On the way to England, the trio pass the armies of Fortinbras, and Hamlet ruminates on their action and his inaction even in the face of overwhelming personal motive. Puzzled by his own failure at the vengeance, Hamlet resolves to act boldly from now on.

Meanwhile, with her father killed and her brother abroad, Ophelia has lost her reason, which shocks Claudius and Gertrude. Laertes hears of his father's death and, suspecting the king of foul play, returns home. He bursts into court, sees what has become of his sister, and is calmed by the king, who privately informs him of all that has happened.

Horatio receives a letter from Hamlet all about how, in a battle with pirates at sea, the prince has escaped from Rosencrantz and Guildenstern and is on his way back to Elsinore. Horatio goes to meet his friend. Claudius finishes his version of events to Laertes and says that he cannot act personally against the prince because Hamlet is his queen's son and he is popular with the people. When Claudius and Laertes learn of the impending return of Hamlet, they plan a friendly fencing match between Laertes and Hamlet, which they intend to end in the prince's death. Laertes will use a poison-tipped rapier, while Claudius makes doubly sure by preparing a poisoned drink for the young prince. The queen interrupts their plotting by announcing that Ophelia has drowned.

Hamlet returns from England and, with his friend Horatio, encounters gravediggers who speak of the prince's madness as a funeral party ap-

278 ■ The Tools of Screenwriting

proaches, including the king and queen and Laertes. Hamlet learns that the funeral is for Ophelia, who probably took her own life. Hamlet reveals himself and his love for Ophelia. Laertes attacks Hamlet, but they are pulled apart.

Hamlet reveals to Horatio that he discovered the king's written request to the king of England, to be delivered by Rosencrantz and Guildenstern, to kill Hamlet when they arrived in England, but replaced it with an order for the pair to be put to death. When they hear that the king would like to wager on a fencing match with Laertes, Horatio warns him of treachery, but Hamlet is fatalistic and agrees to the match. It begins at once, with the king in attendance. They begin with civilities, then Hamlet scores first when the duel starts. Claudius offers him the poisoned wine, but Hamlet refuses it.

Then Gertrude drinks from the cup over the king's protests. Laertes wounds Hamlet with the poisoned rapier, but in the battle, the weapons are exchanged and Laertes is also wounded with the poisoned tip. The queen dies, Laertes collapses and begs Hamlet for forgiveness for the dueling plot, which he says was the king's doing. Hamlet stabs Claudius and then forces him to drink the poisoned wine. In his own death throes, Hamlet forgives Laertes, bids his mother farewell, and asks Horatio to tell the story. Just then, Fortinbras arrives, and as he dies, Hamlet says that he prefers that the Norwegian sit on the Danish throne. An ambassador from England arrives with the news that the king's orders have been carried out and Rosencrantz and Guildenstern have been put to death.

PROTAGONIST AND OBJECTIVE

Hamlet is clearly the protagonist; he is the one who has the problem around which this story is built. His objective is to honor the pledge he made to the ghost of his father to avenge his murder. Because this objective is so firmly and eloquently stated in the aftermath of Hamlet's first visit from the ghost of his father, it makes it possible for Shakespeare to show the young prince procrastinating, wracked with doubts and reluctance to act on his vow. Without such a clear statement of his objective, it would be harder for the audience to follow the very circuitous route from his desire to his ultimate actions to fulfill it.

OBSTACLES

Hamlet is a splendid example of the fact that, although the protagonist can have only one main objective if a story is to have unity, there can be many obstacles. These varied obstacles don't all come from a single line of cause and effect, but rise from a number of different directions.

Few protagonists have been beseiged by more obstacles than unfortunate Hamlet. He is, of course, actively opposed by Claudius, the king presumptive and murderer of Hamlet's father. And he is opposed by all who obey Claudius, especially Polonius. He is also inundated by his own doubts and insecurities, first his doubt about the truth the ghost spoke, but also his inner rage about his mother's hasty remarriage to the detestable Claudius. He loves Ophelia but he fears her betrayal under the sway of Polonius, and he is so shocked by the events at court that he is nearly immobilized with melancholia.

Thus we have a fallible, sympathetic, and tormented central character fighting against both external and internal obstacles, which so test his mettle and courage that this play has endured for centuries and still moves the audience as viscerally today as it did in Shakespeare's day.

PREMISE AND OPENING

Prince Hamlet—intelligent, sensitive, introspective, and already mourning the death of his beloved father—is profoundly shocked by his mother's hasty remarriage to his detested uncle, Claudius, who has become the king. Before the story has begun, Claudius and Hamlet's mother, Gertrude, were adulterers and it was Claudius who killed the king.

Shakespeare might have chosen to open the story with the murder of King Hamlet, Prince Hamlet's return from Wittenberg, and the marriage of Gertrude and Claudius. But his concern in this story was with a man's struggle to fulfill his oath of vengeance, not merely with the facts of the events. Since it is the ghost of the father who reveals the truth of the murder and exacts the promise of revenge against the new king, Shakespeare chose to begin the tale with an appearance of the ghost and the decision to summon the young brooding prince to meet the apparition. In other words, he chose to begin the story closer to the real body of the material and allow us and Hamlet to learn the earlier events in due time.

MAIN TENSION, CULMINATION, AND RESOLUTION

Hamlet swears an oath to the ghost of his father, King Hamlet, and it is that promise, along with the revelation of the murder that prompts it, which creates and sustains this story. But this is no simple tale of revenge. Rather it is a complex psychological study of a bright, sensitive, and deeply troubled man trying to come to grips with not only the impact of the oath, but the crushing events that swirl around him, making his acting on that pledge the urgent question in the minds of the audience. So the main tension might be, "Will Hamlet be able to act on his vow of vengeance against Claudius?" It could also be, "Will he summon the courage, provoke himself to act, break his own inertia?" The important thing to keep in mind is that the real battleground of this story is inside Hamlet himself.

The culmination, the moment when Hamlet finally shrugs off his overlong inertia and leaps into action, comes in the scene where he is viciously berating his mother and telling her of the murder, the nature of her new husband, and the loathsomeness of her marriage. When he hears Polonius behind the curtain and thinks it is Claudius, he finally loses all his hesitation and plunges his sword in to the hilt. The tragedy for Hamlet is that when he at long last brings himself to act, he is mistaken about the man he is killing. This leaves his vengeance still incomplete.

The resolution, of course, comes when the vengeance is complete—that is, when he finally kills Claudius. This is by all means a tragedy and, in the Senecan model of tragedy that Shakespeare worked from, nearly everyone of importance dies. Here we have a prime example: Polonius and Ophelia die before the major climactic scene; then Claudius, Gertrude, Laertes, and Hamlet all die in that scene; and then, on the heels of all those deaths, comes the announcement that Rosencrantz and Guildenstern were also put to death.

THEME

This is a story about revenge. Sometimes the theme is explicit, as it is with Hamlet's promise to avenge his father's murder and Laertes's desire to avenge his father's murder and sister's death against the man he blames for both. At other times it is much more open to interpretation: Is Ophelia's death by presumed suicide her revenge against a world consumed with treachery? Is Gertrude's drinking from the cup intended for Hamlet simply a mistake, or a suicide because she can't bear her part in the horrors of her household, or is it too a revenge on her new and connivingly murderous husband once she has seen him for what he really is? We are left to ponder these questions, and they must be asked by any who stage yet another production of the play, on stage or screen. Still, regardless of the interpretation put on this story, the thoughts provoked by this play still always come back to revenge.

UNITY

Unity of action is carefully observed in this story; it is made all the more necessary because we have a passive central character. Yet even Hamlet's inaction is action. For the story is not simply about his exacting the revenge on his uncle, but about his wrestling with his own inability to act, to get on with his vow, to do the one thing to which he has committed his life. While our protagonist is wrestling with his own demons, he is active after a fashion. At the same time, events are swirling around him that push him to get on with his promised action. Thus, both from the inside and from the outside, the promise of Hamlet's action is what creates unity here.

EXPOSITION

Even Shakespeare was capable of delivering awkward bits of exposition, so there is hope and solace for the rest of us. When Horatio tells Marcellus about the conflict between King Hamlet and the elder Fortinbras, it is unrelieved narrative. It has neither humor nor conflict to help mask the fact that this is information both men should already know. Yet, shortly after this scene, when Hamlet first meets his father's ghost, the scene is so emotionally charged and the enormity of the information is so great for Hamlet that the expositional nature of the scene is fully covered by the horrific changes it exacts in our protagonist.

Other examples of exposition well delivered through a conflict in the scene occur when Gertrude and Claudius implore Hamlet to give up his brooding over his father, and later, when both Laertes and Polonius forbid Ophelia to see Hamlet.

CHARACTERIZATION

There is no more fascinating and complex character in the history of drama than Hamlet. Shakespeare achieves this depth of characterization in part by contrasting Hamlet's encounters with Horatio, whom he trusts, with all those whom he distrusts. The scenes with Horatio give us the key to Hamlet's real nature, the man he would be if it weren't for all these terrible circumstances around him. These scenes are the measure against which we hold Hamlet's dealings with all the other principals in the story. For instance, in all the scenes with Horatio, there isn't the slightest indication the young prince might be mad. The same is true of his soliloquies (or voice-over thoughts in the Olivier film version). These would lead us to believe his purported madness is feigned as a tool in his quest for revenge—or to buy him time in his equivocations.

Hamlet is characterized by his intellect, idealism, imagination, and wit; he is someone who is normally popular and well thought of by other people. But when he is called to action, he delays or procrastinates. Externally there is the uncertainty that the king really is a murderer. Internally, Hamlet is immobilized by his melancholia over all that has befallen him, his mother, and his household. These conspire to keep him from acting on his vow.

Hamlet's first real opportunity to kill Claudius is beautifully placed. Right after the meeting with the players, when Hamlet's rage is most worked up, he comes upon the king alone and unsuspecting. But here his inaction has a very good reason (or a very good excuse?); if he were to kill the man during an act of contrition, it would defeat the purpose of the revenge. In a beautiful irony, it is revealed to us after Hamlet leaves that the king was unable to pray and thus was not in an act of contrition.

The other characters are also expertly drawn. Gertrude is a solicitous and protective mother even after her son's indictment of her. Ophelia, dominated by her father and brother, is an immature girl, but loyal to Hamlet. We know that her love is genuine, and what she does under the influence of her father is done with the hope of helping to cure the prince. Polonius is bumbling, pompous, and windy, but a believable contrast to his hotheaded son, Laertes. Even Claudius, the villain if ever there was one, is given his moment of remorse, his desire to be able to pray, though he is unable. This leaves him a more rounded and believable character.

DEVELOPMENT OF THE STORY

This story develops not so much out of a single want set against a string of successive obstacles as it does from conflicting wants, sometimes of several characters. Hamlet of course wants to avenge his father's murder, and much of the conflict of the story comes from inside him as he struggles to put his vow into action. But Claudius wants to protect himself and his throne, which he murdered to get. Polonius wants to curry favor with the new king and solidify his position as most trusted adviser. Ophelia wants to help the young man she loves, whom she fears has gone insane. Eventually Laertes wants to avenge the deaths of his father and sister. Gertrude wants to believe Claudius's version of events, for Hamlet's version is too horrible for her to bear. Each of these wants presents its own obstacle to Hamlet in his circuitous, two-steps-forward, one-step-back route to his promised revenge.

DRAMATIC IRONY

Uses of dramatic irony abound in this story. From the time Hamlet is visited by the ghost until the play is presented to the king, we know that Hamlet suspects Claudius of the murder, but the king does not. From the moment he realizes that Hamlet knows, Claudius actively plans the prince's death, and we are aware of this while the prince is not. And at the play itself, irony is used masterfully: We know of Hamlet's plan to unmask the king, but the king does not.

When Ophelia comes to Hamlet to return his gifts, we know that she is acting under her father's orders, but Hamlet doesn't know this and it leads him to distrust her, thinking her to be as treacherous as he believes his mother to be.

In Gertrude's bedroom, when Hamlet rails at her with all his fury, we know that it is Polonius behind the curtain, not Claudius, so that when Hamlet thrusts his sword to complete his revenge, we are justly horrified, owing to the irony of our superior knowledge in the circumstance.

And of course the ironies compound in the final scene. We know the tip of Laertes's rapier is poisoned, and we know that the wine the king plans to offer will be poisoned as well. When Hamlet is cut by the rapier, we know he is doomed, but then the sword changes hands and dooms Laertes as well. Gertrude, not Hamlet, ends up drinking the poisoned wine. These events are given all the greater resonance because we know what some characters do not.

PREPARATION AND AFTERMATH

A marvelously ironic preparation is made right before Hamlet's first meeting with his father's ghost. Talking with Horatio and Marcellus, he discusses how a single fault can be the downfall of an otherwise worthy man. He is in fact telling of his own condition, about to come into full being—he has but the one fatal flaw, he cannot provoke himself to action until it is too late. There is also a telling scene of aftermath. Right on the heels of Hamlet making his vow of revenge to the ghost, he refuses to tell his most trusted friends what has just happened. Distrust has entered his life and will stay to the end.

The play within the story also has well-rendered preparations and aftermaths. Of course there is all the preparation for the play and the famous speech to the players, but as a direct preparation for a scene to come, there is the moment between Hamlet and Horatio when the prince asks his friend to watch the king during the performance, setting the stage for the drama to come. After the king has been driven from the audience by the substance

284 ■ The Tools of Screenwriting

of the play, there is a marvelous aftermath when all the others at court flee in horror—both at the accusation and at the reaction of the king.

PLANTING AND PAYOFF

Planting and payoff are not used to a great extent in the play, and barely at all in the Olivier film version. In the play there is all the planting of the Fortinbras character and his proximity to the events of the play. All this is finally paid off when he takes the Danish throne at the end.

Perhaps the best use of planting and payoff in the story has to do with poison. King Hamlet was killed by poison, and this seems to be the form of treachery that Claudius prefers, for he chooses not one but two ways to poison Hamlet in the end. The irony of the payoff is that not only is Hamlet poisoned, but so are Laertes and Gertrude, and finally Claudius himself.

Perhaps a missed opportunity for planting could have been to let us know that Hamlet was an accomplished swordsman who kept up his practice, and that Laertes was studying the sword in France.

ELEMENTS OF THE FUTURE
AND ADVERTISING

There are many effective uses of elements of the future here. Out on the battlements, Horatio speaks to Hamlet about madness right before he meets the ghost of his father. Later, Claudius says of Hamlet, "Madness in great ones shall not unwatched go," indicating his fear of the prince and his unspecified intention to pay close attention.

Even in Hamlet's soliloquies, elements of the future can be found. In his "To be or not to be" speech, he ruminates over losing "the name of action," which helps point us forward by making us worry whether he will be able to act or not.

Advertising is also effectively used. Polonius and Claudius plan to use Ophelia to get Hamlet to talk while they eavesdrop. Laertes and Claudius plan out their poison-tipped revenge for the climactic scene together. And Hamlet makes his plans to unmask his uncle's treachery by using the play. Each of these specific plans of the characters tells us about an upcoming event we can reasonably expect to see.

PLAUSIBILITY

The feeling of inevitability in this story is the result not of Fate, as in the Greek tragedies, but of extraordinarily skillful characterization. Hamlet's inner strengths and inner troubles, when confronted by so many conflicting wants from other characters, lead to an end that we cannot predict, but that seems to be the only way those events could have gone. If Hamlet had been less true to his vow to his father's ghost, he might have abandoned his promised revenge before unmasking the villain at the play. If he had been more impulsive and less thoughtful, he probably would have killed Claudius right after talking with the ghost. In either case, there would have been no story here. Only with the intersection of the character and his circumstances was Shakespeare able to fashion a riveting story that is both clear and plausible throughout.

ACTION AND ACTIVITY

Purposeful action runs throughout this story. Hamlet plays up his madness depending on who his audience is. Polonius and Claudius hide behind curtains to eavesdrop. Polonius sets his daughter up to provoke Hamlet to reveal himself. Hamlet instructs the players to give their play in just such a way as to generate a response from his uncle.

The pageantry of the story, entrances of the king and actions of the court, are activities. So is the digging of Ophelia's grave, though when Laertes flings himself into it, it is an action.

DIALOGUE

What can a merely mortal dramatic writer say in the face of Shakespeare's dialogue? Modern audiences tend to forget that what seems to be stylized language was perfectly comprehensible to the audiences of the day. Any writer would count himself lucky to have written a single phrase that enters the vernacular of his native tongue and lives for a hundred years or more. Yet in this one play alone, Shakespeare enriched the English language with dozens of phrases still used today. Here are just a few of them: "There is something rotten in the state of Denmark"; "Neither a borrower nor a lender be"; "To thine own self be true"; "To the manor born"; "Brevity is the soul of wit"; "There's the rub"; and of course, "To be or not to be, that is the question."

VISUALS

One can only discuss the visuals in terms of a filmed version of this story—in this case, the Olivier version. Despite the formidable sets, marvelous costumes, and considerable expense evident throughout the production, this is still essentially a filmed version of the play. It has not really been taken outside the castle; scenes only alluded to in the play are not dramatized; and, quite understandably, the dependence on the spoken word (but what words!) remains intact from the play. However, the sense of scale that the sets give, the size of some of the pageantry scenes, and the splendor of the costumes, along with the affecting music, do all help to give this more of a cinematic effect.

And there are some expressive uses of visuals, particularly in granting the camera a subjective relationship to Hamlet's inner world. His heartbeat can affect the camera; we can see his thoughts, his visions and obsessions. And there are also some telling moments when the camera and the visuals chosen help to direct our attention. During the play, as Claudius is being repelled by the performance, all eyes in the audience on screen begin to turn toward him and away from the play itself. And in the final scene, Gertrude's fixation on the cup of wine she knows was meant for Hamlet is pointed up. In this case it shows us that she consciously chooses to drink what she cannot help but suspect is poison.

DRAMATIC SCENES

As with dialogue, there is nowhere to begin to discuss dramatic scenes; in Shakespeare in general and in *Hamlet* in particular, no matter where you look, you will find marvelous examples of drama at its best. One fine example occurs when Hamlet and Ophelia meet while Polonius and Claudius hide behind the drapes. There is irony because we know of the eavesdroppers and Ophelia knows as well, yet Hamlet initially does not. There is suspense when we begin to suspect that he may know they are there. There is the use of a prop when she tries to give back his gifts to her. There is revelation when we discover that he really loves her despite all that he has railed on about, leading us to conclude that he has been playing a part, feigning his madness. There's a complete scene of preparation where we see Ophelia come under the sway of her father, and the men hide. And there is an aftermath, when the king and his counselor both use what they have heard to confirm their own personal ideas about what is going on with Hamlet. Who could ask for more in a scene?

Another marvelous scene that plays primarily on the internal conflicts of Hamlet is the one in which he comes upon his uncle attempting to pray. There is preparation where we learn of Claudius's remorse and his desire to pray. There is the moment when Hamlet sees him, and the irony created by our knowing and Claudius being unaware. There is the tussle within Hamlet at this being a perfect opportunity, yet one he cannot take because it would ruin the revenge in the everlasting sense. Hamlet's approach and pulling out his sword are evocative actions showing his intentions; his so-liloquy tells us of his doubts and the reason for his decision; and his retreat makes it final. Then, in an aftermath tinged with irony, we find out that Claudius was unable to pray, and thus Hamlet's reason for not killing him was invalid. The use of irony from beginning to end, the use of staging, props, actions, reasoning, the presence of a difficult and compelling deci-sion—all these contribute to the making of first-rate dramatic scenes.

SPECIAL NOTES

One of the most noteworthy aspects of this story, at least within the dis-cussion at hand in this book, is the fact that Hamlet is the archetypal passive central character. That is to say, he wants to act but cannot bring himself to do so throughout the middle section of the story. He performs a number of actions, most notably the plan of using the play to unmask Claudius, but none of these is *the* essential act that he has committed himself to perform.

In stories where there is a passive—or inactive—central character, we must have two elements, both of which are admirably demonstrated here. The first is that the passivity of the central character is not the result of indifference; the character cares, has passions, but is unable to act, as opposed to not caring and finding no will to act. The other condition nec-essary for a story with a passive central character is that the circumstances of the character's life actively oppose his passivity. That is, there must be strong forces at work that are, knowingly or unknowingly, striving to break the character's passivity, inertia, inability to act. When the character is passive, the obstacles to the character must be active.

Rick in *Casablanca* is just such a character, and Hamlet is the supreme passive protagonist. He cares with every fiber of his being, he has huge passions and every intention of acting. Yet he is filled with doubt, with melancholia, he feels overwhelmed by the recent events of his life, and these all converge to force him into inaction. But the world he inhabits and the circumstances of his life conspire in the opposite direction: he is visited by a ghost exacting a vow of revenge; his uncle is fearful of his every move and makes treacherous plans around him; the woman he loves is under the influence of her dominating father, who is in collusion with his hated uncle; and so on. Everything in Hamlet's world is assaulting his inaction, working to bring his inner conflict—to act or not to act—to a head.

Another noteworthy aspect of this analysis is how many of the tools of screenwriting apply to a story written hundreds of years before cinema was invented. Storytelling has not changed all that much since the Elizabethan days of William Shakespeare, at least not in the principles that govern the quality and effectiveness of a well-told story. Only in the area of planting and payoff does there seem to be anything in our discussion not in active use in this play. Elsewhere in Shakespeare, there is considerably more planting and payoff, but perhaps never quite as much as in film. The nature of a play is such that the audience can look wherever it pleases at any given time, so planting and payoff are somewhat more difficult for the audience to notice—and hence more difficult for the playwright to use.

The ideas we have discussed throughout the book appear in great abundance in this story, commonly considered the best drama of all time. It's food for thought when any screenwriter, whether novice or professional, sits down to create a screenplay.

ADDITIONAL READINGS

Aristotle. *Aristotle's Poetics.* Translated by S. H. Butcher. New York: Hill and Wang, 1961.

Brady, John. *The Craft of the Screenwriter.* New York: Touchstone, 1981.

Chekhov, Michael. *To the Actor.* New York: Harper and Row, 1953.

Clark, Barrett H. *European Theories of the Drama.* New York: Crown, 1947.

Clurman, Harold. *On Directing.* New York: Collier, 1972.

Forster, E. M. *Aspects of the Novel.* New York: Harcourt Brace, 1927.

Raphaelson, Samson. *The Human Nature of Playwriting.* New York: Macmillan, 1949.

Strunk, William Jr. and E. B. White, *The Elements of Style.* New York: Macmillan, 1979.

ABOUT THE AUTHORS

DAVID HOWARD is an active screenwriter, "script doctor," and script consultant, both in Hollywood and in Europe. He is also the founding director of the Graduate Screenwriting Program at the University of Southern California's School of Cinema-Television. In addition to his teaching duties at USC, he frequently lectures and teaches, often in conjunction with Frank Daniel, throughout Europe as well as around the United States. He lives in Santa Monica, California, with his wife, the painter Victoria McClay.

EDWARD MABLEY, besides being the author of *Dramatic Construction,* wrote, among other works, the play *Glad Tidings* and the text of the grand opera *The Plough and the Stars* (after the play by Sean O'Casey). He wrote radio and television plays, directed in television, and taught at the New School for Social Research in New York. He died in 1984.

FRANK DANIEL has been the head of many of the world's most renowned film schools. He was Dean of FAMU, the Czech film school, during the 1960s "Prague Spring." He was the first dean of the Center for Advanced Film Studies at the American Film Institute, then he became cochairman of Columbia University's Film Division with his former student, Milos Forman. He went on to become the first dean of the newly expanded School of Cinema-Television at the University of Southern California. He was also the first artistic director of the Sundance Institute, and artistic director of the Flemish European Media Institute in Brussels. He is currently a professor in the Graduate Screenwriting Program, at USC. and continues with his own extensive screenwriting schedule as well as teaching regularly in Europe.

INDEX